# Propagand

# Propaganda 1776

## SECRETS, LEAKS, AND REVOLUTIONARY COMMUNICATIONS IN EARLY AMERICA

Russ Castronovo

OXFORD
UNIVERSITY PRESS

Oxford University Press is a department of the University of Oxford. It furthers
the University's objective of excellence in research, scholarship, and education
by publishing worldwide. Oxford is a registered trade mark of Oxford University
Press in the UK and certain other countries.

Published in the United States of America by Oxford University Press
198 Madison Avenue, New York, NY 10016, United States of America.

Library of Congress Cataloging-in-Publication Data
Castronovo, Russ, 1965-
Propaganda 1776 : secrets, leaks, and revolutionary communications in early America / Russ Castronovo.
pages cm. — (Oxford studies in American literary history ; 8)
Includes bibliographical references and index.
ISBN 978-0-19-935490-0 (hardcover); 978-0-19-067749-7 (paperback)
1. United States—History—Revolution, 1775–1783—Propaganda.
2. Propaganda—United States—History—18th century.
3. War and literature—United States—History—18th century.
4. Franklin, Benjamin, 1706–1790.   I. Title.
E209.C363     2014
973.3'88—dc23          2014021830

To the Memory of My Parents
Frances Abelson Castronovo
Michael Castronovo

# { CONTENTS }

# Propaganda 1776

# Introduction

Seventeen seventy-six symbolizes a moment, both historical and mythic, of democracy in action. That year witnessed the press release of a document that Edward Bernays, the so-called father of public relations and spin, would later view as a masterstroke of propaganda. Although the Declaration of Independence relies heavily on the empiricism of self-evident truths, Bernays, who had authored the influential manifesto *Propaganda* in 1928, suggested that what made this eighteenth-century public address so "effective" was not sober rationalism but an "inspiring" message that ensured its dissemination throughout the American colonies. This statement of democracy spread among the roughly two and half million inhabitants of British North America, excluding enslaved and indigenous populations, and accrued global significance so that "this day," from Bernays's perspective at the start of the Cold War, it seemingly touches "people all over the world."[1] This sweeping assessment esteems Thomas Jefferson's resolution, though not because it represents the fullest expression of Enlightenment principles or because the Declaration wrests sovereignty from the ancien régime and turns it over to the people. Instead, for the man who defined public relations most of all for its "engineering of consent," Jefferson's innovation consists in penning a rousing document of mass persuasion.[2]

The idea that publics could be easily swayed and managed had interested Bernays, nephew of Sigmund Freud, since he first declared that the unseen "manipulation of the organized habits and opinions of the masses is an important element in democratic society."[3] Far more than placing democracy and propaganda into uncomfortable proximity, this statement raises the possibility that hidden psychological mechanisms might actively warp people's attitudes and beliefs to the point where persuasion and affect become as powerful as abstract political propositions. While the enlightening aspects of print culture—open debate, informed publics, the transparent display of knowledge—are central to our impressions of the Revolution as an unparalleled rhetorical feat, the path toward American independence required above all else the spread of unreliable intelligence that traveled at such a pace that it could be neither confirmed nor refuted. By tracking the movements of stolen documents, satires, and published letters from the 1770s to 1790s, this book argues that media dissemination created a vital but seldom acknowledged connection between propaganda and democracy. Readers have often sidestepped this discomfiting convergence by concentrating instead on the abstract ideas about liberty and equality that impelled the inhabitants of a colonial backwater to challenge an empire. The force of ideas cannot be underestimated, but just as meaningful are the mechanisms as well as accidents that put self-evident truths—along with any number of false reports and unproven accusations—into circulation. By thus shifting the focus from information to communication, this book seeks to understand the extent to which the American Revolution was and, in some respects, still might be revolutionary.[4]

Despite the fact that dispersal and transmission are intrinsic to the notion of propaganda, the stately aura of 1776 often clouds the restive and undisciplined nature of popular pamphlets, circular letters, and other materials of the Revolutionary Atlantic world. The gravitas of the American founding works against this mobility by mining texts for deep significance that befits foundational documents. The Declaration of Independence thus becomes a singular achievement of political theory divorced from less exalted iterations and copies, including the one-page broadside hastily composed by a Philadelphia printer named John Dunlap on the night of July 4, 1776 (fig. o.1). Of the twenty-six extant copies of the Dunlap Broadside, several are marred by creases and dark lines created by folds made before the printer's ink had dried. The offsetting on other copies seems sloppy, betraying signs of a rushed job. Wasting little time after adopting the document, Congress sent this small job to the printer's shop a few blocks away so that it might be disseminated. Dunlap ran off an estimated two hundred copies and when those were depleted, historians surmise, John Hancock quickly ordered another batch.[5] The import of the Declaration encompassed more than the now-famous phrases that supplied information about the supposed

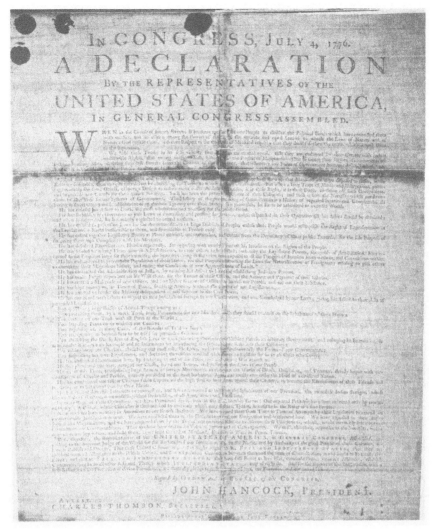

FIGURE 0.1 *One of the surviving copies of the Dunlap Broadside of the Declaration of Independence.*

equality of persons; in 1776, it also entailed the urgencies of communication, which, as the smudges and other imperfections suggest, was rarely an orderly process with clear protocols.

Circulating alongside this broadside were a flurry of newssheets, unauthorized disclosures of confidential correspondence, exposés of disgraced leaders, and samples of republican verse, all whose raison d'être seemed at times to comprise little more than the fact of their circulation. But like a clean and regularized copy of the Declaration of Independence that would eventually take the place of the Dunlap

Broadside, the propaganda of the late eighteenth century has been tamed. In *The Ideological Origins of the American Revolution*, Bernard Bailyn comments that he embarked on his research into pamphlet culture to prove that the patriots' warnings about an enslaving empire were not "mere rhetoric and propaganda."[6] The quest to distill a coherent set of attitudes among the Revolutionary generation leads to a dismissal of propaganda as meaningful political activity. To be fair, propaganda is hardly ever coherent: its proliferation and spread, its dissemination and receipt, its speed and circulation make for a mess of messages rather than canonical statements. The overall effect is a decentralized "sociology of texts" that extends beyond mere reaction by creating a political culture of contestation and contradiction.[7] Such ganglia of communications enable and indeed, to a certain degree, constitute democratic activity by widening access to debate while broadening its scope and range.

Of course, expanding the bandwidth of eighteenth-century communications may have amplified the quantity of pamphlets, broadsides, and letters without enhancing their quality. Arguments against propaganda rest precisely on the suspicion that mass persuasion saps people of their free will and tricks them into adopting unproven opinions and making irrational decisions. The critique of propaganda often imagines a submissive citizenry held in thrall by a political sorcerer who alternately threatens, cajoles, and deceives. According to this perspective, propaganda distorts reality, reducing social complexities to easily digestible narratives and replacing facts with convenient half-truths. The taint of propaganda, it would seem, might jeopardize the meanings of 1776. In responding to Progressive-era historians who had interpreted founding documents of the American Republic as propaganda for class interests, Bailyn counters that "real fears, real anxieties, a sense of real danger" lay behind the Revolutionaries' heated rhetoric. Rather than seeing the flood of pamphlets in the wake of the Stamp Act (1765) as targeting the "inert minds of an otherwise passive populace," Bailyn presents an image of an engaged citizenry whose deep commitment to political (and polemical) ideas imbued radical thought with real substance. The vitality of democracy in this view depends on its distance from propaganda. After Walter Lippmann and other Progressives launched withering critiques of government propaganda during World War I, it often seemed wiser to associate the patriot rhetoric of 1776 with rational argument and measured debates. "The more I read, the less useful, it seemed to me, was the whole idea of propaganda in its modern meaning when applied to the writings of the American Revolution," writes Bailyn.[8] But textual meaning and political interpretation are not only a question of "more" reading; how these texts are read is just as crucial. For the *printscape* of early America with its public sharing of private letters, its pirated editions and quick production of pamphlets, its intercepted communiqués and its clever forgeries, its broadsides and plagiaries, meaning inheres in how documents circulate and travel, how they become lost and then reappear, in short, how they move.

*Propaganda 1776* invokes "printscape" instead of the more familiar "print culture" because the term resonates with the shifting formations that characterize other "scapes" such as landscapes and mediascapes. Landscape frequently entails dynamic geographies where the unevenness of physical features, the pull of the horizon, the interplay of weather and environment, and other effects create a sense of movement in otherwise static representation. For Arjun Appadurai, who first developed the notion of mediascapes, "the suffix -scape allows us to point to the fluid, irregular shapes" in which people, capital, technology, images, and texts move.[9] So irregular is printscape that it includes handwritten letters and other artifacts not prepared by a printing press. Always hungry for the latest intelligence, printers and publishers took delivery of penned correspondence that they then laid out in galleys for their newspapers. Print shops, often doubling as post offices, were important hubs in a loose media infrastructure that received, transposed, and distributed communications.[10] Besides this shuttling between writing and type, the most significant irregularity of printscape entailed distribution, which ebbed and flowed in response to the availability of writing materials, impassable roads, dangerous seas, and a host of other accidents introduced by the sorts of human scheming (theft, forgery, plagiarism) archived by the epistolary novel.

So fluid is this terrain that information, along with the distortions and manipulations commonly associated with propaganda, spread widely because printscape facilitates horizontal communication. Admittedly, print usually follows hierarchical channels carved out by religious and state officials, starting at the top and center and radiating "outward and downward."[11] Yet this textual traffic plan lacks breadth, which is why Natalie Zemon Davis adds the spread of pamphlets to the map of popular politics. Unlike the realm of the fine arts, where a sculpture or other oeuvre might take months to design and complete, the outpourings of printscape—newspaper verse, letters, and pamphlets—often seemed to require little thought or skill.[12] A lowly immigrant proved how quickly print could radiate upward and across when he authored *Common Sense* less than two years after setting foot in America. Pamphlets such as Thomas Paine's are but one recognizable feature of a decentralized information grid. Over the course of forty years as a group of colonies in the Atlantic world transformed into a republic, newspaper verse, scurrilous exposés, circular letters, and, of course, declarations all provided alternative—and not always reliable—media for expressing and shaping public opinion. As much as print sowed knowledge and enlightenment, it also created "conditions of distrust" in which the quick production and circulation of texts eroded the virtues of patience and moderation deemed so important to the prospect of a republican society.[13]

Print nurtured the growth of republicanism in eighteenth-century America. People entered the public not only in such concrete settings as taverns and village greens but also in virtual spaces via the "pamphlets and broadsides [that] were a familiar and normal feature of politics," as Michael Warner observes.[14] Because publics are "text based," circulation and dispersion enable people to identify common interests.[15] But the speed and variability of such movement also suggest that the classical republicanism that took root in the New World was not so classical, after all. The pursuit of public happiness envisioned in "an organic state joining individual citizens together into an indissoluble union of harmony and benevolence" often seemed out of step with the fast pace of data across a printscape riddled with crevasses of calumny and distrust.[16] By 1774 Loyalists had undammed "torrents of…billingsgate" while "propagating thousands of the most palpable falsehoods."[17] John Adams lodged this complaint (in an anonymous series of newspaper essays attacking the administrative clique of colonial Massachusetts) even as he and his colleagues in the Continental Congress were contributing daily to the flood of propaganda. Decades later, Ben Franklin's grandson would censure members of Adams's party for deliberate misrepresentations even as he was busy printing up falsified documents about George Washington. Despite an impetus to resolve these tensions and anchor early American culture in self-sacrificing ideals of civic virtue, the era of the Revolution and its aftermath witnessed the onset of a "new rhetoric of persuasion," to use Jay Fleigelman's phrase, that tested the rationality of the public sphere.[18] Instead of pinning meaning to Enlightenment principles or national precepts, propaganda infused the Revolutionary printscape with the ferment of transatlantic republicanism to widen political knowledge beyond either the strictly empirical or official public opinion.

Dissemination served as a principal aim of printscape, facilitated by such common practices as reprinting newspaper essays in pamphlet form or copying and circulating letters among committees of correspondence. The spirited rejoinders to Paine such as James Chalmers's *Plain Truth: Addressed to the Inhabitants of America, Containing Remarks on a Late Pamphlet, Entitled "Common Sense"* or Charles Inglis's *The Deceiver Unmasked; or, Loyalty and Interest United: In Answer to a Pamphlet Entitled "Common Sense,"* both published in 1776, provide a measure of how texts increased and multiplied in early American printscape. Even though Inglis predicted that Paine's "pamphlet, like others, will soon sink into oblivion—that the destructive plan it holds out will speedily be forgotten, and vanish, like the baseless fabric of a vision," it was his *The Deceiver Unmasked* that nearly disappeared without a trace when members of a Revolutionary committee ransacked a printing house and destroyed all copies of Inglis's rebuttal to Paine before they could be distributed.[19] The tumult and quick reversals witnessed in this episode reveal that printscape is less a zone of orderly communication than an expanding jumble of accusations, counterthrusts, and ripostes.

Proliferation is the overriding logic of printscape. Franklin and the Sons of Liberty copied and spread stolen British documents up and down the Atlantic coast; Mercy Otis Warren fashioned her plays so that others could continue and extend the Revolutionary drama; first Loyalists and then Democrat-Republican printers published counterfeited Washington letters so that they kept circulating for decades; Paine and other American pamphleteers strove to imagine colonial insurrection on a global scale; and, finally, Philip Freneau experimented with poetry and prose to see which medium best diffused democratic values throughout the population. A common thread among these thumbnail descriptions of this book's five chapters is the idea that across printscape the propagation of a message is as significant as the message itself. In printscape, content loses some of its prominence as different concerns—dissemination, movement, and velocity—emerge to play a role in the production of meaning. Propaganda exploits this kinetic nature of texts.

Not merely information but also communication, not simply content but also diffusion, propaganda may be defined as publicly disseminated knowledge that serves to influence others in belief or action.[20] Typically, however, propaganda gets reduced to deceit and dishonesty in ways that impoverish the concept, ignoring the four-hundred-year history of its modern usage that began with the Vatican's establishment of the Congregatio de Propaganda Fide in 1622. Only in the twentieth century, during World War I, did the term become associated with the transmission of fraudulent information, seen most infamously in the 1917 atrocity story that the Germans were operating "*Kadaververwertungsanstalten*" or "corpse-utilization factories."[21] By treating propaganda as a false message, historians of early America have concentrated on falsity at the expense of messaging, disregarding the erratic but complex system of communication that is intrinsic to the concept.[22] Classic senses of propaganda were more neutral, suggestive of increase or spreading. Cicero employed *propagare* in the context of *bellum*, alluding to military conquests that extend territory and spread one's influence.[23] In its nominative form (*propago*) denoting the practice of reproducing plants by means of slips and cuttings, propaganda often came to entail consideration of the networks, formal as well as informal, that propelled texts and ideas across public and private spaces. The connections between propagation and horticulture gestured to vines, whose tendrils enlarge and extend a plant's range. By this means, plants spread across landscape in ways that prefigure how texts spread across printscape. Plants are rooted, to be sure, but the sending out of shoots allows them to move. Texts are certainly written and imprinted, but propaganda makes them mobile.

These meanings, especially those associated with *bellum* and conquest, remained active during the church's pastoral crusade to extend Catholicism among the wayward flocks of Europe that had fallen under the sway of the Reformation and to the heathens of the New World. When Pope Gregory XV employed the gerundive form, *propaganda*, the term took on a fresh sense of urgency, acquiring an active sense of purpose and exhortation. The true doctrine must be propagated. The faith ought to be disseminated. The gerundive functions as a future passive participle, perhaps best seen in the English use of *agenda* (from the gerundive of *agere* or "to do"), which carries the connotation of things that "ought to be done or acted upon." By this reckoning, propag-*anda* is the stuff that ought to be spread. The matter of propaganda signifies incompletely if it is considered apart from its mobility.

Along with mobility, propagation and emotion are indispensible components of propaganda. Accordingly, beginning with propagation, the following three sections place each of these components in historical and theoretical context. The final section rounds out the introduction by providing an overview that suggests, in part, how the printscape of 1776 offers critical leverage for creating convergences with later historical moments.

## Propagation

As ruler of a global empire, King George III had plenty of opportunity to observe how communications, both official and unofficial, propagated across colonial networks. In a proclamation best remembered for first referring to the breakdown in American affairs as a "rebellion," the British sovereign described the commotion in the colonies as a psychological symptom fed by propaganda.[24] Measuring the disobedience spreading across "the divers parts of our Colonies and Plantations in North America," the king held the view that treason sprang from what skilled manipulators gulled people into wanting and believing. A century and a half later, Bernays put the matter in commercial terms: as opposed to a predictable pitch such as "please buy a piano," the trick is to get the consumer to say, "please sell me a piano."[25] But this insight into the unconscious habits of twentieth-century consumers does not adequately explain the Crown's perspective on the motivations of American patriots in 1775. Where Bernays saw propaganda as a necessity for managing the chaos of modern society, George III contended that the proliferation of texts—"traitorous correspondence"—across colonial printscape facilitated disorder and sedition. The public relations expert adhered to a top-down model in which consumers and other citizens lap up strategically placed propaganda. King George, in contrast, confronted a much more diversified landscape. The erosion of American obedience was not the work of a single deceiver on the order of Milton's Satan, although Bernays would later credit Sam Adams with pioneering the propaganda techniques that he and his colleagues at the Committee on Public Information used to sell World War I to the U.S. public.[26] George III did not single out any traitors by name,

but he alluded more than once to the media communications—
letters, pamphlets, and statements of support and sympathy—that
were traducing the once loyal subjects of British North America.

Whether or not the king and his court advisers grasped the complexity of Anglo-American correspondence networks, the proclamation of August 23, 1775, ultimately fails to address this fundamental
fact: propaganda is not so much the work of agent provocateurs as an
unsanctioned, decentralized, and often disorganized flow of information. By royal reckoning, "dangerous and ill designing men"
are encouraging rebellion in the colonies, but what this assessment
misses is that writing also spreads treason.[27] Yes, the realm must be
on guard against rebels, but the real worry was a baggy, harder-to-
pin-down network of "traitorous correspondence." George III's directive charged officers of the king to ferret out anyone engaged in
"carrying on correspondence with...the persons now in open arms
and rebellion against our Government, within any of our Colonies
and Plantations in North America."[28] For the sovereign authorities at
the Court of St. James, the threat of propaganda lay in its capacity to
propagate ideas and information that served as the basis for seditious alliances.

This insight might be expressed still more simply: the threat of
propaganda is that it propagates. The content of Philip Freneau's
antimonarchical verse, Benjamin Rush's essays on the "dreadful
evils" of tea, or John Dickinson's warnings about the East India
Company—to name just three of the many items of propaganda
examined in the following pages—was surely cause for concern, but
what proved far more worrisome was that ideas and opinions were
being disseminated in the first place.[29] The fact of transmission was
as significant as the content of what was circulating. Whether the
context is the eighteenth-century world of epistolary exchange or
our more familiar one of electronic communication, propaganda is a
vector that ramifies, begetting extensive, elongated, and branching
chains of communication. Media practices of proliferation and scattering were not limited to transatlantic luminaries such as Benjamin
Franklin or Tom Paine. As they exchanged, produced, and consumed
both handwritten and printed sheets of paper, "ordinary Americans"
entered a "huge political network" in which the "key to expanding
the insurgency was communication."[30] Early American printscape
entailed propagation every bit as much as a contemporary mediascape with its links and threads forwarded in viral fashion, but

ultimately what matters more are the differences between 1776 and an era of electronic communication. As the king's misapprehensions in "A Proclamation...for Suppressing Rebellion and Sedition" make clear, eighteenth-century hierarchies could not fully appreciate the extent of propaganda and its implications for personal agency. Even so, the web of colonial communications was hardly worldwide and information moved across its surfaces at a rate that could often be excruciatingly slow. The epistolary novel dramatizes the hand-wringing of more than one heroine who is sentenced to await the languid pace of letter writing.

Comparisons between Revolutionary propaganda and modern media practices just as often remind us of the unbridgeable gulf that separates Atlantic republicanism from contemporary notions of citizenship. And yet this distance also speaks to the vitality of printscape. Although a handful of American printers enjoyed comfortable relationships with the Crown as the king's official printers, today's media conglomerates were unknown in the colonies. Via the horizontal integration of printers with their counterparts in other towns and cities, with the postal service, and with the several committees of correspondence, a loose network sprang up in which recipients quickly became transmitters. Readers clipped and forwarded news items, discussed the latest publications in public houses and taverns, or even turned writer themselves by composing essays and letters for local newspapers. Alongside these eighteenth-century communications, pulpit oratory, celebrations, parades, and town meetings added to the range of broadcast sites.[31] In this context, letter writing, pamphleteering, and other print activities offer an important contrast to the homogeneity of twenty-first century corporate journalism and media.

Media infrastructures of the eighteenth century are not those of the twenty-first. Nonetheless, without a dramatic increase in the number of newspapers operating in the colonies, expanding print runs, and the recruitment of new craftsmen and, in some cases, craftswomen to the printing trade, propagation would have been a less momentous feature of the American Revolutionary printscape. Between 1763 and 1775, the number of colonial newspapers doubled from twenty-one to forty-two in part because more master printers had set up shop.[32] It seemed to Peter Oliver, a high-ranking Loyalist, that Americans, behaving like "Witches" who took the Lord's Prayer and "read it backward," had transmogrified printer's devils—the common term for an apprentice in a printing house—into devil printers.[33] In 1781, as Britain was coming to terms with the scale of its military defeat in America, Oliver diagnosed the unrest in the Thirteen Colonies as a contagion first planted by printers and radical clergymen whose tales worked to "stimulate the Seeds of this Rebellion to a progressive Vegetation." In his view, it was not the fields that were sown but the wind: printers and pastors had so "worked up" the people that "to attempt to undeceive them was talking to a Whirlwind."[34] Back in the early 1770s Oliver had learned full well how engulfing this storm could become when some of his dispatches, enclosed with a packet of correspondence from Massachusetts Governor Thomas Hutchinson, were stolen and passed on to American printers. Like kindling to the flames of rebellion, Oliver's and the governor's letters were soon condemned from New England to the Carolinas.

Their problem was not the letters but rather copies of the letters. Like many supporters of British rule, Oliver and Hutchinson suffered the effects of increased print production. Pamphlets like *Common Sense* went through multiple editions; newspapers expanded their print runs several fold. Meanwhile, the type of material that contributed to "the ever-broadening public sphere created by print" shifted to a more secular nature.[35] Historians calculate that by 1776 the output of religious tracts declined to just one of every ten items published, as political items crowded out sermons and religious tracts. Whatever their sins, these printers could not be accused of sloth since they were churning out more pamphlets in more editions and newspapers by the thousand. In the dozen years leading up to 1776, "231 separate pamphlets dealing directly with the dispute between Britain and the American colonies came off American presses."[36] But it was not enough to print more material or make it more inflammatory: this outpouring had to be mobilized.

## Mobility

The spread of revolutionary material in the form of newspapers, pamphlets, broadsides, letters, songs, and poems across British North America (and later the United States) created multiple networks that spawned new and often radical ideas about political communication. Mobile and shifting, these networks also encompassed the Caribbean and France after 1789, which became flash points for reflecting on the changing meanings of the American Revolution. Across the late eighteenth-century Atlantic world, communication itself became revolutionary.

Even though ocean calms and muddy post roads slowed the rate at which Revolutionary pamphlets such as *Common Sense* circulated, the propagation of messages still depended on the mobility and movement of texts. The formatting of so many political arguments from John Dickinson's *Letters from a Farmer in Pennsylvania* (1767–68) to Edmund Burke's *Reflections on the Revolution in France* (1790) as virtual letters, not to mention the actual letters that traveled eighteenth-century correspondence networks, speaks to the importance of mobility in printscape. In *Speed and Politics*, Paul Virilio contends that movement and circulation drive revolutionary activity. Jumping from feudal Europe to the era of nuclear weaponry, Virilio identifies the city, itself a place modeled after the medieval fortress designed to outlast a siege, as a bulwark against the mobility associated with deserters, wanderers, and roving bands of marauders. Yet these same cities and the printing presses that they housed, as in Zemon Davis's account of sixteenth-century Lyon and Paris, provided the setting for the people's entry into politics. More modern urban centers—Virilio's example is Paris in 1968—often hum with a dynamic energy that defies the protocols of the state, or, quite simply, stasis.

But only up to a point: totalitarian regimes of the twentieth century also utilized propaganda to shorten the response time needed to mobilize and ultimately manage people. For Virilio, this quickened political velocity becomes ominous in the threat of nuclear war in which an ICBM can reach its target in a matter of minutes. The rough analogue in the realm of civil society is Nazi propaganda minister Joseph Goebbels, who relied on speed to outmaneuver the masses, often bypassing the print sphere to deploy audiovisual techniques that quite simply do not allow time for rational deliberation and judgment. "Reading implies time for reflection, a slowing-down that destroys the mass's dynamic efficiency," writes Virilio of Goebbels's propaganda techniques.[37] A steady diet of images, in contrast, helps keep the masses at fever pitch but always under the direction and control of the party. Everywhere in his diaries from 1932–33, Goebbels speaks of the velocity of National Socialism, propelled by an untiring propaganda machine, in taking over the German state: "Motor to

Potsdam at eighty miles an hour"; "[p]lacards and pamphlets hastily being designed and dictated"; "[a]t the office. Everybody is working at full speed"; and finally, as he looks back on events, "[t]he Revolution was achieved with a celerity hitherto unknown."[38] The demands to make Nazi ideology circulate faster and wider would absorb radio and film into a propaganda apparatus that already included newspaper articles, speeches, and mass rallies.

In contrast, the world of American Revolutionary propaganda often moved at a glacial pace, although Whig activists knew how to use effigies, cartoons, drums, and parades to muster popular sentiment. A printing house with a diligent compositor and helpful apprentices could run off a newspaper or broadside within a few hours. Still, correspondence in the eighteenth century could take weeks and often months to reach its destination.[39] When tidings at last arrived, patriot leaders might hesitate to publish or otherwise make known the contents. In 1773 when incriminating letters written by prominent Loyalists fell into the hands of the Sons of Liberty, the Massachusetts legislature revealed the contents only in closed session, delaying a public airing in the house chambers. Not until weeks after the seal was first broken on this confidential correspondence were copies of the letters printed in newspapers. Goebbels, in contrast, took pride in never waiting but a moment to strike. Any comparison between the Nazi coordination of media and the loose network of eighteenth-century essayists, letter writers, and printers is without doubt tendentious, and not only because of the hate and unquestioning obedience required by the fuhrer cult. Still, the comparison remains important for illuminating the kinetic aspects of propaganda.

Although it is hard to shake off the toxic aspects of propaganda that surfaced during World War I and that Goebbels's work at the Ministry of Propaganda and Public Enlightenment fully confirmed, rallying public opinion and securing consent remain vital to popular rule. Assuredly, people can be manipulated enough that their consent becomes an illusion, yet the dissemination of ideas, circulation of viewpoints, and mobility of information (even it is ultimately misinformation) do connect people across time and space. Historian Philip Davidson in *Propaganda and the American Revolution* long ago construed the propaganda activities of colonial leaders as evidence of a profound commitment to democracy: "The more democratic a community, the more need for first marshaling opinion."[40]

This history would inspire no less a champion of propaganda techniques than Bernays, who cites Davidson's study in recounting how "press agents" of the American Revolution such as Sam Adams and Tom Paine early on recognized the importance of print media to pitch the idea of revolution to the British subjects of North America.[41]

Nor was Bernays the only theorist of propaganda who returned to 1776. In their sparring over the future of public opinion, John Dewey and Walter Lippmann in the 1920s each looked back to the origins of American democracy. Their debates about propaganda are punctuated by nostalgic references to the American Revolution. In his review of Lippmann's *Public Opinion* as "perhaps the most effective indictment of democracy as currently conceived ever penned," Dewey appealed to Jefferson and other eighteenth-century thinkers as a breakwater against the high tide of information distortion.[42] Yet he also believed that intelligent public opinion depended on dissemination. No supporter of propaganda itself, Dewey still believed that democracy could thrive only when ideas and information are mobilized in intelligent ways. "Dissemination is something more than scattering at large," he cautioned, stipulating that the goal of an educated public demanded a scientific approach.[43] Scientific did not mean mechanistic: instead of Bernays's "engineering of consent" or Lippmann's "manufacture of consent," Dewey relied on organic metaphors that hearken back to the ideal of the independent yeoman farmer. When ideas and information like "seeds are sown," not in wild fashion but after a logical plan, they will surely "take root and have a chance of growth." In opposition to Lippmann, who seemed to trust the invention of consent to a few technocrats, Dewey urged that experts work to make social inquiry a widely shared public aptitude. In the next breath, however, he expressed anxiety that "there is too much public, a public too diffused and scattered.... There are too many publics."[44] The worry was that the very techniques of propagation required to create a public would be derailed by their own excessive proliferation.

The concerns over propaganda thus lay bare the fragility of democracy, which at one moment demands the circulation of ideas and information but at the next is endangered by manipulative communications. Almost all studies of propaganda begin with the supposition that rhetoric and mass persuasion put publics at risk. People are too gullible to withstand the sophisticated techniques that create "epistemic deficits" and seduce them into making rash decisions and

accepting unfounded opinions.[45] As the title of one history of propaganda puts it, people are "easily led," prone to surrendering free
choice and rationality when they fall under the spell of everything
from broadside ballads to radio broadcasts.[46] Propaganda entails the
"management of collective attitudes"; it originates in a "failure to respect the autonomy of those with whom one communicates"; it seeks
"a diminished role for citizens"; it views people as "an all-too-easy
mark for the flimflam," as has long been observed.[47] Ranging from
communications theorist Harold Lasswell's pronouncement in 1927
to *New York Times* syndicated columnist Frank Rich's take on post-
9/11 politics, these conclusions echo one another in their disquiet
over democracy. But this concern for democracy ironically rests on
the antidemocratic assumption that propaganda always acts on people but that citizens never act through propaganda.

The notion of propaganda that takes shape is one that views the
masses as passive recipients of messages orchestrated by privileged
interests. It is "an elitist phenomenon," writes Terence Qualter, an
"attempt by the few who have access to the media to influence the
many."[48] There is more than enough history to bear out this conten-
tion. From Pope Gregory's 1622 papal bull about disseminating the
gospel to Secretary of State Colin Powell's 2003 speech before the
United Nations Security Council falsely asserting that Saddam
Hussein had acquired yellow cake uranium from Niger, propaganda
has often seemed to be perpetuated by a small but crafty set of publicists. Messages flow only in one direction, outward from an agency
such as Rome's Congregatio de Propaganda Fide, the Committee on
Public Information during World War I, or the Third Reich's propaganda ministry to captive audiences. During the Cold War, this impression was strengthened by the mentality of détente, which imagined
propaganda following a vector much like that of Virilio's ICBM—
fateful, unstoppable, and fully weaponized. Even the American
Revolution could be retrofitted to this model: in the 1961 idiom of
one historian, when colonists in Canada seemed on the verge of sid-
ing with the rebels to the south, the British tried to cordon off an
"eighteenth-century 'Iron Curtain' to halt the movement of American
agitators and propaganda into that uneasy territory."[49] Overall, in
this understanding of propaganda as tightly controlled communication, the phenomenon is like the static subject of a still life.

But when seen amid printscape, propaganda reveals dynamic and
mobile properties. Its practitioners no longer appear limited to a select

group of spin artists upholding entrenched interests. Likewise, its arrow-like vector splits into multiple trajectories that are more suggestive of a network or web. In his proclamation condemning the American rebellion, George III confronted the abundance of sedition spilling out from the "correspondence, counsels, and comforts of divers wicked and desperate persons" in "divers parts" of the empire. The document reluctantly acknowledges that propaganda neither emanates from a single source nor is confined to one location. As the king and his ministers were discovering, correspondence could erupt from just about anywhere. At one moment targeting the thirteen colonies and at the next directed at rebel sympathizers in Britain, the royal proclamation issues a transatlantic communications advisory. Propaganda, were it embodied as a lone malefactor, would not sit still for its portrait. Indeed, propaganda cannot be reduced to the propagandist, but is instead a distributed system of proliferation, transmission, and receipt. The diversity of sedition in 1775 makes it seem unlikely that the multiple vectors of correspondence and print could be "brought together within a single conceptual scheme" that befits Robert Darnton's description of a "communications circuit."[50]

An influential model in book history, the communications circuit diagrams the various positions within a book's journey through culture from the binders who stitched together the final product to the agents who shipped it to the consumers who read it. Whereas the "disparate elements" of print culture "operate in consistent patterns" within a communications circuit, the "divers" people and texts populating the Crown's view of Revolutionary printscape achieved no such coherence.[51] The difference between the consistency of a communication circuit and the jumbled nature of the late eighteenth-century printscape stems from the fact that Darnton's account depends on physical objects that made up only a fraction of what printers produced and sold: books. "Printers do not print books," asserts Peter Stallybrass.[52] Instead they print sheets, a broad category of ephemera whose history includes everything from papal indulgences to handbills to broadsides. In a world of inexpensive sheets that could be passed hand to hand or even discarded and blown by the wind, mobility, not King George, reigns supreme. Something like a conservation of creative energy underlies a communication circuit in which the words, messages, ideas, and themes of books eventually make their way back, albeit in radically altered form, to authors and publishers. In contrast, the sovereign, looking out on the multiple disturbances that would soon lead to the disintegration of British North America, saw only the increasing proliferation of propaganda. Call it the entropy of an empire.


## Emotion

The Revolutionary committees of correspondence that formed in the 1770s, along with the seizure of the postal system that soon followed, encouraged a vast cooperative network designed to establish, in the words of Sam Adams, "a free Communication with each Town...to ascertain...that we are united in Sentiments."[53] Dubbed a "pioneer in propaganda" by the title of a 1936 biography, Adams was a canny strategist whose most enduring insight might have been to recognize that communication entails "making common."[54] Still, it would be misleading to single out Adams from a "divers" movement. Acts and expressions of defiance staged by the Sons of Liberty were never limited to "a handful of agitators," and "the movement against Britain was largely decentralized," as Pauline Maier writes.[55] As the king's proclamation has it, the prevalence of contaminating influences meant that everyone, not just officers of the realm, had to guard against rebellion because it seemed that everyone was spreading it.

From the collective grief voiced in funeral orations commemorating the Boston Massacre to the "popular rage" that Paine elicited at the end of *Common Sense*, the specific emotions marshaled by propaganda vary. But the crucial factor, as Adams realized in his appeal to "Sentiments," was that there be "Unanimity" with respect to whatever the people were feeling. Facing divisive rumors in the fall of 1772 that the "timid sort of people are disconcerted, when they are positively told that the Sentiments of the Country are different from those the City," Adams believed it imperative that the duties of committees of correspondence be "executed with Spirit."[56] The historical importance of making emotion common raises a theoretical question that is beset with its own emotional difficulties: might propaganda have a connection to democracy? This possibility has generated some rather jaundiced conclusions about popular sovereignty as little more than a cleverly managed zone of consent. "In a democracy you have to control people's minds. You can't control them by force," says Noam Chomsky to explain why democracies depend so heavily on mass persuasion to secure the acquiescence of the governed.[57]

Chomsky here follows a path blazed by Jacques Ellul, who described propaganda as a sort of shared emotional synapse linking citizens to the democratic state. Without propaganda, citizens would be lost, deprived of symbols and other signposts that orient individuals within the complexities of modern communities. At the same time, democracies require propaganda to connect people, who would otherwise be nothing other than disaggregated atoms, to the state. The "citizen," according to Ellul, "craves propaganda from the bottom of his heart," and newspapers, radio, and other incorporative technologies gladly sate this desire by providing a solution to the existential crisis that haunts modern subjects: where do I belong?[58]

People implicitly consent to propaganda because without its cavalcade of symbols, myths, and ready-made narratives they would have to confront soul-wrenching questions about their own estrangement from the rest of humanity. For Ellul, propaganda thus underwrites an illusion of popular sovereignty. The trick consists in making the will of the people take shape around policies or other measures that have been narrowed in advance. "The point is to make the masses demand of the government what the government has already decided to do," writes Ellul.[59] Once the glitz of popular sovereignty wears off, it would seem that the connection between propaganda and democracy is fundamentally a relation of hegemony in which a ruling class or other elite presents its values as a matter of free choice. Yet Ellul is not a conspiracy theorist who sees citizens as mindless dupes at the mercy of master manipulators. All studies, from those that view rank-and-file Nazis and Communist apparatchiks as "poor victims" deluded by authority figures to those that treat consumers as unsuspecting "prey" fleeced by advertisers, seriously underestimate the extent to which people actively participate in propaganda.[60]

Warnings about "intellectual slavery" like those found in *The Propaganda Menace* (1933) later set the stage for Cold War paranoia about brainwashing and mind control as the logical but terrifying outcome of mass persuasion.[61] In this way, studies of propaganda tend to ignore people's agency in producing, receiving, spreading, and consuming media. "Individuals collaborate in their subjection," writes Mark Wollaeger in a helpful gloss on Ellul that explains propaganda as a response, one often deeply rooted in pleasure, to "cultural desires" for meaningful inclusion.[62] Citizens mediate sociopolitical environments via "scapes": the daily newspaper, for instance, provides "the thousand little strokes, the variations of color, intensity, and dimension" that render the world as a recognizable landscape.[63] The print media canvas is not equivalent to just any panorama, however. Invoking a suitably French reference, Ellul likens the newspaper to a pointillist artwork that assembles a multitude of old-fashioned data pixels, which resolve into a coherent image only when the viewer steps back. Emotional investments make it difficult to attain this detachment. Efforts to gain perspective entail some necessary distance, but because new disasters occur every day, the landscape changes with each new edition. And so propaganda becomes a daily ritual, an obsessive emotional interplay of distraction and detachment offset by attention and engagement.

*Propaganda 1776* highlights the nexus of eighteenth-century media of dissemination and the emotional register of popular politics in early America. While organizations such as the Boston Committee of Correspondence ensured that politically sensitive material traveled from colony to colony, irregular patterns of communication such as intercepting letters and falsifying or plagiarizing other documents also played important roles in establishing shared sympathies and common ideological positions among men and women separated by both time and distance. Yet the paradoxical counterpoint is that a literature designed to promote "common sense" and unity relied heavily on the vilification of political opponents. A critical focus on propaganda enables an understanding of how expressions other than those grounded in deliberation and reason—impassioned reactions, heated accusations, and declarations of shared injury— provided a basis, but surely an ambivalent one, for democracy. The sobering realization made after World War I by Dewey, Lippmann, and other Progressive intellectuals that liberal rationality did not inoculate citizens against mass persuasion comes laced with the insight that affect is just as important to democracy as any set of self-evident truths. Declarations and other texts travel the printscape not merely because distributing information is a civic virtue but also because a range of emotions from the need for reassurance to the bite of resentment demand it. Moving from Ben Franklin's scene of humiliation before the British Privy Council to Philip Freneau's despairing republicanism, this book's attention to printscape reveals how quickly shifting emotions—as opposed to any stationary meaning— amount to political activity that, however unreliable and suspect, is political nonetheless.

Tom Paine's short-lived career as a poet exemplifies how the emotional charge of propaganda inheres in its movement. In 1775, a year before *Common Sense* burst onto the colonial scene, Paine published a rather unremarkable poem entitled "Liberty Tree" about the unifying power of symbols. Its list of grievances is familiar and its rhymes now seem stilted by alternating lines of alexandrine verse. But familiarity, not originality, was the desired effect. The headnote to the poem instructs readers, or what is more likely in this case, tavern singers and auditors that recitations of "Liberty Tree" should be set to the tune of "The Gods of Greece."[64] Patterned after the 1771 composition "The Origin of English Liberty," Paine's verses echo the meter, number of stanzas, and theme of this earlier work, which opens, "Once the gods of the Greeks, at ambrosial feast...."[65] "Liberty Tree" is as much a recognizable jingle as it is a poem. In the same way that television commercials wrap a hit song around dish soap or other commodity, Paine adapted a popular ballad in an attempt to ensure the catchiness of his Revolutionary political message. The fact that *propagare* is the source of the Spanish word *propaganda*, meaning "advertising," intensifies the comparison between Paine's poetic take on liberty and the efforts of a Madison Avenue publicist. For each, the circulation of the message is indistinguishable from its emotional appeal.

## Converging on 1776

While primarily concerned with eighteenth-century dissemination, *Propaganda 1776* reaches out to a number of twentieth- and twenty-first-century contexts. In doing so, I establish continuities as well as discontinuities between the celebrated era of 1776 and more current moments. Instead of purely historicist work on the eighteenth century, the project takes various steps in a temporal back-and-forth in order to provoke a discussion about communication and the limits of consent.

While Franklin's unauthorized transmission of confidential documents provides the most resonant parallel (to WikiLeaks), war also makes up a major chord that emphasizes the enduring presence of propaganda's past. How do states manufacture consent for war? When official communications are given over to militarism, how do people communicate heterodox truths? How does the imagined threat of terrorism, sometimes called propaganda by the deed, curtail the proliferation of information or argument? These and other questions are treated in chapters that address the fate of radical republicanism in post-Revolutionary society from the perspective of printers like Benjamin Franklin Bache, satirists like Mercy Otis Warren, and poets like Philip Morin Freneau. More important than these and other historic personages are the copies, memes, and networks that accelerate the flow of information across printscape. This book is about the tempo of Revolutionary communication.

Insofar as this book explores continuities between eighteenth-century media and contemporary modes of transmission and circulation, it draws critical comparisons while preserving the contingency of discrete historical moments. Assertions of unbroken patterns over time can take on "an overdetermined feel," as Robert Levine writes, "in which contingencies go by the wayside and historical actors are subsumed to the history that has already happened and thus is conceived of as inevitable."[66] After all, if the propaganda of 1776 is just like the history of spin after the torpedoing of the *Lusitania* in 1915 or the destruction of the World Trade Center in 2001, we have little left to learn about any of these moments. Clearly Paine devised propaganda tactics to assail a global empire in the late eighteenth century, but his innovations do not make him a distant cousin of Dick Cheney or Donald Rumsfeld, who used propaganda to initiate a global war on terror after 9/11. Such historical asymmetries remind us that Revolutionary communications in the eighteenth century remain distinct from a later communications revolution. Some readers may find my occasional engagement with modern media jarring, just as others may not expect to see scattered references to the French Revolution—to say nothing of World War I and II or the U.S. invasion of Iraq—appearing in a book that begins by considering Bernays's comparison of the Declaration of Independence to a public relations coup. Such convergences, however, can pry open historical moments by providing new and perhaps unexpected angles of comparison.

*Propaganda 1776* situates American Revolutionary activity amid the ebbs and flows of French Jacobinism, slave revolt in Saint-Domingue, and atrocities in British India. Because it spreads and expands, propaganda provides tools for an incipient global analysis that competes with the conventional wisdom that would restrict the meanings of the Revolution to national significance. The project puts eighteenth-century experiments with paper and ink into conversation with electronic communications in order to reassess the connections among media, war, and revolution. Exposés of secret British administrative documents and the rapid transit of broadsides, for example, have continued relevance for our understanding of "hate radio" in Rwanda, digital activism in Egypt and Tunisia, and other sites where the techniques, patterns, and vectors of mass persuasion affect social and political change.[67] By focusing on Revolutionary communications, *Propaganda 1776* both reconsiders the role that printscape plays in historical transformations and reexamines the widely relevant issue of how information circulates in a democracy.

The focus on the propagation, mobility, and emotional register of texts, whether as handwritten letters or printed declarations, fits with the book's arc from the anticolonial propaganda of the 1770s to the anti-Federalist propaganda at the end of the century. This trajectory encompasses the retooling of Revolutionary propaganda in a society, which, at least by the time of the Constitution, had steadily retreated from the more radical premises of republicanism. By the late 1780s, according to Larry Tise, signs of a counterrevolution seemed rampant, and nothing better illustrates this retrenchment than the Massachusetts state government's plan to raise revenue by implementing measures that recalled British policies that had been so roundly detested by American colonists twenty years before. When legislators passed a tax on newspapers and other printed materials, the Massachusetts *Centinel* cried foul, decrying the scheme as a throwback to the notorious days of the Stamp Act that would "deprive the people of political information."[68] Edmund Morgan writes, "By the end of the eighteenth century popular sovereignty, originally invoked in England to justify resistance to government, had proved equally useful in securing submission to government."[69] In the first days of the early Republic, the propaganda of 1776 was again pressed into service not to attack the British empire but to stir up opposition to an American federal state that turned its back on the French Revolution, ratified the controversial Jay Treaty, and passed the Alien and Sedition Acts. Colonial governor Thomas Hutchinson, whose name in the patriot lexicon of the 1770s was synonymous with rapacity and corruption, reappeared in Mercy Warren's 1788 pamphlet arguing against the proposed federal constitution. Tory propaganda designed to undercut General Washington, thanks to the efforts of Democrat-Republican printers, circulated once more to impugn

President Washington as a secret Anglophile. A letter of John Adams seized by the British in 1775 made its rounds again during the partisan feuds of the election of 1800. In each instance, the discursive field surrounding sensitive information altered and at times reversed its political charge. Not unlike the magnetic field of the Earth that flips every several hundred thousand years, the printscape of early America seems subject to similar variations, which, while coming at shorter intervals, are also momentous. One might say that the pamphlets and letters that stoked the Revolutionaries' dissent were within a very short time directed against the new nation's suppression of internal conflict. The only exception to this proposition—and, as we will see in later chapters, it is a significant caveat—is that Paine and others often activated propaganda for political purposes that extended beyond the nation.

For these reasons, this book moves forward from the 1770s to the fractious era of the 1790s in an effort to track how the propaganda of the American Revolution kept circulating well after military operations had ended. Because the activities of writers such as Mercy Warren, Philip Freneau, and even Benjamin Franklin Bache, who claimed his grandfather's mantle, span these years, it is instructive to examine how their uses of and attitudes toward Revolutionary propaganda were updated to meet the needs of a new crisis in republicanism.

Entering printscape could be dangerous business, however. After James Otis, Jr. (often credited with the slogan that "taxation without representation is tyranny") sent the *Boston Gazette* a letter criticizing the Massachusetts colonial regime, he was severely beaten in a local coffeehouse by a government official who resented the public censure. Otis suffered the debilitating effects of the attack for the rest of his life. His sister, Mercy, neither forgave nor forgot the assault and, like other radical Whigs, she recognized the inflammatory potential of public letters. Chapter 1 ("State Secrets: Ben Franklin and Wikileaks") begins with the British Empire's consternation over letters and other writing that propagated new ideas and oppositional viewpoints. Eighteenth-century men and women utilized correspondence networks to spread seditious ideas, and discovered in the process how the collaborative work of writing and committee meetings provided a "technology for a revolution."[70] Looking in particular at the stolen letters of colonial governors and Franklin's role in leaking these communiqués, this chapter shows that the threat of propaganda is precisely that it propagates. If dissemination implies a masculine mode, chapter 2 ("Memes, Plagiarism, and Revolutionary Drama") turns to the prolix writings—newspaper satires, letters, poems, rebuttals to the Constitutional Convention of 1787—authored by Mercy Warren. The problem, however, is that her work contains numerous interpolations and plagiaries. This chapter contends that unauthorized contributions to her corpus facilitated its movement across and heightened its significance in Revolutionary America.

Warren received letters thanking her for forwarding copies of the most popular pamphlet of the day, *Common Sense*, and accordingly the next chapter ("From East India to the Boston Tea Party") examines a series of neglected pamphlets by Paine. While his writings are often placed in a nationalist context, chapter 3 instead stresses how Paine, among other patriot propagandists, engaged the policies of the East India Company in Asia and the Caribbean to reveal the workings of an expansive military-mercantile complex. This international focus continues in chapter 4 ("Epistolary Propaganda"), which traces the connections among radical republicanism, French Jacobinism, and slave rebellion in Haiti. By considering counterfeit letters of Washington that were part of a British propaganda scheme, I make the case that unofficial documents such as private letters and secret histories can communicate unofficial truths. But what is the best medium for communicating those truths? The final chapter ("Aftermath: The Poetry of the Post-Revolution") examines the work of Philip Freneau, who critics have long described as a poet-propagandist. In expressing uncompromising attachments to republicanism, Freneau alternated between poetry and prose, correlating each medium with a different political valence. For Freneau, who was sharply critical of post-Revolutionary society, poetry served as an oppositional form in a prosaic world of Federalist consensus.

The first three chapters track how loss of authorial control—as a traditional locus of identity—within Revolutionary printscape could heighten the mobility of messages. By jumping forward to the early Republic, the final two chapters extend this focus to examine how notions of authority remained under pressure in post-Revolutionary society. Counterfeits and other unauthorized texts emitted a critical charge in political debates during Washington's second administration, as chapter 4 shows. But the ungovernable nature of this printscape also generated the cynical realization that perhaps authors and propagandists—was there much of a difference, after all?—no longer had a meaningful role to play in the shaping the course of public opinion. Taken together, these chapters examine eighteenth-century media and public persuasion in order to explore the necessary yet disquieting relationship between propaganda and democracy.

The study of propaganda has long occasioned a mix of antiquarian and modern registers. So volatile was eighteenth-century American propaganda against the British that certain items, it seemed to one post–World War I historian, "might have been written in 1918" when anti-German feeling and war fever were at their height.[71] Meanwhile, American emissaries in Europe after 1775 began seeding the Continental press with stories favorable to the rebels' cause as part of an effort that during the Cold War began to look like an early proto-type for the propaganda broadcast agency, the Voice of America.[72] Reflecting on a similar collision between the ethos of an earlier time and modern forms of knowledge, Henry Adams wrote that he felt his "historical neck broken by the sudden irruption of forces totally new."[73] Convergences between the Revolutionary moment of 1776 and the media of mass persuasion may produce this sort of whiplash, and yet the archive of not-so ancient communications also has the potential to teach us that a broken neck need not result in paralysis.

# State Secrets

## BEN FRANKLIN AND WIKILEAKS

By the eve of the American Revolution, the secret correspondence of the colonial governors of Massachusetts, New York, Maryland, Virginia, and North Carolina had been stolen, and its compromising contents soon turned up in colonial newspapers. As the confidential business of imperial administrators entered the public thoroughfares of printscape, the British Empire's control over communication seemed fragile and incomplete. More than two hundred years later, state secrets of the American empire have been exposed across digital superhighways, thanks to the insouciant journalism of WikiLeaks. It is perhaps more predictable than ironic that the twenty-first-century nation-state that emerged from those eighteenth-century colonies now finds itself unable to regulate the dumping of confidential cables involving everything from military operations in Iraq and Afghanistan to unguarded statements from Tony Blair and Hillary Rodham Clinton. To date, the most damaging material released by WikiLeaks has been decrypted video footage of a U.S. Apache helicopter firing on and killing a Reuters journalist and several others in a public square in Iraq.[1]

The point of this historical collision is not to make WikiLeaks appear old fashioned nor is it to make eighteenth-century correspondents out to be precursors of digital activists. Rather, by drawing together the handwritten letters of mercantilist functionaries and electronic communiqués from what Manuel Castells calls "the network society," this chapter seeks to open a critical wedge in the history of the relationships among media, networks, and revolution.[2] Specifically, the linkage between the violations of eighteenth-century epistolary confidence and the disclosures of WikiLeaks invites a meditation on the revolutionary capacity of liberal subjects, who, as it turns out, may be most revolutionary when they cease to be identified or act as subjects at all. But revolutions are uneven and incommensurate, as Hannah Arendt observed some time ago of the colonial rebellion of 1776, which failed to address social misery with the same terrible force of France in 1789, to say nothing of the Haitian Revolution of 1791–1804 that is nowhere mentioned in *On Revolution*.[3] So, too, it would be misleading to lump together the opposition that erupted in 2012 in places as far-flung as Tahrir Square and Zucotti Park simply because media networks such as Twitter and YouTube played a role in each. Nonetheless, the enduring fantasy of a sovereign subject provided *Time* magazine with enough encouragement to name "The Protestor"—and the singularity of this designation bears scrutiny—as "person of the year" for 2011 (fig. 1.1). If news organizations were initially frustrated that no identifiable spokesperson stood out from Occupy Wall Street, *Time*'s annual stunt provided reassurance that a consistent subject existed "from the Arab Spring to…Occupy Wall Street," one who could be represented by an iconic cover image of a presumably Arab woman, her eyes fixed in heroic defiance.

Whether it is the hagiography that began with Parson Weems's *The Life of Washington* (1808) and continues with contemporary biographies of the founding fathers or *Time*'s creation of "The Protestor," oppositional activity loses a good deal of its incalculable ferment when it is keyed to a recognizable subject. Against this sort of fixation, a critical approach that tracks how texts proliferate and speed across multiple geographies from private to public and from colonial periphery to imperial center and back again resists the artificial condensation of identity that is often a staple of histories of revolution. "The manifest secret of a discourse network that places ultimate value in the individual is never to inscribe the individual," writes Friedrich Kittler, describing how eighteenth-century novels refrained from burdening their protagonists with specific physical attributes.[4] By yoking together American colonial propaganda and the digital "hacktivism" associated with WikiLeaks, this chapter suggests how the unauthorized circulation of state secrets and other official information has potentially revolutionary implications for political identities. These implications are bound up with patterns of textual dissemination and circulation, which, because they often propagate information and rumor quickly and continuously, try to safeguard network secrecy by not revealing an individual at the end of a paper (or digital) trail.

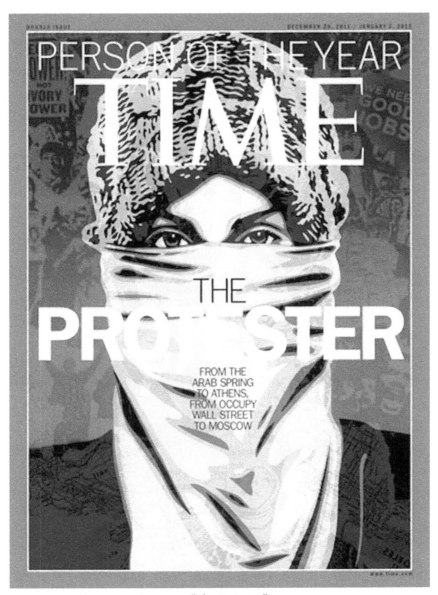

FIGURE 1.1 Time *magazine cover, "The Protestor."*

The interpretative charge here is to resist lavishing attention on content and thereby setting up texts as static artifacts as opposed to mobile materials. It is not always easy to study objects in motion, but readings that pin down texts—like butterflies under glass—risk missing how everything from handwritten letters to rashly sent e-mails do not simply signify but circulate. Indeed, meaning is bound up with movement, especially the propagation of messages and other texts across epistolary, print, and digital cultures. The contents of eighteenth-century letters subject to theft, interception, and other vicissitudes of transatlantic exchange, like the mixture of revelation and diplomatic sniping contained in the document dumps facilitated by WikiLeaks, are surely noteworthy. But an exclusive focus on content can obscure the networks that relay and spread information, diffusing agency to the point where familiar notions of political identity eventually dissolve.

To put this concern in the concrete terms of this chapter's title: if networks like WikiLeaks disperse information via a connective tissue of links, relays, and nodes, what happens when Ben Franklin is viewed as a network hub that disestablishes agency so as to speed the propagation of information? One outcome is that Franklin's attempt to render himself insignificant appears as a revolutionary take on identity. But another and contrasting conclusion is that networks reanimate notions of subjectivity that remain consistent with conventional political identities. Different technologies, architectures, and protocols shape networks, but a consistent feature is that the manner in which networks propel information is just as significant as the information itself. The content of propaganda does not exist apart from its transmission. It is not the single piece of propaganda that requires analysis. What matters instead are the modes of dissemination, including planned raids as well as unforeseen accidents, that set state secrets moving along networks of printers and newssheets or Internet servers and websites.[5]

This chapter works its ways backward, beginning with a discussion of how the network presence of WikiLeaks paradoxically recuperates heroic and celebrity versions of subjectivity, tethering politics to some rather stable coordinates. The final two sections examine colonial propagandists who participated in epistolary networks, often effacing their own roles, in order to propel the idea of revolution beyond the limits of identity.


## Mobile Messages

The real disclosure of WikiLeaks is not a cache of secret government cables. Nor are pronouncements that the unrestricted flow of state secrets facilitated by a stateless organization has ushered in an era of global transparency particularly surprising. Foremost in trumpeting these claims about the significance of WikiLeaks is its controversial founder, Julian Assange, who views open access to information as integral to a new type of network activism. Yet for all its newness, such networked agency seems cast in the familiar image—the liberal subject of American democracy. The highest principles are cited in defense of this subject: the press defends the release of confidential diplomatic communiqués as an example of Western openness opposed to fundamentalist terror; Assange frames his activities with reference to Thomas Jefferson and landmark U.S. Supreme Court decisions; even former insiders who have become disillusioned with "the world's most dangerous website" dedicate their efforts to the First Amendment of the U.S. Constitution.[6] Ultimately, the debate over WikiLeaks—does democracy require full transparency? are confidentiality and secrecy indispensable to honest communications? at what point does public access to information become a national security risk?—orbits an unexamined position. "What isn't questioned," as Slavoj Žižek writes, "is the democratic-liberal framing" of the WikiLeaks affair at the outset.[7]

So what then is the disclosure of WikiLeaks? Potential meanings of WikiLeaks have been confused by ancillary events, ranging from accusations that Assange had unprotected sex with and raped two women in Sweden to celebrations of Assange as "rock star of the year" that appeared in *Rolling Stone* magazine (the Italian edition). When Sarah Palin targets Assange as an "anti-American operative with blood on his hands" who should be hunted down with "the same urgency [used to] pursue al-Qaeda and Taliban leaders" and when a Democratic pundit advises that "a dead man can't leak stuff" so why not "illegally shoot the son of a bitch," extremist rhetoric masks the fact that these assessments lavish attention on a fairly recognizable political entity who may or may not be a villain but is always the subject of American-style liberal individualism.[8] Media coverage appeals to armchair psychology to "explain" this subject, as the *Guardian* did, by noting that Assange, like many brilliant hackers, comes from a broken home. Therapeutic narrative becomes relentless in background profiles that "explain" the actions of Bradley Manning—the low-level Army specialist alleged to have downloaded over 250,000 confidential documents to a rewritable CD of Lady Gaga tracks—as stemming from his outcast status as a gay subject serving in the military. Manning has since announced that she is female, changing her first name to Chelsea and requesting that she be referred to with female pronouns. In resurrecting subjects, even transgressive ones, such explanations resurrect the juridical force of the law that makes them subjects in the first place.

In short, the lesson of WikiLeaks may be a counterlesson. At the end of this network of "a high security anonymous drop box fortified by cutting-edge cryptographic information technologies" stands an identity conventional enough to be recognized by everyone from Sarah Palin to the celebrants of digital democracy.[9] This conclusion at first seems contradictory. Encryption, digitally untraceable sources, and the use of mirroring sites would seem to mask individual identities, after all. Yet such technological misdirection encourages not the evaporation of identity but its protection from government reprisal. Likewise, electronic protocols of anonymization used by WikiLeaks do not render identity irrelevant but instead establish individuality as an endangered and therefore cherished political resource. In effect, networks frequently do not so much disperse agency as consolidate and safeguard it. This counterlesson not only deflates some of the optimism that WikiLeaks signals the emergence of a new type of network actor, one whose digital subjectivity defies state inscription, since in the end this subject claims a legal and rhetorical status that closely resembles that of the traditional "person" of liberal democracy. It also implies that the interdisciplinary endeavor among physicists, computer scientists, and communications theorists on the complex relationships within systems, which has become known as network theory, may recuperate older forms of identity that slow down and obstruct the dissemination of information that is often touted as a primary feature of networks.[10]

"Who Is Julian Assange?," asks *the New York Times'* doorstop volume on WikiLeaks, *Open Secrets*. Similar biographical queries that motivate efforts like *WikiLeaks and the Age of Transparency* (associated with the Personal Democracy Forum) and *Inside WikLeaks* (associated with OpenLeaks), whether depicting Assange as an "egomaniacal, crypto-anarchic destroyer of diplomatic traditions" or an activist in the mold of Daniel Ellsberg and the *Pentagon Papers*, seek to inscribe an individual who stands apart from and in opposition to state power.[11] Despite the mobility of classified cables that were first transmitted, then downloaded and leaked, and finally published worldwide, individuality remains a fixed feature across this fluid terrain of circulation. "Has technology decisively now tipped the balance of power away from governments and toward individuals?"

muses one of the reporters whose articles are collected in *Open Secrets*.[12] The unconfirmed public knowledge implied by "open secrets" sounds a lot like the "manifest secret" described by Kittler as a primary feature of discourse networks but with this critical difference: instead of keeping individuals hidden within the folds of the network, assessments of WikiLeaks conclude with the recognition of political actors, who are brought into sharp focus by the presumably democratizing power of technological communications.[13]

But it is not only journalistic punditry that returns compulsively to a democratic "person." Even theoretical discourse devoted to disestablishing the subject of bourgeois liberalism becomes fascinated with the individuality cloaked by the computer mirroring sites, volunteer servers, and links that characterize digital networks. To get specific and name names, this attachment persists in Žižek's commentary on WikiLeaks. Franklin, as we will see in a bit, offers an important counterexample in his many personae let loose across Atlantic epistolary and print exchanges, but first it is necessary to chart how even though Žižek and others herald WikiLeaks as the fortunate demise of an autonomous subject, their accounts of the phenomenon revert to heroic forms of individuality.

The significance of WikiLeaks to democracy became visible as a media event in summer 2011 when Assange, Žižek, and Amy Goodman of Democracy Now! appeared together on a London stage to discuss the political, ethical, and philosophical dimensions of information networks under global capitalism. Websites across the world streamed the forum live, as Žižek was introduced as "the Elvis of cultural theory."[14] At one point Goodman even turns to Žižek and asks him about rumors that he and Lady Gaga are dating. It would seem that just being associated with WikiLeaks invites rock star celebrity, which is strange for an organization that prides itself on its anonymization of sources. Žižek, of course, was well known before Cablegate, but he emerged as a salient figure in the debate when first in the *London Review of Books* and then in *Living in the End of Times* he heralded WikiLeaks as the fortunate end of a knowing, empowered subject. No longer does snooping follow a familiar ideological screenplay—Žižek's examples are *All the President's Men* (dir. Alan J. Paluka, 1976) and *The Pelican Brief* (dir. Paluka, 1993)—in which "a couple of ordinary guys uncover a scandal which reaches right up to the President, forcing him to step down."[15] While many commentators and critics have sought to tame WikiLeaks by co-opting its media insurgency as evidence of Western journalism's progressive values, in effect, setting up this stateless organization as "the darling of liberal freedom-fighters," Žižek is adamant that its meaning not be reduced to a feel-good script.[16] Despite this refusal to accede to "the liberal appropriation of the WikiLeaks saga" demanded by cinematic depictions of network politics, the role of the heroic political individual has been reprised to great media fanfare by not just Assange but also Žižek. This fantasy of individual agency resurrects itself at the Democracy Now! forum at which the two shared top billing. Žižek asks the audience to imagine a scenario in which his daughter has been kidnapped with Assange as a malefactor—since "somebody has to play this role"—with knowledge of her whereabouts. Enter Žižek and Goodman to play the role of torturers who will use an array of ghastly medical techniques to extract information.

Žižek is seeking to illustrate a point about the legalization of torture, but Goodman stops him in his tracks. "Speak for yourself, Slavoj," she tells him twice, good-naturedly resisting his attempt to make her adopt the role of a hypothetical torturer. Žižek counters by turning to actual persons, namely Private Manning, to declare him (now her) "the hero" of the entire episode for placing a fundamental ethics before a questionable legalism and objecting to a system that normalized torture. The Nobel Peace Prize should be bestowed on this communications dissident, Žižek asserts to the applause of the audience. The forum gets routed into a discussion of recognizable actors who are legible because of their cinematic status: the daughter as damsel in distress, the quiet man pushed to the edge, the hero. This performance of the political is hardly new.[17] Express moral outrage. Display principle. Face an ethical dilemma. Act on conviction. That is, consolidate an image of politics as simultaneously expanded and limited to the power of the individual. The resolution is that even as Cablegate makes a knowing subject obsolete, the critical phenomenon of WikiLeaks also witnesses the reemergence of a plucky individual who revitalizes ethics.

Data spillages of diplomatic cables and war logs are hardly irrelevant.[18] A complex network of thousands of volunteer global computer servers, using encryption protocols first developed by the U.S. Naval Research Laboratory but since adopted by hackers covering their tracks, has earned WikiLeaks notoriety as a secure hub for relaying confidential messages. Known as "The Onion Router" or simply Tor, this software relies on onion-like layers to protect against

electronic eavesdropping, enabling users like WikiLeaks to demate-
rialize in a stateless flow of information.[19] But the reverse seems
more likely: the network produces WikiLeaks as a recognizable digital actor with Assange as its ultimate embodiment. In an ironic
twist, this entity alarms commentators who are usually the first to
defend individual agency as a cornerstone of neoliberal freedom.
Thomas Friedman worries that WikiLeakers are "super empowered
individuals" whose emergence the United States should monitor
closely, much as it keeps tabs on superpowers like China.[20] In other
words, it is fine to promote individuality unless those who embody it
agitate for causes that the United States opposes. Media exposés focusing on a single networked agent dominate to the point that newspapers were mining Assange's Internet dating profile from 2006 for
clues because, as the *Guardian* put it, "it is impossible to write this
story"—a story of how networks shred government secrecy to bits—
"without telling the story of Julian Assange himself."[21]

Refusing to dwell on personality in this way, Saroj Giri looks past
the fetish of identity to search for the significance of "WikiLeaks beyond WikiLeaks."[22] For Giri, a political scientist at the University of
Delhi, WikiLeaks provides an "exceedingly abstract notion of power"
that falsely attributes agency to a narrow set of players. Call such
players *Time* magazine's "the protestor," Friedman's superempowered
individual, or the profile of Assange that emerged in places like the
*Guardian* and the New York *Times*: the consistent feature remains
the sovereign actor. The backdrop is appropriately feudal, as power is
held on high by a small set of agents conspiring to keep the veil
drawn over state secrets. Meanwhile, WikiLeaks is outside the castle,
battering at the firewalls for the truth. "We are the underdogs," says
Assange.[23] But the significance of WikiLeaks does not consist in the
disclosures that some hardy band of Internet marauders brings to
light. Instead, as Giri argues, WikiLeaks "challenged power by challenging the normal channels of challenging power." What matters
are the pathways for getting at content and then spreading it. Marshall
McLuhan famously downplayed content to focus on the medium,
arguing that a fixation with the obvious blinds us to the social impact
of media's transmission and spread.[24] If McLuhan concluded rather
ominously by wondering about our enslavement to media content,
critical observers of WikiLeaks express guarded optimism that the
network mode of spilling secrets—more than the secrets themselves—carries insurgent potential. "WikiLeaks' action is therefore

at one level a purely formal gesture, the audacity of the act, which stands on its own irrespective of how damning the actual contents of the leaks have been for the US and other governments," writes Giri.[25] Žižek echoes this position by arguing that while WikiLeaks exceeds liberal formations of subjection, "we should not look for this excess at the level of content."[26]

Where then should we look? To form, not in a traditional literary sense but as a matter of circulation and the diffusions created by network flows. Critical interest in networks seen everywhere from the distribution of social connectivity in Dickens's *Bleak House* to the web of relationships in films like *Syriana* (dir. Stephen Gagan, 2005) and *Babel* (dir. Alejandro González Iñárritu, 2006) allows us to see presumably static texts as moving targets that propel objects, information, and other types of content across geographic space.[27] Texts do not just mean or signify; they also travel from site to site, their transit and amplitude enhanced by technologies of conveyance, which include everything from envelopes and sealing wax for letters, ink and printing presses for pamphlets, and computer servers for e-mail. Although hardwired with different levels of technological sophistication, such networks can propagate content relentlessly so that a single message frequently reproduces itself in different forms, generating responses, counterclaims, and links. But the content of communication often pales in comparison to the significance of its propagation. More revolutionary—as politics becomes indistinguishable from communication—is the mobility of the message, its propagation and dissemination.

## Networked Propaganda

Propaganda is the preeminent mode for spreading and scattering. Its functions elicit institutions and patterns of dissemination: correspondence networks, print networks, digital networks. Back in the 1920s when Edward Bernays inaugurated the study of mass persuasion, he defended propaganda by anticipating the biological metaphors that frequently crop up in network theory. He describes propaganda as a living organism that is connected at a cellular level. Rather than isolating the individual, propaganda targets the individual "as a cell organized into the social unit." Bernays describes a hypothetical citizen, one John Jones, a lodge member, churchgoer, regular golfer, professional man, and a supporter of the local chamber of commerce. Each of Jones's social connections is a marker of middle-class existence, but viewed collectively they become nodes of propagation. Less a person than an information hub, Jones "will tend to disseminate" the opinions that he receives from other hubs, creating an "invisible, intertwining structure of groupings and associations."[28] Jones appears relatively insignificant compared to the network that allows him to receive and send opinions. Now imagine multiple numbers of John Joneses linked together by churches, professional organizations, country clubs, and so on. Bernays calls this vast network "the public mind," and the singularity of his expression here should not go unnoticed, for the point of *Propaganda* (1928) is to manage and control this flow of opinion.

The "meaning of a message cannot be isolated from its mode of propagation," writes Steven Shaviro in *Connected, or What It Means to Live in Network Society*.[29] Propagation, however, seems inherently sinister, akin to a contaminant or virus that "harasses...attacks...or parasitically invades" its hosts.[30] Americans circa 1776 no doubt felt harassed by government policies, but they also discovered revolutionary possibilities within the transatlantic correspondence networks that the empire maintained. Letter writing and espionage were always proximate activities.[31] Even though King George III and his ministry sat at the center of this web, its filaments often behaved independently of any sovereign center. Correspondence networks formed a decentralized communications grid that existed alongside—indeed, often inside the very same envelope as—the more regular and linear set of exchanges that flowed between the metropole and its North American colonies. More significant than the sending and receipt of private letters between individuals, correspondence encompasses a range of public activities, including the recitation of letters aloud, the printing of handwritten letters in newspapers, the transmission of pamphlets, and the sending of circular letters by local governments.[32]

Characterized by quick bursts but also the delays that dogged all transatlantic communication, epistolary networks of the eighteenth-century Revolutionary world did not behave much like today's advanced technological networks. Still, letters were never dead on arrival. They were sent and exchanged, opened by third parties and forwarded without permission, shared in social circles and reprinted in newspapers. At issue is how communication spreads and metastasizes, how ideas proliferate and take root, how views and opinions propagate themselves. This biological resonance takes us back to the derivation of propaganda from *propagare*, meaning to reproduce (plants) or to produce (offspring) with the implication that such activities extend a species' range and assure its survival. While Bernays believed that mass persuasion provides mechanisms to solidify and singularize democracy on a large scale, the tempestuous print-scape of British North America suggests a decentralized terrain in which propaganda makes colonial society not manageable but erratic, not coherent but herky-jerky, not consensual but splintered by conflict.

Extensive epistolary networks were perhaps the most important technology for administering a vast trading empire and for making far-flung British subjects feel that they belonged to a transatlantic community. Bridging gaps of time and space, letters helped maintain vertical loyalties that radiated governmental power outward from London to the provinces in England, Scotland, and America. But correspondence "also permitted lateral communication among the king's subjects independently of the London authorities."[33] As a pathway for transmitting rumor and accusation in addition to tamer forms of knowledge and information, correspondence never congealed into a unitary system. Transatlantic communication supported a "multiplicity of epistolary networks" that relayed information, official and unofficial, sanctioned and unsanctioned, public and private.[34] Along the shoals of the Eastern Seaboard, packet ships were entrusted with petitions to Parliament, observations about New World flora and fauna, protestations of love, speculations about trade, tidbits of gossip, and news. Although American letter writers often felt insecure about their location on the empire's periphery, as Susan Scott Parrish shows, they just as often assumed "a mutual sense of dependence and a necessary laterality" when addressing English correspondents.[35] Long before assorted predictions that the Internet will usher in virtual democracy, extend communicative capitalism, or ratchet up government and corporate surveillance of citizens and consumers alike, eighteenth-century men and women entered epistolary networks in ways that transformed and, at times, severely strained identity. As letters and print traveled the Atlantic, their passage slow and uncertain, much more than information and rumor were diffused. Identity and authority got caught up in correspondence networks, enlarged across imperial time and space but also spread thin and attenuated. This simultaneous expansion and weakening of agency reveals a contradictory and, in the context of the times, a potentially revolutionary form of political agency that had little use for familiar notions of identity itself.

In theoretical accounts of networks, whether composed of digital bits or foolscap and India ink, individual agency becomes unmoored from stable locations and is set adrift along an interconnected web of tendril-like links and nodes. In the anxious "geoscape" of twenty-first-century depictions of terrorist networks, as Patrick Jagoda observes, accident and unpredictability expose human agents to radical contingency.[36] New media do not have a lock on disaggregation. A baggy nineteenth-century form, like a sprawling Dickens novel, discloses a complex social world that replaces "the centrality of persons with the agency of networks," according to Caroline Levine.[37] As primary conduits not just for news and information but also for spreading invective and fueling outrage, for sharing grievances and creating sympathy, for promoting Revolutionary identifications and spurring emotions that gave colonial American politics its unremitting psychological edge, eighteenth-century epistolary networks were hardwired for propaganda. With its public sharing and unauthorized exposure of private letters, its pirated editions and quick production of pamphlets, its reprinting and plagiaries, all encouraging more writing and printing, the printscape of early America prefigures a contemporary mediascape with its propagation of threads, links, and digital nodes. As a network, the significance of transatlantic propaganda lies not so much in specific documents as in the tangle of connections among them.

Circulation, distribution, and, above all, propagation emerge as the defining features of network forms, changing the way readers approach texts. Whether participants in eighteenth-century epistolary networks appreciated the wayward and contingent nature of the mails is somewhat beside the point since it was frequently at the moment when writers and intended recipients lost control of handwritten missives that letters became most sensitive and politically productive. Rather than parsing the single letter, pamphlet, or other document, the interpretative charge is to read its strange travels and look for the connections it creates. Out of such correspondences publics congeal. If, as Michael Warner argues, "no single text can create a public," it is also unlikely that some magic number—one hundred books or a thousand letters—will do the job either.[38] Instead something of a paradox exists in which the dispersion of texts across a network draws people together.

When British sailors boarded a Newport ferry and intercepted correspondence from the Continental Congress, the letters were doctored to include a lewd reference about procuring "little Kate the Washer-woman's Daughter" to satisfy General Washington's fancy.[39] While in Philadelphia attending the Continental Congress in July 1775, John Adams had entrusted a packet of correspondence, also containing letters written by fellow delegate Benjamin Harrison, to a fellow Massachusetts resident named Benjamin Hitchborn. Having come under suspicion as a Tory, Hitchborn hoped that he could dispel doubts about his patriotism by returning to the Boston area and announcing to neighbors that he was carrying Adams's confidential letters. But neither Hitchborn nor the letters made it to their destination. Apprehended by the British navy, Hitchborn was imprisoned on the British flagship, and the letters were turned over to the squadron commander and passed to General Thomas Gage in Boston. Adams's grandson later faulted Hitchborn for "singular want of courage or presence of mind" for not destroying the letters or tossing them overboard before British officers searched him.[40] The British supposed that they had discovered incriminating documents and hastened to publicize their contents—but not without first adding a bit of salacious detail to Harrison's letter about Washington's prurient interest in a working-class girl. For the remainder of the embarrassing material in the letters—namely, a reference to a colleague in the Continental Congress, John Dickinson, as a "piddling genius"—Adams had only himself to blame since in a moment of vexation he had penned an incautious line, although he would also later assert that the "British printers made it worse than it was in the original" in an effort to portray the Congress as petty and bickering.[41] The smear campaign seemed to work for a while, as Benjamin Rush remembered Adams's colleagues meeting him with "nearly universal scorn and detestation."[42] Meanwhile in the Tory circles of Boston, poetasters were soon "versifying" the letters confiscated from Hitchborn, turning Adams's indiscretion to their satirical advantage.[43]

The bigger scandal proved to be evidence of political infighting that Loyalists thought they had uncovered in Adams's letters. When a Tory newspaper announced in a headline, "Genuine Copies of the Intercepted Letters Mentioned in Our Last," it sought to depict

Adams as overreaching in his plans for establishing a navy, devising a new constitution, consolidating legislative and executive powers, in short, for rashly urging a separation from England.[44] "I had explicitly avowed my designs of independence" in the letters, Adams recalled.[45] The British considered the intercepted letters a "great prize," and they hoped to sow dissension within the Continental Congress and among the colonies by publishing their contents widely. But the efforts of the Loyalist press backfired, according to Adams, since it was the circulation of his intercepted letters that first popularized the idea of independence. If the British made him into an inadvertent but willing propagandist for an independent American state, then it was an idea that dates back to these letters and "not from the publication of 'Common Sense,'" as Adams took care to correct the historical record after his own fashion in his diary.[46] In claiming priority over *Common Sense*, which would not appear until the next year in 1776, Adams implicitly challenged Paine for the title of American propagandist.

Aside from revealing a touch of Adams's egotism, the incident suggests how in his estimation letters disseminate ideas and shape public opinion as effectively as any pamphlet. But for that popular impact to be felt, Adams had to become but one link in an epistolary chain. While Adams writes the letter, he is not the author of its picaresque travels through a transatlantic printscape. That power is instead borne by each node—the suspected Tory trying to clear his name; the seized ferryboat; Admiral Samuel Graves, who sent the correspondence to the British high command in Boston; General Gage, who sent the originals back to the ministry in London; Margaret Draper, who published the letters in her *Massachusetts Gazette*—in an epistolary network far more complex and unpredictable than a simple communication from John to Abigail.

Pinning down the contours of epistolary networks can be difficult— although in the Atlantic world access to heavily taxed commodities such as paper and stamps as well as more intangible resources like leisure time to cultivate literacy gave the printscape some rather clear boundaries. Both diplomatic circles and the patrician world of polite republican exchange that Adams participated in demanded sizable degrees of refinement, to say nothing of the rudiments of literacy that were denied many women, slaves, and working-class persons. Although the republic of letters created possibilities for people to enter the public sphere as faceless and depersonalized actors, in the realities of eighteenth-century writing and print, the markers of identity were quickly uploaded by a network that privileged white masculinity and property owning. This world contrasts starkly with views that see contemporary networks as porous and unstopping. "Literally there is nothing but networks, there is nothing in between them," writes Bruno Latour.[47] By getting rid of the "between," Latour refuses standard geographies of social space that assume stable centers or fixed points. Instead there remain only continuous connections that refuse centralization so that what becomes important are not individual Web pages but the links that direct users from one Internet site to another, not strong friendships but the weak personal associations that expand social worlds, not commodities like a single laptop but the interconnectivity of multiple computers that makes them useful and valuable. And so we might add: not the packet of confidential correspondence that Hitchborn ineptly carried on behalf of Adams but the wider net of a printscape that amplified and widened the notion of American independence expressed in the intercepted letters. In this way, dissemination emerges as propaganda's most important content.

## Revolutionary Correspondence

The network of colonial correspondence maintained by inkwells, quill pens, and couriers no doubt lacks the complexity and sophistication of WikiLeaks. But the routes and relays exploited by American propagandists also often lacked the accretions of personality and celebrity that have emerged from the critical commentary over Cablegate. As a network phenomenon, WikiLeaks also reassembles not the social, as Latour would have it, but the subject.[48] Unlike observers of WikiLeaks who peg content to familiar signs of identity, Ben Franklin tried to diminish his agency, at least temporarily, so as not to impede the flow of propaganda. Surely, though, Franklin is as much a rock star in his day as Assange is in ours, making him every bit if not more of an identifiable node as Assange, his agency amplified by the epistolary, scientific, and diplomatic networks of the Atlantic Revolutionary world. It is for this reason that Franklin's unburdening himself of identity represents a crucial juncture in the transit of Anglo-American correspondence.

In 1773, the letters of Thomas Hutchinson, royal governor of Massachusetts Bay Colony, were leaked to the American press and touched off a public relations nightmare for the British Empire. No stranger to colonial conflict, Hutchinson had narrowly escaped a mob that ransacked his mansion during the Stamp Act crisis in 1765. But this scrape little prepared him for the public relations fiasco that would erupt when copies of letters he sent to a London politician, after lying dormant for a number of years, were surreptitiously conveyed to the Sons of Liberty. Once-innocuous private reflections on the colonial crisis became a public liability when retransmitted and propagated across correspondence networks. In their dispersion across the printscape, Governor Hutchinson's handwritten epistles changed form—and meaning—when they were typeset in newspaper columns and later circulated as a pamphlet. In the eyes of American radicals, the publication of the governor's correspondence revealed evidence of the attack on colonial liberties that British authorities had been covertly planning all along.

Mystery still surrounds the means by which these letters were sucked into the wider currents of transatlantic epistolarity. Hutchinson's correspondent, Thomas Whately, could not clear up the mystery since he had died the previous year. In an attempt to resolve matters, the deceased's brother challenged the man whom gossip identified as responsible for the theft to a duel. On the field of honor, as it was called, Whately's brother was wounded and a second duel seemed imminent after charges of an unfair swordfight carried over from the first contest. At this point, Franklin spoke up in the London press and revealed his role in channeling the letters to Massachusetts, an act, he claimed, he committed with the best intentions and certainly not with an eye toward publication. Yet some enmity and payback were surely involved since Franklin charged that Hutchinson had "procured copies" of his letters first and conveyed them to British governmental authorities.[49] Franklin, however, never revealed who had rifled through a dead man's papers and forwarded the politically sensitive but private letters to him.

For Hutchinson, the fallout was nothing as dangerous as swords and pistols at dawn. But the consequences were nonetheless severe, as his reputation and ability to govern a colony suffered an irreparable blow. By the end of the affair he would leave Massachusetts, his native land, for England, where he asked the ministry to replace him since he believed his effectiveness as colonial governor had come to an unceremonious end. What had Hutchinson written to ignite such controversy? Not all that much, according to historians. Back in

1768–69, Hutchinson sent a packet of correspondence to England that laid out his take on American affairs. Hutchinson's communiqués, in particular, show restraint, an attitude consistent with his previous efforts to defuse the heated animosity and suspicion that tainted Anglo-American relations. For Hutchinson's biographer, the governor is a tragically misunderstood figure, who was powerless to stop the patriot propaganda machine once it made him its target. Hutchinson's confidential letters "were mild as mother's milk," according to one nineteenth-century historian's metaphor.[50] This perspective of the Hutchinson affair has generally prevailed, and readers such as Bernard Bailyn and Gordon Wood have sought to explain how the governor's intended meaning so quickly got away from him. But the issue is not and likely never was simply confined to the content of the letters. The more crucial factor is their dissemination.

Colonists latched onto a single phrase embedded in a letter of January 20, 1769, which, with Franklin's assistance, leaked out in 1773: "There must be an abridgement of what are called English liberties" (20:550). These eleven words spread through the Whig press and from colony to colony at a steady pace. The content of the letters paled in comparison to the scandal of their circulation. First reported in the *Boston Gazette* on June 7, 1773, the letters made their way to other publications and by August had been printed in full in South Carolina. A pamphlet version soon followed, and by December, ten different printings were circulating in both North America and England. Yet just as many Whig-leaning newspapers refrained from typesetting the letters, not out of delicacy, but so they could cut to the chase and denounce the governor without wasting time repeating all the incriminating details that had become common knowledge. An oddity of the colonial printscape is that news of Hutchinson's treachery, as Americans viewed matters, continued to proliferate even when the text of the letters was withheld. The true sensation was not merely the facts *in* the stolen letters but rather the fact *of* their existence, a secret that had become public.[51]

Even before the actual text of the letters started appearing in mid-June, newssheets were planting seeds of outrage by hinting at "some extraordinary discoveries" in which "the characters of some men in power would appear infamous in the highest degree."[52] When Benjamin Edes and Jonathan Gill lobbed this accusation from their offices at the *Boston Gazette*, they never mentioned the governor specifically, opting instead for a veiled reference to "tyrannical rulers," who would soon enough "tremble" once the letters became public. Pinpointing the players involved might have been overkill since the newspaper was reporting on a rumor that Boston residents were already talking about.[53] The tactic was to let the governor incriminate himself: directly beneath this vaguely worded press item, the paper printed a message from "T. HUTCHINSON" protesting that he never wrote any letters that advanced a plan for undermining colonial rights. But he did acknowledge the existence of "certain private Letters said to be wrote by me," which was confirmation enough that the Crown's chief executive in Massachusetts had little control over the printscape of the colony he governed.[54]

Hutchinson seemed to anticipate what would happen if candid assessments of the strained relations between Britain and its American colonies were widely propagated. In the letters, he urged his acquaintance in London, "I must beg the favor of you to keep secret everything I write, until we are in a more settled state" (20:551). Perhaps as a descendent of Anne Hutchinson, he had a keen appreciation of persecution. By his own words, Hutchinson looked back to "the time of witchcraft" to draw an unflattering comparison between the reign of superstition in seventeenth-century Salem and "the deception" in late-eighteenth-century Boston through which "the body of the people...have suffered themselves to be made such dupes."[55] Hutchinson was not alone in his anxiety: the packet of stolen correspondence also contained several reports from American Loyalists that expressed nervousness over patriot propaganda. Multiple media incurred their condemnation, as the governor and his associates sought to explain the increase of sedition in the colonies. Hutchinson complained that the town of Boston had sent circular letters to surrounding communities to organize and coordinate protest efforts. A supporter of the Stamp Act found the "rapid deep impressions" made on the populace by John Dickinson's *Letters from a Farmer in Pennsylvania* (1767–68) so disconcerting that he took the liberty of forwarding the eighth and ninth letters to Whately (20:566). The lieutenant governor, not wanting to abet the dissemination of the colonists' propaganda, refused to enclose any specimens of the newspapers that from his alarmist perspective had seized control of public opinion. Besides, he assumed that copies of the *Boston Gazette* regularly completed the ocean crossing—"I imagine they somehow or other find their way to you" (20:556)—effectively negating any efforts he personally might take to slow down the spread of patriot opposition.

Given these complaints about an unregulated printscape, it is no small irony that Whately, a secretary to the Treasury under Lord George Grenville who had drafted the Stamp Act (1765), was the original recipient of the letters. Imposing a tax on printed paper in- cluding newspapers, tracts, notices, licenses, legal documents, even playing cards, the measure collected revenue from Americans to offset the costs of the Seven Years' War, which, after all, had been fought to defend the borders of the British holdings in North America. Its secondary aim was more insidious since the surcharge on paper threatened to drive up printers' costs, in effect, decreasing both the amount of printed matter in the colonies and the speed at which it circulated. Irony might be added to irony: Benjamin Franklin, although a printer himself, urged Americans to economize and pay the tax as a fair price for the military benefits they received from being part of the British Empire. Meanwhile, Hutchinson tried his best to dissuade Parliament from passing an act that he thought likely to worsen an already tense colonial situation. He even circu- lated a treatise in London against passage of the Stamp Act. Not Franklin, the most celebrated American of his day, but Governor Hutchinson, soon to be reviled for his supposed assault on American liberties, had the more accurate reading of public opinion in the colonies.

In his capacity as colonial agent for Massachusetts, Franklin re- ceived the letters and, despite their private nature, in 1773 leaked them to the Sons of Liberty. The packet came with the express pro- viso that the letters not be copied or, even worse, printed and circu- lated. As Franklin likely anticipated, however, the Boston Committee of Correspondence, with Sam Adams at its helm, ignored this stipu- lation and arranged for printers to typeset and bind the letters into a pamphlet. Debates over Franklin's intentions continue to this day.[56] But his intentions are beside the point. Focusing on his agency obscures his mobile location along a web of transatlantic epistolary connections. Of course, Franklin is not just any relay: his reputation as a philosopher, diplomat, inventor, and printer make it clear that he is just the sort of hub through which sensitive letters would pass. But this dignified reputation—some of it invented by Franklin him- self and the rest repeated by biographers—fixates on individual achievement while ignoring the conduits that enable information and rumor to spread. When networks come into view, "the social actor of traditional social theory is not on the agenda.... Actors are not conceived of as fixed entities but as flows," argues Latour.[57] Instead of actors, the emphasis is on action, which flows through nodes—and Franklin, by virtue of his connections and his reputation as the most famous cosmopolitan of his era, was an especially rich node for creating still more connections.[58] Conventional understandings of identity are inadequate for mapping networks, whether it is a heavily visited website or the conduits of letter writing. We might instead view Franklin as a sort of hyperlink that facilitates the transmission of information—much of it unauthorized—across the complex network of Britain and its North American colonies.

This printscape furnished Franklin the opportunity to deploy his fictional personae such as Poor Richard, Count De Schaumberg, or the more generic "a correspondent." By Gordon Wood's count, Franklin used at least forty-two different pseudonyms during his residence in London.[59] This excess of subjectivity is also its strategic attenuation. Authorship gets lost in the shuffle of rhetorical masks that variously echo one another in ways that partially anticipate how Internet mirroring sites provide exact copies of sensitive information in the event that the original site is blocked or denied service. Yet this array of personae, thanks to the diligent efforts of editors and archivists, represents a merely temporary deferral of identity since all these textual roads eventually lead back to the historic figure of Franklin. The full revolutionary import of the Hutchinson affair instead consists in Franklin's relinquishing of subjectivity so that what stands forth is not a personality or even an individual but the printscape itself. He empties himself out to increase the bandwidth of information (as well as innuendo and accusation) that flows through his agency. As any good horticulturalist knows, the defining feature of propagation is not the original plant that sends out shoots but rather the entire ground that supports and replicates the species. So, too, for the propagator of ideas and information: it is not identity that takes center stage (here one might imagine *Time* magazine, if it existed in the eighteenth century, putting Ben Franklin on its cover as "person of the year" for 1773) but rather the networked flow of secrets that stretch across the Atlantic. Most crucially, though, there is no center stage since the deepest political charge lies spread out across the background with its hum of ideas and chatter in which no single actor seems distinguishable.

In his account of the role he played in the Hutchinson affair, Franklin chose not to enact any one of his scores of avatars but took a more radical course by minimizing his own agency altogether. "When I see that all petitions and complaints of grievances are so odious to government, that even the mere pipe which conveys them becomes obnoxious, I am at a loss to know how peace and union is to be maintained or restored between the different parts of the empire," he wrote, still smarting from the blows his reputation suffered from his involvement in the Hutchinson affair (21:93–94). Parliament rebuked Franklin personally for the role he played in transmitting the ill-gotten private letters back to America. Casting himself as a "mere pipe," Franklin downplays the charge that he has stirred up trouble between the colonies and the England. But if we take him at his word—always a risky proposition when dealing with this early American ironist—then it also appears that a real but incalculable threat lies in the possibility that a person, without exercising any particular volition or agency, can relay political critique. Anyone could be a node of transmission, everyone a spreader of information. Even the innocent among us, Franklin seems to be saying, is a potential propagandist. Keeping with the terms of Franklin's metaphor, we might say that smoke is only a danger sign and that the true menace is the seemingly inert mechanism—the "mere pipe"— that transmits it. Not all pipes are for smoking, and it is likely that Franklin also intended to invoke a musical wind pipe, which here seems to make noise independently of any player.

In locating himself along the epistolary connections that broke the seal on the Hutchinson letters and returned them to Boston, Franklin cast himself as but one link in an extended chain of correspondence. He claimed never to have authorized publication of the letters. His protestation of innocence was more than self-serving. In a perhaps uncharacteristic move, Franklin refuses to occupy the center, instead preferring to sit back in the shadows where, after all, the shadowy work of espionage gets done. The diminishment of agency supplies a tactical advantage. Writing from London in July 1773, he explained that the "great Reason of forbidding their Publication, was an Apprehension that it might put all the possessors of such Correspondence here upon their Guard, and so prevent the obtaining of more of it" (20:270). Channels of transatlantic correspondence, Franklin warns, could become clogged with precaution and slowed down if the network becomes too public. Rather than focusing on any single node—such as himself—Franklin advised that colonial propagandists take heart in the diffused nature of the network itself. Despite its private nature, Hutchinson's treachery in undermining Anglo-American relations will "spread thro' the Province" since in their networked form his personal letters radiate outward from each member of the committee of correspondence who, courtesy of Franklin, gained access to the originals (20:271). This interlocking set of links exposes the perfidy of Hutchinson and his cabal, and "demolish[es] effectually their Interest and Influence" more thoroughly than the action of an isolated whistle-blower. Propaganda flows unchecked if it can avoid being gummed up with individuality.

The impossibility of pinning down a sprawling correspondence network perhaps explains why the British ministry singled out Franklin. London officials took pains to publicly humiliate the colonial agent for Massachusetts by pinning the entire blame for the scandal on him. On January 29, 1774, the Privy Council summoned Franklin to a hearing to consider the colony's petition that the governor and lieutenant governor be recalled. Only nine days before, however, news of the Boston Tea Party had reached London to provide seeming confirmation that Americans respected neither property nor sovereign authority. Why should they be any less scheming and lawless when it came to dealing with a gentleman's letters? Jeers greeted Franklin as he walked into the council chamber, at one time an arena for cockfighting, known appropriately enough as the Cockpit. Echoes of the building's former uses were not lost on Franklin, who likened the scene to a "Bull-Baiting" and noted that "all the courtiers were invited as to an entertainment" (21:92,112). For over an hour, Franklin sat silent as the solicitor general, Alexander Wedderburn, excoriated him for violating an unwritten gentlemanly code by trafficking in stolen letters. The attack confirmed what Franklin had suspected all along, namely, that government officials would now exercise vigilance over their correspondence lest it, too, be intercepted as fodder for a public propaganda campaign. Once the world learns of Franklin's trespass, "men will watch him with a jealous eye; they will hide their papers from him, and lock up their escritoires," charged Wedderburn, calling on government officers to exercise greater control over the epistolary traffic that Franklin had so shrewdly exploited (21:49).

In his speech at the Cockpit, Solicitor General Wedderburn invoked another kind of traffic—the slave trade—in order to check the freedom that Franklin enjoyed as a conduit in a dishonorable correspondence network that propagated American opposition to British policies. Alluding to Edward Young's *The Revenge* (1721), a tragedy about forgery and deception, Wedderburn racialized Franklin by comparing his role in the Hutchinson affair to that of Zanga, "the captive Moor," of the play. To appreciate the extent of Franklin's culpability, Wedderburn quoted the following lines spoken by Zanga as he gleefully reveals how he has manipulated the flow of correspondence to exact his revenge:

> Know then 'twas—I.
> I forg'd the letter—I
> Dispos'd the picture—
> I hated, I despis'd, and I
> Destroy. (21:50)[60]

While it is bad enough that Franklin has acted like Zanga, his guilt is compounded by the fact that his villainy is itself but a copy, a plagiary of the black slave's behavior. In a London pamphlet that circulated a version of—and made some adjustments to—the scene at the Cockpit, Wedderburn is reported to have prefaced these lines by saying that "what poetic fiction only had penned for the *breast* of a cruel African, Dr. Franklin has realized, and transcribed from his *own*. His too is the language of a Zanga" (21:49–50). Not only has Franklin disregarded the prohibition against copying the letters but he has also copied or "transcribed" immorality from his own inwardness, which is presumably as savage as the resentment lurking within a faithless African slave. In the more official version of events preferred by the editors of Franklin's papers, Wedderburn simply asks the Privy Council if "the wily American" is not like "the bloody African" (21:50). The allusion to Zanga is more than a flourish: it is a move to locate, personalize, and restrict the diffused system of transatlantic correspondence. Here is the guilty party: Ben Franklin, the most respected American of the era, not some diffused assemblage of intimates, correspondents, and printers, which would surely be more worrisome. The reference to Zanga converts the now very public Hutchinson affair into a matter of interiority so that it appears as nothing more than the visible symptom of Franklin's scheming, "black" character. Confronted with the sprawling nature of correspondence networks, the ministry responded by singling out the agent for the colony, reverting to a narrative of "binary enmity," to use Patrick Jagoda's terms, that simplifies "network antagonisms."[61] The fantasy is that the propagation of revolutionary material emanates from a lone agent and not a public interlinked and excited by expressions of dissent. Attributing malice to Franklin is, above all, an attribution of identity, which acts as a drag on the propagations of an Atlantic epistolary network.

While this network lacks electronic drop boxes, what it most lacks are cumbersome accretions of personality—the brilliant hacktivist, the cyberterrorist, the digital defender of free speech—that the network phenomenon of WikiLeaks engenders and sustains. Networks, it seems, can produce not just connections but also identities that interrupt an otherwise undifferentiated dimension of links. Latour proposes that within networks "actors are not conceived of as fixed entities but as flows" in order to multiply the possibilities for action.[62] Yet this emphasis on total connection can "end up seemingly oddly anti-connexionist," as Sianne Ngai writes, because it envisions a host of individual actors, each supreme in its separate hub or node.[63] If networks thus facilitate the reemergence of individualism, then surely Franklin, as the perhaps preeminent American individual of the eighteenth century, would seem to confirm this counterintuitive lesson of networks. But in his role as a transatlantic propagandist, his temporary evacuation of identity also removes a major obstacle to the continued spread of seditious media. By disabling, however momentarily, the linkage between democratic practices and his own liberal identity, Franklin essayed to propagate revolution far more widely than he ever could by individual action.

If the scene of public censure at the Cockpit was part blood sport and part theater, Franklin would neither take the bait nor play to the audience. He listened without protest or objection as the gallery applauded and laughed in response to Wedderburn's speech, although by one account Franklin did break his silence when he left the chamber by whispering to Wedderburn, "I will make your master a LITTLE KING for this."[64] What appears more certain is that Franklin, adopting the persona of a Londoner shocked by the Privy Council's behavior, sent a letter to the *Pennsylvania Gazette* that explains the attack on the good doctor as motivated by the ministry's annoyance over communications that it could not control. From behind the screen of epistolary imposture, Franklin vacates his specific identity to claim the generic status of a "Public Messenger" who facilitates communication indiscriminately, without regard to regions, custom, or the niceties of confidentiality. The correspondent expresses embarrassment that among the thirty-five lords at the Cockpit, "not one of them had the Sense to reflect on the Impropriety and Indecency of treating, in so ignominious a Manner, a Public Messenger, whose character in all Nations, savage as well as civilized, used to be deemed sacred."[65] Like Franklin's self-representation as a "mere pipe," the sentiment here runs toward the notion that the propagation of information is potentially more volatile than information itself or the agents who set it in motion.

## Unauthoritative Texts

Unlike the fallout from WikiLeaks that casts Julian Assange as villain and Chelsea Manning as victim, Franklin would not cop to either role. The ministry certainly tried to paint him as a black villain while American national mythology idolizes him as the cagey progenitor of liberty along with liberal individualism. No stranger to the self-divisions created by what Warner calls his "untempered pursuit of print negativity," Franklin sought to keep both his private self and many public personae out of the affair.[66] Only later did he seek to settle the matter in a tract, but it was an account that he abandoned and never published during his lifetime, which is where the uncertain movements of printscape take over. The "Tract Relative to the Affair of Hutchinson's Letters" exists only as a draft with two copies, one mutilated and the other missing pages. The copies are not in Franklin's handwriting and the surviving texts, his editors surmise, stem from Franklin's now lost transcriptions of the revised original draft. "Which text is the most authoritative[?]" Franklin's editors ask (21: 415). It is a question generated and at the same time made unanswerable by the mobility of textual copying, transmission, and circulation. This hardly definitive document comes to light only posthumously, that is, after the human has entered the ground and "the person" sinks back into the very networks of print and propaganda that first produced it.

The day after the show trial in the Cockpit, Franklin received notice that his services as deputy postmaster general of North America would no longer be needed. Still, the damage had already been done, and the stream of propaganda did not come to an end with Franklin's dismissal. The epistolary network, while neither secure nor dependable, had made identity, to a certain extent, superfluous. Or rather identity had been diffused along a communication network while decoupling, if only temporarily, transatlantic republicanism from more traditional understandings of identity. Likewise, Manning does not want to be a link. In a chat room exchange that eventually led to her arrest and detention, she typed that he does not want to be associated with WikiLeaks, especially Assange. "I just want the material out there. I don't want to be part of it." Manning, as Franklin might view the situation, sees herself as a "Public Messenger." Of course, Manning now has been identified as the crucial link in the dissemination of secret state and military information, and for months she had been held in solitary confinement for twenty-three hours a day, denied even the most basic physical freedom to move or sleep when she wanted to. In summer 2013, a military court convicted her of violating the Espionage Act. Not long after being dishonorably discharged and sentenced to thirty-five years in a federal penitentiary, Private Manning issued a statement that reads in part as a simultaneous abrogation, affirmation, and redefinition of identity: "I am Chelsea Manning."[67]

# Memes, Plagiarism, and Revolutionary Drama

As news of Governor Hutchinson's private opinion of colonial liberty—he favored abridging it—spread across British North America in 1773 and led to a showdown between Ben Franklin and Parliament back in London, the governor seemed to realize that it would be impossible for his political reputation to rebound after the disclosure of his confidential correspondence. Nor could Hutchinson, or at least in the opposition's view of him, refute the authenticity of classified documents that had been leaked to the public. "Original—The Hand! The signature": the governor's staccato cries tied him to the incriminating letters that were the topic of protest and heated public discussion.[1] Although Hutchinson and members of his family had a lock on official administrative politics in Massachusetts since throughout the colony "almost every department of high trust...was filled by some relation or dependent of governor Hutchinson," as Mercy Otis Warren later charged in her political history of the American Revolution, neither nepotism nor cronyism could transform the printscape into safe terrain.[2] "Why these reprints[?]," he wondered, referring to copies of the stolen letters that appeared in Whig newspapers and several pamphlet editions. In dramatic fashion, Hutchinson conceded defeat: "Is the game up? Can I deceive no more?"[3]

The voicing of these self-incriminating questions in iambic pentameter indicate that Hutchinson's vexation was indeed dramatic. It also makes clear that the historical Thomas Hutchinson is not in fact speaking these lines, but rather that this confession about "my art, my sophistry and guile" is spilled by a literary character only modeled on the governor. What's more, this character is not even named Hutchinson but Rapatio—and yet readers of the *Boston Gazette*, where these guilty proofs first appeared in the summer of 1773, had no trouble recognizing Rapatio as the embattled leader of the colony of Massachusetts Bay. Rapatio speaks these lines in *The Defeat*, a farce by Mercy Otis Warren that constitutes some of the most dramatic—in both senses of the word—propaganda that the patriot cause would produce. Spanning Revolutionary-era dramatic satires and a two-volume history of the new nation fashioned from personal memories, letters, and official documents, Warren's literary-political oeuvre anticipates Marx's famous adage that history first appears as tragedy and then as farce. Yet for Warren who, according to Nina Baym, excelled at producing "patriot propaganda," it might instead be said that history appears the first time as farce and then as tragedy.[4] For a woman who saw her compatriots and herself as modern exemplars of a republican ethos that flourished in ancient Rome, the farce was that slack functionaries of a British administrative class were trampling on the "English liberties" of American citizens who displayed far more virtue than they did. The tragedy came years later in her *History of the Rise, Progress and Termination of the American Revolution* (1805), which despite its rosy invocation of "rise" and "progress," is ultimately about the decline ("termination") of republicanism in the United States.

Warren's ardor for an independent America would cool in the post-Revolutionary era with the ratification of the Constitution in 1788, which to her signaled the eclipse of republicanism and the concentration of federal power under the sway of a newly emergent aristocracy beholden to the interests of a merchant class. Despite this sense of decline, her considerable literary output, including plays, poems, and volumes of letters, remains unwavering in pitting an Americanized version of Roman civic virtue against government corruption, whether represented by Hutchinson and his cronies in the 1770s or, as she would come to feel about the Federalist consensus of the 1780s, the new national order that began with Washington's presidency. Rapatio had already confessed his chicanery with a previous performance, a 1772 newspaper drama entitled *The Adulateur*, this time calling on oratory, pageants, and other media of the Loyalist spin machine to shore up his crumbling reputation. The subtitle given by the play classifies it as a "tragedy," but Rapatio's scheming with Dupe, Gripeall, and other lackeys suggests its true nature as farce. Meanwhile, the dramatis personae lists a cast of "patriots" with names such as Brutus and Cassius inspired by Joseph Addison's tragedy *Cato* (1712), a source for all things Roman in revolutionary America. The commingling of farce and tragedy distills a clear political lesson: it will be tragic for American liberty if Hutchinson's farce of government continues. Ben Franklin, no stranger either to Addison or the uses of satire, echoed this conviction when he reviewed British policy in North America and concluded that Parliament had behaved scandalously during the long-simmering crisis. Reflecting on the ministry's attempt to pillory him while handsomely rewarding Hutchinson for his years of service in the colony, he archly summed up the situation by saying, "But this they call government."[5] Government was not government but a farce when Americans were compelled to pay—through the levies and imposts that they send to London—for such abuse.

While Franklin named names after he was publicly shamed by the Privy Council and stripped of his deputy postmaster's office, Warren masked events in a political allegory that "is now acted in Upper Servia." The timeliness of the setting ("now"), however, indicates the urgency of the situation just as the name of Rapatio, in its evocation of voracious greed, defines the governor's true character. In case the personages in her closet drama remained opaque, a handwritten footnote on the manuscript version of *The Adulateur* in Harvard's Houghton Library reads, "written on the discovery of Hutchinson's and Oliver's letters."[6] Her portrait of the Massachusetts governor stuck: shortly after her plays appeared in Boston newspapers, "Rapatio" began circulating as a thinly veiled code name for Hutchinson in the correspondence exchanged among John and Abigail Adams, James and Mercy Warren, and other opposition leaders of the day. Warren and her epistolary partners "sometimes wrote partially in code or left their letters unsigned for fear of their seizure."[7] This precaution made good sense since the letters of Warren and her set fell into the hands of colonial authorities on more than one occasion. Despite this fear of exposure, it is Rapatio in *The Defeat* who expresses frustration that his letters have reversed course across "the broad Atlantic" to supply "guilty proofs / Of our perfidious, bold and black designs."

Exposing nefarious deeds was only half the battle. For an ardent supporter of American independence such as Warren, the more crucial task was cultural transmission. The constraints that often relegated Revolutionary women to the political sidelines scarcely made this objective any easier. Letter writing constituted an important activity of cultural transmission, but even with the circulation, copying, and forwarding of personal correspondence that formed the mainstay of epistolary culture, handwritten communication only went so far. There was a limit to how many letters Warren could write a day (when her eyesight diminished, one of her sons acted as her amanuensis)—and the hundreds of letters she leaves behind are a memorial to her prodigious efforts. A more efficient unit of dissemination than the personal letter was needed. Surely some means for amplifying and replicating messages existed other than the daily work of maintaining the vibrancy of an epistolary network. Warren solved this problem by using memes to transmit oppositional politics, packaging ideas in ways that replicated their appearance across multiple sites. From the Greek μίμημα for "that which is imitated," a meme "conveys a unit of cultural transmission" that assures propagation by passing on ideas and information. Memes store bits of cultural code in convenient forms that travel quickly and easily.[8] While *mimeme* would be truer to the original Greek sense of imitation, *meme* in its compactness also resonates with *gene* and the processes of self-replication. Coined by the evolutionary biologist Richard Dawkins, the term *meme* suggests how cultural materials, such as an infectious tune that gets taken up by others or an inexplicable clothing style that becomes a fashion trend, "propagate themselves in the meme pool by leaping from brain to brain."[9] Or in the printscape of the American colonies circa 1776, memes jump from personal letter to shared conversation, from newspaper column to public discussion, and from the work of a single author to the status of an oft-repeated catchphrase, theme, or point of critique.

Memetic techniques rely on scraps of catchy data as a sort of cultural DNA that evolves across different media. Like genes, memes have a capacity to self-replicate. Yet memes are not biological but rather thoroughly cultural, depending on music, print, and pixels for their movement. Nor does their self-replication always come off without a hitch since changes and adaptations to an original cultural message are part of the transmission process. Take "Rapatio" as elegantly penned by Mercy Warren in the manuscript version of *The Adulateur* (fig. 2.1). This devilish code name for Governor Hutchinson caught fire with Warren's correspondents, who repeated it in their letters. It soon traveled more broadly across printscape after the initial publication of the newspaper drama in Boston (fig. 2.2). In the year prior to the publication of *The Adulateur*, there were just six uses of "rapacity" and three of "rapacious" in the colonial press (fig. 2.3). But after Warren engineered the appearance of Rapatio, these words

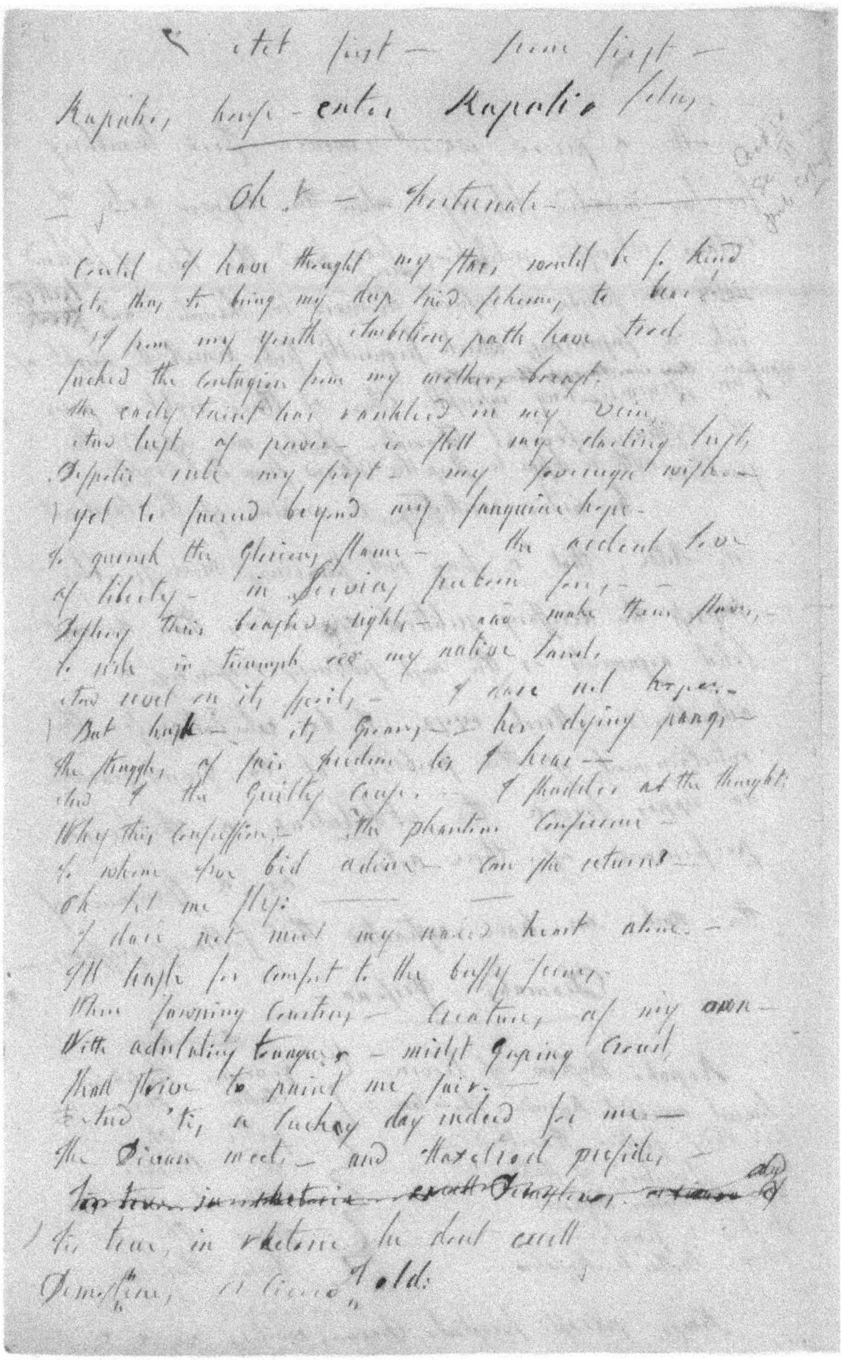

FIGURE 2.1 *Mercy Otis Warren's handwritten manuscript of* The Adulateur. *Bold emphasis has been added to highlight the "Rapatio" meme. Image courtesy of the Massachusetts Historical Society.*

By all that blood, that precious blood they fpilt,
To gain for us the happieft boon of Heaven :
By life--by death--or ftill to catch you more,
By LIBERTY, by BONDAGE.  I conjure you.
*Junius.* Nor is it vain. We fwear, e'er we'll be flaves,
We'll pour our choiceft blood.  No terms fhall
    move us.
Thefe ftreets we'll pave with many an human fkull.
Carnage, blood and death, fhall be familiar,
Tho' Servia weep her defolated realms.
    *Brutus.* 'Tis bravely fpoke. And now thou power
        fupreme !
Who hateft wrong, and wills creation happy,
Hear and revenge a bleeding country's groans ;
Teach us to act with firmnefs and with zeal :
'Till happier profpects gild the gloomy wafte.
  While from our fate fhall future ages know,
    Virtue and freedom are thy care below. [*Exeunt.*

## S C E N E  II.

*A Chamber in* Repatio's *Houfe.*

**Enter** RAPATIO, *folus.*

HAIL happy day ! In which I find my wifhes,
    My gayeft wifhes crown'd.  Brundo retir'd,
The ftage is clear.  Whatever gilded profpects
E'er fwam before me—Honor, places, penfions—
All at command—Oh ! my full heart ! 'twill burft !
Now patriots think, think on the paft and tremble.
Think on that gloomy night, when, as you phras'd it,
Indignant juftice rear'd her awful front,
And frown'd me from her—when ten thoufand
    monfters,
Wretches who only claim'd mere outward form,
To give a fanction to humanity
Broke my retirement—rufh'd into my chamber,
And rifled all my fecrets—then flung me helplefs,
Naked and deftitute, to *beg* protection.
                                            Hell

FIGURE 2.2  *The first scenes of* The Adulateur *as a pamphlet drama. Bold emphasis added to stage directions. Image courtesy of the Massachusetts Historical Society.*

## *The Adulateur:* March 26, 1773 (*The Massachusetts Spy*)

| In the year previous to publication | | From date of publication through 1777 | |
|---|---|---|---|
| "rapacity" | 6 instances | "rapacity" | 138 instances |
| "rapacious" | 3 instances | "rapacious" | 118 instances |
| | | | |

(results from America's Historical Newspapers database)

FIGURE 2.3 *Table showing the frequency of "rapacity" and "rapacious."*

exploded across printscape and were frequently used to characterize church officials, kings, and, of course, governors. When the *Boston Gazette* of June 15, 1772, spoke of Hutchinson as "the rapacious and lustful governor," it represented but one small drop of printer's ink in the deluge of "rapacity" unloosed in American newspapers.[10]

Yet the most significant phase in its memetic replication began when sympathetic plagiarists adopted and adapted Warren's characters and settings for new pieces of Revolutionary drama that extended as well as altered her original message. While memes certainly replicate themselves, they also mutate, spawning creations, which, while not entirely original, were nonetheless proof that messages of political opposition had multiple authors. Original art was never the point; instead art suitable for imitation and propagation formed the basis of a public aesthetic.

### Mercy Otis Warren and the Committee of Correspondence

The historical Hutchinson may not have avowed his schemes as boldly as the fictional Rapatio, but Warren eventually found a way to make him confess his worry that correspondence networks threatened the Crown's control over colonial affairs. After the Revolutionary government of Massachusetts confiscated Hutchinson's country home in Milton, Warren and her husband purchased the property in 1781 (fig. 2.4). The decision never made good financial sense for the couple and their family, who were often in debt and had enough

FIGURE 2.4 *Watercolor of Thomas Hutchinson's "Unquity," later purchased by James and Mercy Warren. Painted by John Ritto Penniman in 1827. Image courtesy of the Milton Historical Society.*

difficulty maintaining just one home in Plymouth during and after the lean years of the war. Yet the Milton estate overlooking the Neponset River seemed to suit the lifestyle of a gentleman farmer. For James Warren, who served as president of the Provincial Congress of Massachusetts and paymaster general of the Continental Army, the residence offered the vague promise of providing the financial in-dependence that underwrote the ideals of disinterested republicanism. The fantasy was fundamentally patrician, a more exalted version of what Jefferson had in mind when he celebrated the yeoman farmer. For Mercy, who described Hutchinson as "dark, intriguing, haughty and ambitious," occupying the seized estate of Rapatio must have seemed a fitting combination of political and poetic justice.[11] The man-sion surrendered secrets that the governor had kept close. Squirreled away in "a secret corner of his house at Milton" lay Hutchinson's letter book, left behind in 1773 after his quick departure for England as the colonial crisis intensified.[12] For Hutchinson who, four years before the signing of the Declaration, had caviled in his letter book that "our newspapers publickly announce this independence every week," off-the-record opinions in his letter book would wind up in the official record. Domestic space supplied Warren with a tactical advantage, as she turned private documents into public records—much as Franklin, with help from a network of influential Bostonians and printers, had done with the letters of Hutchinson and his lieutenants. Hutchinson's stipulations in the letter book that "I consider this a private letter…and wish it may go no further" were now out in the open.[13] The irony was something to savor: private correspondence had become public record. In appending these letters to her *History*, Warren made the single but significant interpolation of affixing the heading "Private" to several of the governor's communiqués. The discovery of secret documents in which Hutchinson privately reveals his anxiety over publicity confirms Rapatio's concerns over letters and pamphlets that Warren had penned in dramatic fashion years earlier.

In the papers stashed away in Hutchinson's letter book, Warren chanced upon reference to communiqués notifying the governor of "his majesty's express disapprobation of all *committees of correspondence*."[14] King George III formalized this displeasure in the August 1775 proclamation of the colonies' rebellion, which, as we saw earlier, condemned "traitorous correspondence" for promoting sedition far and wide. In the governor's forgotten letter book, Warren unearthed a smoking gun of sorts, revealing that several years before the king officially clamped down on correspondence as unlawful propagation (Hutchinson resigned his post and decamped to England in 1773 but George III did not issue his proclamation until 1775), the monarchy had been pressuring its officials in America about abridging the traditional rights of colonists. The Loyalist cabals and double-dealing that Warren depicted in her dramas of the 1770s are corroborated and confirmed by her *History*: Hutchinson appears as a Crown puppet who secretly and consistently undermined colonial communications. Although Hutchinson in the letter book enjoins his correspondents "my sudden thoughts…I must pray you not to communicate as coming from me," his own house divulged the truth.[15] Domestic privacy surrendered its closeted secrets to the American woman who wrote closet dramas to spread Revolutionary enthusiasm among other elite Whigs of her set.

Warren had a personal stake in defending the committees of correspondence since, according to a bit of patriotic lore probably inspired by the details of her own *History*, the plan to create these organizations for oppositional media was hatched in own drawing room. During a visit by Sam Adams to the Warrens' home in Plymouth (they had not yet purchased Hutchinson's Milton estate), her husband suggested that the exchange of communications between Boston and other locales would speed the "spread" of sympathy and intelligence "from town to town, and from province to province."[16] If Mercy Warren played a role in this conversation, her part was obscured by a combination of feminine modesty and the distance she cultivated as one of the first historians of the new nation. (David Ramsay preceded her work with his *History of the American Revolution* published in 1789.) Whether patriot women saw themselves working from the political sidelines or somewhere nearer the center, the "gendered meanings of virtue" shifted during the Revolution in profound ways that converted the traditional female stations of wife and mother into civic roles.[17] When Tom Paine in 1777, writing on the second anniversary of the skirmishes at Lexington and Concord, alleged that the prostitutes in New York City were all Tories, he was merely putting a scandalous finish on a well-established set of connections between sexuality and American independence embraced by Mercy Warren, Abigail Adams, and other chaste matrons allied with the patriot cause.[18]

By claiming the status of the republican mothers, American women invested domestic labors such as childrearing, boycotting imports, and letter writing with political significance. Groups calling themselves the Daughters of Liberty resolved to forsake tea and other commodities in support of the patriot cause.[19] Yet lest they invite accusations of immodesty for "unnatural" participation in the public political world, republican mothers kept their politics private, according to Linda Kerber. Wary of reaching out beyond the traditionally feminine confines of domesticity, women "brought public perceptions to their private world" by sprinkling their letters and diaries with observations about the upheavals going on around them.[20] Warren reversed this trajectory, redirecting supposedly private forms of writing—for example, the letter and the closet drama for circulation among friends—toward the public good. Disputing accounts of republican motherhood as a tame ideology that failed to challenge the fundamental limits of domesticity, Kate Davies views women's "reading and writing as social rather than private phenomena."[21] The multiple outlets of the printscape that included handwritten letters and poems first sent to intimate acquaintances and then forwarded along a network of readers, respondents, and, in some cases, printers diversified women's access to public debate in the Revolutionary era. With the stretching of epistolary chains, political space opened up for women. As Warren's satires about Rapatio that John Adams arranged to have printed in the Boston newspapers suggest, women's correspondence amplified Revolutionary politics by extending its message to other print media.[22]

Even in their traditional roles as helpmates, as the biblical culture of the day might have circumscribed their identities, women created and sustained environments conducive to demonstrations of (male) political engagement. Warren's comfortable home at Plymouth served as a portal to the semipublic world of epistolary exchange. For eighteenth-century women who used letters and homes as spaces for connecting the momentous politics of the day to gendered notions of virtue, "their heterosexual relationships provided the supportive backdrop for a culture of patriotic homosociality," as Davies observes.[23] Never fully public but so much more than merely private, the physical manifestations of epistolary culture encompassed letters as well as the settings where those letters were composed, read aloud, and answered. The Revolutionary printscape, rather than upholding clear-cut distinctions between domestic intimacy and public politics, infused gender and femininity into the practices of republicanism.

While women gained meaningful influence in generating ideas and communicating opinions through their correspondence, they enjoyed this influence not as principals but "as social companions, wives, and mothers" who "assumed a major role in instructing men to be virtuous."[24] In one of his last letters to Mercy Warren written just a few months before her death in October 1814, John Adams esteemed her reputation as "the historical, philosophical, poetical, and satirical consort of the then Colonel, since General James Warren of Plymouth."[25] In case this identification through a husband was not complete, Adams added a line about her status as sister to "the great, but forgotten, James Otis," an early opponent of parliamentary policy whom admirers dubbed "The Patriot" and whom Mercy used as a model for the noble partisan who defies Rapatio in *The Defeat*. As Otis's mental competency declined, a disability possibly worsened by a blow to the head he received during scuffle with a British customs official, his sister stepped up her propaganda activities by using her many friendships, her husband's connections, and her proximity to

Boston publishers to transmit and spread patriot communications. Despite being construed as an appendage to husband and brother, she was a major hub of her epistolary network, joining Franklin from across the ocean as one of the important conduits who relayed news of Hutchinson's letters among Revolutionary committees of correspondence and the printing presses of North America.

In an epistolary network that included John and Abigail Adams, Hannah Winthrop, Martha Washington, and Catharine Macaulay, Warren's correspondence acquired "a range far beyond that of the sender and receiver."[26] Never just a writer or reader, Warren strengthened and extended the links of a communication chain by copying and forwarding letters, enclosing political pamphlets, retransmitting news clippings, and even destroying letters deemed not worth the risk of falling into unfriendly hands. Taken separately, each of these literate activities does not measure up to the stuff of traditional authorship but their sum, the aggregate of multiple interfaces with epistolary media, represents much more. This range of communication practices corresponds to the several roles that Warren inhabited at a time of social and political upheaval: informant and relay, archivist and critic of empire, confidante and historian of American republicanism. Because she and her allies handled letters in so many different ways and had access to the medium at several points in letters' dissemination from escritoires to more public settings, they had frequent opportunity to influence the messages that the network spread. Her letters mix domestic tidings, military intelligence, public policy, and political theory by imparting tidbits about children's illnesses along with news about British troop movements, inquiring after spouses while reporting on people's anxiety during wartime, and making polite requests for more letters and continued correspondence along with less polite demands that republican women such as Abigail Adams and Warren be given some say in the new government that was forming so that it could be truly representative.

Signing their letters "Marcia" and "Portia" to allude to the wives of Roman senators and consuls, Mercy and Abigail joined "a sentimental-political network that extended beyond Massachusetts across the Atlantic."[27] Their circle functioned as a robust but informal committee of correspondence that thrived well before her husband ever suggested the idea to Sam Adams during a visit to their Plymouth home. Not long after hatching the plan for a committee of correspondence,

Adams and James Warren were soon drafting letters on behalf of the town of Boston, alerting outlying communities to the threat posed by the East India Company's monopoly on tea. In addition to unmasking the sweet deal that Parliament had cooked up with this giant trading concern at the expense of American interests, the pair wrote more broadly about the committee's mission to foster "common rights" and "united efforts."[28] Decades later, Mercy Otis Warren drew still broader conclusions by viewing the formation of the committees of correspondence as the single most significant step toward continental unity and the goal of independence. Yet these exalted claims remain grounded in intimate, domestic spaces. Her husband "first proposed the institution to a private friend [Sam Adams], on a visit to his own house."[29] This domestic space both contrasts with and recalls the "secret corner of [Hutchinson's] house at Milton" that later surrendered up evidence that the governor had long rejected any fellow feeling with his countrymen by condemning the committees of correspondence in obedience to his majesty's sentiments. And yet, as Warren tells it, the "connexion of interest" and "union of action" shared by patriot correspondents surpassed the cozy relationship of monarch and appointed governor, giving the colonials the upper hand to "defea[t] the machinations of their enemies throughout all the colonies."[30]

As communications exchanged across the colonies, letters from the committee of correspondence performed and enacted the concord that their writers urged. At first glance, their origin was domestic and intimate, emerging from a bond between Warren's husband and a "private friend" that seems to confirm older views of epistolarity as "essentially a private affair."[31] But the implicit protocols of women's sentimental correspondence networks made for mixed messages, blending personal information with matters of public significance. Such a combination does not mean that these women anticipated a later era of feminism by claiming the personal as political. Although Abigail famously urged John in 1776 to "Remember the Ladies" in the declaration that the Continental Congress was drafting for a July release, she and her compeers did not insist on politicizing private events. During the war when Mercy and Abigail each compared how smallpox had affected their respective families, for instance, the moment did not become an occasion to broach a discussion of public health as a women's issue. They nonetheless used these same letters to weigh in on a wide range of public matters on everything from the limits of satire in providing social critique to diplomatic relations between the newly declared independent states of America and foreign powers. Letters were varied communications in which abrupt transitions from household news to thoughts about Roman exemplars of virtue reflected the strained and uncertain position of patriot women, whose ardent interests in public affairs were often in tension with their relegation to a feminized private sphere. The lines that Warren wrote on octavo sheets and sent alike to friends in neighboring Massachusetts towns and Ambassador John Adams in France doubled as a "form of private address" and as "semi-public performance."[32] Her epistolary output, in Davies's assessment, constitutes "a forum of political debate" that "enabled the circulation of supportive information which bolstered feelings of resistance...as it connected and consolidated dispersed wartime communities."[33] When the committee of correspondence first emerged as an "institution" in Warren's parlor, to recall the language of her origin story in the *History*, it followed a trajectory already established by the informal culture of women's epistolarity.

Expectations of publicity accompanied the letters that Warren sent out across her correspondence network. Not only did she assume that Abigail shared her news with John, but she also knew that it was customary for letters to be summarized or copied and forwarded along a chain of correspondents, which, given the accidents of the printscape, also potentially included the opponents of colonial self-rule and other Tory sympathizers. Letters safely sent could come back to haunt years later. Consider the captured letter of John Adams (discussed in chapter 1), esteeming a colleague in the Continental Congress as a "piddling genius." Mercy's husband, James, had been among the intended recipients, but the letter never arrived, or rather, it arrived in an all-too public fashion after a British warship seized the packet from a Newport ferry and turned it over to a Loyalist newspaper. Mercy took up her pen to reassure Adams that any information he sent by post—should it arrive safely—would be guarded in close confidence by his trusted friends. She also wondered about the fallout from the leak: "I want to know if certain intercepted letters had any consequences at Philadelphia," the site of the Continental Congress. "Was any umbrage taken by any genius great or small?" she wrote on February 7, 1776.[34] Thirty years after the initial embarrassment that this stolen dispatch created for

Revolutionary leaders, Abigail complained to Mercy that the letter was still causing public relations problems. In 1803 Abigail wrote to her longtime friend and confidant that "the Intercepted Letter" had once again been "draged [sic] to light." The slight about a "piddling genius" reemerged as the point of controversy, but this time around the letter was construed so that the phrase applied not to John Dickinson, Adams's erstwhile colleague in the Continental Congress who back in 1775 had advocated reconciliation with the Crown, but to George Washington. It seems that even after Jefferson defeated Adams for the presidency in the so-called Revolution of 1800, the partisan press kept up its attacks on Federalist positions by implying, in Abigail's reading of the scandal's resurgence, that her husband had supposedly belittled the soon-to-be father of his country as part of "a plot to get him removed from the command of the Army."[35] The attempt to discredit Washington a generation ago, according to this latest invention, should discredit Adams now. Aside from revealing the factional divisions that settled in after independence, the incident confirms what Mercy and Abigail knew about epistolary culture all along, namely, that its conduits for creating sympathy and accord could also be exploited to sow enmity and discord.

The interception of confidential correspondence surfaced as a frequent source of annoyance and anxiety in Mercy's exchanges with John and Abigail Adams. The danger of personal communiqués being captured by the enemy (or tossed into the sea in order to prevent their capture) hit close to home. When a British frigate apprehended Warren's son, Winslow, along with letters he was conveying from his mother to Adams during a transatlantic crossing in 1780, her worry was palpable. While Winslow's detention as a spy was cause for concern, Warren observed that her son, in sharp contrast to the courier Hitchborn, showed resolve and quick thinking by destroying the letters before naval officers searched his person. Concern was not for her son alone. As Abigail wrote to her friend, "the Enemy kidnapt them both," linking the fates of Winslow and Mercy's handwritten letters.[36] Writing letters constituted an important activity in the sphere of literate white women, yet as this incident reveals, this sphere was never simply domestic but military and political as well. As epistolary networks merged with wartime communications, the sending, receipt, and safeguarding of correspondence—above and beyond the nature of its contents—became patriotic political activities.

## The Patrician Author as Producer

Letter writing corresponds to a political orientation that values open debate and the circulation of informed opinion as indispensable to republicanism. When James Warren enclosed a manuscript containing his wife's dramatic forays into the realm of patriot propaganda to John Adams, he may have thought little about publication. The couple expressed some concern over her possible public exposure, but Mercy was flattered that Adams had passed along her handwritten pages to the *Boston Gazette* for publication. In a follow-up note of her own, Mercy thanked Adams for bringing her work to "the public Eye," and went so far as to hope that "it might in some small degree be beneficial to society."[37] Warren's *History* counterpoises this openness to the insiderism of British colonial rule, symbolized by Governor Hutchinson's awarding of key judicial and administrative posts to his brother, brother-in-law, and other relatives. From her perspective, matters of public interest had been redirected into the pockets of one elite family. By imaginatively eavesdropping on the conversations that these men had behind closed doors in such plays as *The Adulateur*, *The Defeat*, and *The Group*, Warren effectively gained entry to an exclusive bastion of male political privilege and class entitlement. Her dramas thus follow the public trajectory of her personal letters: domestic scenes and backroom deals are exhibited to a wider audience. Anything less would reinforce the concentration of power into a small set of hands.

In the swirl of letter writers, printers, copyists, readers, and plagiarists who moved across the printscape of the Anglo-American world, texts were often the product of several hands. For activists such as Sam Adams and James Warren, the drafting and approval of letters by committee reflected—at the material level of composition—the unity of purpose idealized by American Revolutionary leaders. Commenting on the fleeting possibilities of a very different sort of revolution, Walter Benjamin in the 1930s linked the dispersal of authorship and collective sharing of literary labor to progressive political tendencies. Revolutionary ideas become woven into the materiality of print culture when readers transition from waiting around as mere consumers of print to taking active part as writers. Employing an industrial idiom designed to resonate with workers, Benjamin called these readers become authors "producers." Warren's epistolary network of the late eighteenth century lacks this prole-tarian accent, and her politics, like those of the Boston committee of correspondence, are a far cry from the strains of European and Soviet socialism that Benjamin explores in his classic essay "The Author as Producer." Whereas Benjamin cheered "the decline of writing in the bourgeois press" as a necessary step toward broadening the appa-ratus of revolutionary expression, writing for Warren and the corre-spondents in her network remained more or less limited to a patrician network.[38] Even as more white women found ample room for polit-ical and social expression in the epistolary culture of the 1770s, access to literacy, costly paper, and the leisure time to write were beyond the reach of most enslaved, poor, indigenous, or uneducated people in British North America. Within Warren's circle, the possibilities for literary expression may have seemed as wide as an idealized republic of letters, but for those who could not enjoy the connections of being sister to John Otis or wife to James Warren, entrance remained restrictive.

Still, the comparison between a German-Jewish intellectual's mus-ings on the socialist newspaper and the mannered letters of New England matrons remains instructive in at least one significant re-spect. In epistolary culture, each reader is also a writer. In situations where "the reader is ready at all times to become a writer, that is, a describer, but also a prescriber," multiple roles transform once unidi-rectional communications into dialogic media. For Benjamin, the diversification and extension of authorship results in a trade-off since "writing gains in breadth what it loses in depth," sacrificing one kind of literary quality for a flatness that enables expression to spill across a communications landscape.[39] While it is unlikely that Warren, steeped in the idiom of neoclassical republicanism, saw her-self as a popular writer bent on spreading the idea of revolution at the expense of political gravitas, it is surely the case that her writing was productive, enabling readers to become writers—and not always with her blessing. She fully expected that recipients of her letters would take up quill pens and become writers to exchange news and provide intelligence in return. The epistolary network, after all, sus-tains reciprocity by activating the circuits of public discussion. But plagiarizing her newspaper dramas was not something she expected of her readers. After her sketch of Rapatio appeared in Boston pa-pers, new scenes were added—but not by Warren. This unforeseen extension and propagation of her message converted her patrician critique of colonial corruption into a participatory medium based on anonymity instead of authorship.

Polite expectations of letter writing are not what Benjamin had in mind when he imagined turning passive consumers into cultural producers. After all, he intended a seizure of the apparatus of literary production that would transform the printscape into a truly proletarian environment. In the socialist newspaper, for example, "the conventional distinction between author and public" disappears, converting a once-stratified literary milieu into "public property."[40] Just as it would be a stretch to consider Warren's output as public material in this sense, it would be fruitless to propose that she sought to extend literary access to anyone other than propertied white persons. Yet her correspondence and plays did become public property in a different sense when it was expropriated by the Revolution, not unlike the way that Governor Hutchinson's estate was confiscated by the Revolutionary government of Massachusetts. Unknown hands took up her initial portrait of Rapatio and added multiple scenes, enlarging the work into a pamphlet. Readers became authors by interpolating new characters, speeches, and settings into *The Adulateur*. This simultaneous weakening and proliferation of authorship grew out of an epistolary culture where letters and other documents were routinely seized and confiscated, printed and made public, and even altered by persons other than the intended recipients.

Without a doubt, the basic scaffolding of *The Adulateur* comes from Warren's pen, and the Massachusetts Historical Society has her handwritten manuscript to prove it. But its location also lies within the sociology of texts that comprised the postal system, print shops, newspaper columns, and groups of readers that variously augmented, amplified, and disseminated her original meanings.[41] Within this network, she is joined by multiple collaborators: James Warren, who first enclosed her dramatic sketches with one of his letters; John Adams, who then conveyed the manuscript to a publisher and printer; Isaiah Thomas, who set the galleys of *The Adulateur* in his *Massachusetts Spy*; the uninvited plagiarist(s), who built on the newspaper columns to publish a pamphlet- length Revolutionary satire. The transmission of her text is precisely its production of meaning. As the manuscript moved further away from her immediate setting, it acquired new breadth because of its incompleteness and lack of authorial control. A weak sense of authorship supplied tactical importance. Not long after Warren's *The Group* appeared in newspapers, her husband, writing elliptically so as to keep Mercy out of the picture, expressed concern to Adams that a clergyman was spreading the report that a "certain Lady of your Acquaintance" was the play's author.[42] Where did the gossipy parson get his information? How was this rumor circulating? Adams responded with news of still wider dissemination, observing that different versions of the drama had been published in New York and Jamaica and that a Philadelphia edition was imminent. As an author, Warren is merely a singular figure, but as one of a series of collaborators she serves as a propagandist who circulates and makes available the republican critique of colonial government.

Was it Warren or an admiring imitator who on June 7, 1773, published a mocking poetic soliloquy that seems spoken by Rapatio? This day the *Boston Gazette* broke the news that "*original Letters*" written by Hutchinson had been read in the legislature, and then printed the governor's response that he could not recall ever writing any document that would have had "*such an effect*" as to fuel suspicions that he was plotting against the people of Massachusetts.[43] In a cunning bit of stagecraft, the editors also printed "A Soliloquy" that has its speaker wondering "Who, has my Treach'ry thus betray'd!" in the same column in which the actual Hutchinson gave his first official reaction to news of the letters' existence.[44] The Privy Council, as we have seen, provided one answer by indicting Franklin for the theft of the letters. But who wrote this poem about a rueful politician who complains that the "*adulating* Tongue no more / Shall . . . trumpet my unrival'd Zeal / And Ardor for the Common Weal" now that everyone knows that such fulsome praises are nothing more than puffery?[45] The theme and characters are Warren's, yet the poem does not appear in her works and I have not been able to locate it in her papers. Perhaps, however, it does not matter: in a printscape that had little regard for traditional authorship, anonymity made it conceivable that anyone might have continued to propagate Warren's intimate portraits of disgraced rulers. The possibility that she may or may not be the author of Rapatio's soliloquy indicates how the uncertain and unverifiable contours of authorship opened up space for others to try their hand at producing Revolutionary propaganda.

A few months before her death on October 19, 1814, at age eighty-six, Warren contacted Adams to verify her authorship of *The Group*, a play she had written back in 1775. Such clarification seemed a straightforward matter. Dismayed that the pamphlet copy housed in the Boston Athenaeum listed one "Samuel Barrett" as the hand behind *The Group*, she trusted Adams to remember that she had first sent him the satire.[46] Since Adams had arranged for publication of her dramatic sketches and bestowed praise on her efforts, he could well testify to her literary role during the Revolution. Although Adams complied with her request, the question of authorship long had been rendered murky by the interpolations of printers and subsequent writers who encountered her work. (The gender conventions that had kept Warren anonymous behind a veil of modesty did nothing to clarify matters, either.) After her work appeared in Boston, new scenes were added by unknown hands, while later propaganda plays of the Revolution were attributed to her. *The Blockheads; or, The Affrighted Officers* (1776) is credited to her (a recent Kindle edition continues the error) even though it is unlikely that Warren, who borrowed language and themes from neoclassical standards like Addison's *Cato*, would have switched from blank verse to prose and then stooped to have a timorous Loyalist in this farce exclaim that he "would rather shit my breeches" than leave the security of British lines for a bit of privacy.[47] While Warren may not have written *The Blockheads*, her characters from her previous drama reappear in this 1776 farce, expertly continuing the corrupt parts that Warren first set as a pattern for their characters.

A contemporary analogy to this reactivation and retransmission of elements within Warren's satires can be seen in the memes that drive fan fiction. Like the devotees of *Star Trek* who created *Spockanalia* as a tribute to the original televisions series, imitators latched onto *The Group* and *The Adulateur* as a way of prolonging and intensifying her initial critique. The abundance, range, and diversity of fan fiction are truly staggering, and, like many subgenres, it has thrived with the advent of electronic communication. The specific points of comparison are not what matter here, especially given the obvious asymmetries between the printscape of 1776 and the viral nature of Internet fan culture. After all, the writers who extended Warren's scenes and characters likely had very different aims than the aficionados who imagine steamy interspecies romances between Spock and Kirk or the fans who invent new Quidditch matches on the grounds of Hogwarts. Instead, the important commonality is the unit or pattern that enables and speeds the replication—as well as deviations—of characters and contexts: the meme. For partisans imitating Warren, "Rapatio" is a potent meme, which, as it moves across personal letters, newspapers, and pamphlet satires, condenses the critique of corrupt government into a single figure become a catchphrase, a bit of aesthetic and political code that gets replicated by and distributed among sympathizers.

When in *The Adulateur* Rapatio vows, "I'll trample down the choicest of their rights," his words seem cribbed from Hutchinson's letters, specifically the incendiary phrase about abridging English liberties in America that already had been circulating to such notoriety for months. Nowhere evident is the scatological humor that steers republican sentiment toward the latrine in the sequel, *The Blockheads*. Instead, Warren takes her inspiration for *The Adulateur* from *Cato*, invoking Addison's lines about "Roman bravery" as an epigraph. The play opposes the principled declarations of the "Patriots" to the brazen scheming of Rapatio and his crew. When the action unfolds and Cassius (most likely modeled on Mercy's brother, James, who is often cited as the originator of the slogan "taxation without representation is tyranny") and Brutus (here suggestive of Sam Adams) recall "our ancient sense of freedom," the style and sentiment point to Warren. But rhetorical appearances can be deceiving. The publication history of *The Adulateur* comparing the installments that appeared in the *Massachusetts Spy* to the subsequent pamphlet version strongly indicates that several scenes of Revolutionary demagogues calling for heroic resistance to tyrants are not in fact the product of Warren's pen.[48]

The first to express doubts about the play's composition was Warren herself. As she tells the story, sympathetic readers of the initially published scenes jumped the gun and "before the author thought proper to present another scene to the public it was taken up and interlarded with the productions of an unknown hand. The plagiary swelled the Adulator [sic] to a considerable pamphlet."[49] It is this composite form that makes Warren a lively propagandist—perhaps even despite her best intentions. Poetic creation no longer appears as an individual act; production instead becomes copulative, increasing in size, like a pregnancy. This "swelling" has caused problems for readers who rely on traditional signposts about authorship in order to safeguard art from the taint of blatant politicizing. Few plagiaries are considered works of art, most probably because of familiar valuations about originality, and still fewer are the number of highly partisan plagiaries that meet recognizable aesthetic criteria. Hardly surprising are assessments of

*The Adulateur* as "essentially a propaganda piece...more weapon than work of art."[50] And so critics give the writer a pass since "even a talent like Mercy Warren's could not concern itself with art for art's sake in the America of 1773."[51] In this view, political necessity trumps artistic considerations, leading to complaints that pasteboard characterization and turgid verse make *The Adulateur* more of a historical curiosity than an aesthetic achievement.

Since the 1770s the sharpness of the satire has worn off and the identities of Dupe, Bagshot, Gripeall, and the rest of Rapatio's henchmen have dulled with time as well. When some forty years after the appearance of *The Group* Adams in 1814 confirmed the work as Warren's production, he admitted that verifying her authorship "has convinced me of the decay of my memory more than anything that has yet occurred" since he could no longer match up each figure in this closest drama to his historical counterpart. "Help! Oh, help my memory!" he exclaimed.[52] The years have similarly dimmed the epistolary practices that propelled Warren's writing beyond her parlor. "Her verses were passed from hand to hand, long before publication...to receive no small meed of praise," as her earliest biographer wrote in the nineteenth century.[53] Seemingly light years away from the modern technologies of radio, film, and Internet marshaled for propaganda, Warren's writing propagated itself via the crude medium of epistolary exchange. Yet long after the sheen of their critique fades, Revolutionary communications echo. What reverberates is the memetic quality of propaganda that establishes not originality but replication as an engine of dissent. While the specific barbs and allusions have grown indistinct, *The Adulateur*'s reflections on the nature of political transmission remain as keen as ever.

### "Modern Composition"

Even if memes such as "Rapatio" lent themselves to easy adaptation and quick reproduction, Warren worried that American propaganda could not compete against a stable of state-supported writers. British propaganda was often better financed than American efforts. Tory writers were in some cases subsidized by the Crown, and Loyalist newspapers like the *Massachusetts Gazette* and *Rivington's New York Loyal Gazetter* received lucrative contracts as the king's printer in their respective colonies. John Adams fretted that lavish sums were doled out to "every scribbler who has taken up the pen on the side of the ministry" compared to the proponents of liberty, whose only reward was honor and virtue.[54] Warren was not an investigative journalist so she could not track the flow of monies from imperial coffers to "Poplicola," "Mentor," and other hirelings who rallied around the preservation of English rule in the colonies. But she could imagine one of Rapatio's toadies in *The Defeat* issuing an explicit summons for a hack to bolster the agenda of the colonial administration:

> We must call in to Aid the tottering Cause
> Some wretched Scribbler, Bartering for Gold,
> Truth, Freedom Peace and Honor, sacred Ties,
> Confounding all Things with Sceptics [sic] Art,
> And...prostituted Pen

A candidate readily comes to Rapatio's mind, one Philalethes, whose lax sense of civic virtue equates to a willingness to court sexual immorality. At the time, Adams and others in the know identified this Tory mouthpiece as Jonathan Sewall, a Loyalist supporter mistakenly believed to have authored a series of pro-British letters under the name "Massachusettensis." In the eyes of this defender of the Crown, Parliament oversaw enlightened rule in the colonies, and Boston and other hot spots would be wise to learn obedience to proper authority.

In his third letter, Massachusettensis takes aim at the committees of correspondence, deploring how they have spread depictions of Hutchinson's supporters as "base wretches...who had been sacrificing their country in adulation of him."[55] Warren's meme about the "adulating Tongue" that had been sprinkled into the columns of Boston newssheets now seemed to have insinuated itself unconsciously into the idiom of rival propagandists. Soon to be redubbed Philalethes by Warren, Massachusettensis could easily have been talking about the scene of Rapatio surrounded by his tribe of sycophants appearing in *The Adulateur*. For the real identity behind the pseudonym, Daniel Leonard, the committees of correspondence embodied the "foulest, subtlest, and most venomous serpent, that ever issued from the eggs of sedition."[56] Propaganda proliferates with every iteration: each batch of traitorous communications begets more. Even rebuttals written on behalf of the Crown were sucked into this rhetorical torrent, as the shared language of the fictional Philalethes, the pseudonymous Massachusettsensis, and the historical Leonard suggests. Leonard, who had been handpicked by Hutchinson to serve on the Governor's Council of the colony after he suspended elections to this representative body, correctly saw that the problem of propaganda is its generation.

Warren responded by sexualizing such Loyalist publicity as the product of a "prostituted Pen." Her conceit leverages classic notions of political virtue against gendered meanings of moral virtue. It does not blunt her satire that the string of pseudonyms and allusions from Massachusettensis to Philalethes found the wrong target (the Loyalist behind the mask was Leonard, not Sewall) since American propaganda was rarely about tracing messages back to their original roots. Instead, as a loose network of patriot writers, printers, copyists, plagiarists, and interpolators recognized, the task was to sow beliefs and disseminate opinions by sending out shoots—what botanists call propagules—of an initial message.

Like a dissolute rake who finds pleasure by paying for sex, Rapatio/Hutchinson hires "scribblers" to fawn—to adulate—over his corrupt administration characterized by self-interest and nepotism.[57] This compulsive need for flattery to satisfy private interests, as opposed to stoic appraisal of the public good, is the true target of *The Adulateur*. The first installment printed in the *Massachusetts Spy* of March 26, 1772, opens on Rapatio, governor of Servia, unburdening himself in a soliloquy. Lest "the phantom conscience" accuse him of trampling the rights of his subjects, Rapatio resolves to fly this private space and seek reassurance from an entourage of bootlickers. The drama takes its title from this moment where Rapatio enters the public sphere in search of "adulating tongue." Although this play would never be acted, the original stage directions printed in the *Spy* pack the dramatis personae with "waiters, pimps, parasites, sycophants, dragoons, &c. &c." as though the procession of spaniels and minions in Servia—and Massachusetts—was unending. The governor seizes control of public space in an attempt to blazon his actions with the veneer of popular consent:

> I'll haste for comfort to the busy scenes,
> Where fawning courtiers, creatures of my own,
> With adulating tongue, midst gaping crowds,
> Shall strive to paint me fair....

Adulation replaces enlightened discourse: a combination of puffed-up oratory and spectacle unleashes a flood of government misinformation. When this opening scene in Warren's drama became the second scene of act 4 in the pamphlet versions that soon followed, the shift created space for contrasting speeches delivered by the cast of patriots—but not written by Warren. The one-sided satire of Rapatio elicited a patriot response composed by an "unknown hand." Rather than an intrusion, this unauthorized interpolation reveals *The Adulateur* as a shared endeavor, much as the communiqués, resolutions, and dispatches from the committees of correspondence required collective effort.

To his dubious credit, Rapatio wonders whether the "fawning courtiers" who praise him as "the paragon of virtue" will appear over the top and strain credulity. The governor thus may have to stoop to act as a copyeditor and take "A speech prepared, but what I must correct, / If interlarded with profuse encomiums." Rapatio here employs the same distinctive word—"interlarded"—that Warren used to describe the emendations that an anonymous sympathizer made to her play after its first appearance in the *Spy*. Yet there is an important difference between plagiary and interpolation. Whereas Rapatio intends to mute any over-the-top flattery in his flunky's speech, Warren chose not to excise the lines that have been "interlarded with the productions of an unknown hand." Generosity is the principle of her composition: Warren herself invited interpolation by sending out covert signals about where and how her drama might be embellished. Following this speech by Rapatio, the pamphlet version contains a scene not found in newspaper installments, and yet it is a scene clearly anticipated by the original stage directions that call for a chamber "highly pleasing to the creatures of arbitrary power, and equally disgusting to every man of virtue." But rather than fill in the action, the playwright immediately instructs her readers that "we pass over several interesting scenes," in effect, leaving space for others to add to, adapt, and extend her dramatic extract. She literally sets the stage for "interlarding." This strategy makes propaganda central not just to the meaning of *The Adulateur* but also to its proliferation: the meme-like offshoots cultivated by this brief satirical sketch incite the composition and continued propagation of more antigovernment discourse.

Added scenes, multiple versions, unclear authorship, unknown hands: this evidence of textual jerry-rigging amounts to what Rapatio calls "modern composition." The phrase is uttered with a sneer. Rapatio is, after all, contemptuous of the false praise that his waning authority requires. The puff piece that a government apparatchik prepares to deliver to the public, even though Rapatio can barely tolerate it, may well satisfy the fashionable tastes of courtiers. The governor also knows that "modern composition" is often short on classical political virtue. What he does not know, however, is that the memes associated with "modern composition" would enable the play to expand and spread. Propaganda gave *The Adulateur* a second act or, more exactly, new scenes of patriot resistance in acts 1, 2, and 3 in the plagiaries that Warren described. "Interlarding" and interpolation extend and magnify the scope of the original scenes, offsetting the closeted soliloquies and private counsels of Rapatio and his publicists. This contrast encapsulates the difference between propaganda and adulation. In the play, the spilled blood of partisans visibly suggests this spreading, as the patriots predict that from the gore that "stains thy streets shall spring a glorious harvest." In a scene meant to evoke the Boston Massacre, the citizens mowed down by government troops are disfigured by wounds that "speak expressive language." Figurative language is like blood: rhetoric flows across public space with sanguinary potential to nurture a new crop of patriots. As the blood runs, Brutus exclaims, "Oh! Patriots rouse" and then invokes the Liberty Tree, which, although now dormant, awakens at its roots in preparation to send out new growth. The quick succession of metaphors perhaps suggests an author who lacked full control over her "expressive language." But such instability may be the fortunate fate of "modern composition" that makes critique accessible to others, especially plagiarists and interlarders. The failure of *The Adulateur*, we might say, is Warren's success in becoming a producer who set the stage for multiple and repeated acts of dramatic propaganda.

These repeat performances hearken back to a much older type of meme: the enthymeme. Defined by Aristotle as "the most effective of the modes of persuasion," an enthymeme tasks listeners with filling in details and information that a rhetorician has purposely withheld in a bid to involve audiences at an emotional level.[58] Enthymemes "excite the louder applause" because the orator communicates a message, one purposely designed as incomplete, that asks his or her auditors to conclude the thought.[59] This rhetorical invitation to participate and finish the message is, of course, also the moment of interpellation that is an indispensable element of all propaganda. *The Adulateur* first appears in newspapers so that it can be completed in pamphlet form by readers become writers. The drama gestures to its gaps, pointing the way for "unknown hands" to participate in the drama that is unfolding, not just on the page but across Revolutionary America. Warren's sketches are enthymemes outlining "an argument completed by the receiver," according to Sandra Sarkela, who links this Aristotelian figure to the raw, unfinished aspect of the original newspaper installments featuring Rapatio.[60] An artifact somewhere between the memes of "modern composition" and the enthymemes of classical rhetoric, *The Adulateur* understands replication as persuasion. As its messages get repeated and adapted, a process coincident with its movement from pen-and-ink manuscript to newspaper columns to expanded pamphlet, the satire invites textual participation as a form of political participation.

But the strange effect of such replication is limited circulation. "Adulation" and "Rapatio" propagate principally among audiences predisposed to the meanings that such memes carry. As a code word for Governor Hutchinson and a synonym for colonial graft, "Rapatio" at once extends Warren's critique while also circumscribing its reception to those who are already receptive. Media theorists describe this phenomenon as "narrowcasting" to indicate the dissemination of information to specific slices of a population instead of the public as a whole. If memes travel widely because of a capacity to strike chords of common interest, they nonetheless tend to create niches, reinforcing existing beliefs and values without reaching across the aisle or outside the network. Memes seem skittish, avoiding "the uncertainty associated with opposing, conflicting or even just different ideas," as Gary Marshall writes. The overall effect is "social fragmentation and the production of incompatible social segments"—an unpleasant irony for the proponents of republicanism.[61]

Mercy Otis Warren tasted this bitterness firsthand, becoming increasingly isolated in post-Revolutionary America, where she seemed out of step with an emerging Federalist consensus. In this way, her *History* is really about the present, closing with a jeremiad about the erosion of classical republican valor in a new nation where people are now "corrupted by wealth, effeminated by luxury, impoverished by licentiousness," and "intoxicated" by "ambition."[62] These leanings had made her an Anti-Federalist who saw the ghost of Hutchinson in the woodwork of the bitterly debated plan for a federal constitution. In an anonymous pamphlet (for years it was incorrectly attributed to Elbridge Gerry), she wrote as a "Columbian Patriot" to protest a constitution that seemed to enshrine order at the expense of basic democratic procedures. Case in point: the proposed constitution calls for the biennial elections of representatives, and, as anyone who had been around in the 1770s knew, this stipulation accords with the "views that Mr. Hutchinson once acknowledged himself."[63] The allegation rested on a letter—how could it be otherwise?—Hutchinson had sent to Lord Hillsborough, urging that annual elections in the colonies should be abolished and replaced with elections once every three years. The Hutchinson meme comes back to life, but by 1788 had it played itself out? For Warren, the reference to the historical prototype for Rapatio was a sad indication of the recrudescence of consolidated authority in America. That the farcical Rapatio reappeared in the new federal order was a tragedy for liberty.

In the end, circulation of the Hutchinson meme registers political fragmentation and factionalized division. A sign of the narrowcasting that set in with the strife between Federalists and Democrat-Republicans, this rallying point for colonial unity now signaled an open schism in the country's future. Feeling thus at odds, Warren responded by calling for continued dissemination, a new round of propaganda that would offset the very nation that her letters, poems, and plays had helped to imagine into being. While Warren would not be the last historian of American independence to allege a conservative retrenchment after independence, she was the "first reporter of the counterrevolution" whose stance against the Constitution made her something of "an anti-Federalist guerilla."[64] As her *History* takes stock of the present, it becomes sorely evident that "there has been a conspiracy formed against the dissemination of republican opinions" in a reactionary climate where parties eager for advancement and wealth are colluding with aristocratic interests in Europe to roll back the Revolutionary tide.[65] If the printscape no longer supported a robust range of oppositional critique, Warren shared some of the blame. Her polite epistolary mode seemed an anachronism in the post-Revolutionary context. Anti-Federalist committees in upstate New York that received copies of her anonymous *Observations on the New Constitution* for distribution judged "the style too sublime and florid for the common people in this part of the country."[66] Whether or not she was right about a new tyranny "more formidable than kings" taking shape, her language of conspiracy marked her distance from mainstream opinion. Decades before Alexis de Tocqueville ever visited the

United States, Warren looked at the fading of her epistolary networks and the narrowing of public discourse, and warned of a
coming "tyranny of opinion."[67]

In this new society, Mercy Otis Warren discovered that she had
gained the freedom to articulate a message that was out of step
with the governing consensus. What she had lost was the ability to
propagate it.

# From East India to the Boston Tea Party

## PROPAGANDA AT THE EXTREMES

Despite her disillusionment with a proposed federal system of checks and balances that seemed ready to rein in radical republicanism, Mercy Otis Warren failed to avoid the nationalist rhetoric that glorified the newly independent states of America. She ultimately acceded to the exceptionalism that would leave no ground for the very sort of critical dissent she had practiced for most of her adult life. Her *History* (discussed in the previous chapter) comes to a close by reflecting on the bounty that divine providence is sure to provide for "this last civilized quarter of the globe."[1] The other three quarters of the globe had not been insignificant terrain to either Warren or her comrades-in-print, who waged a propaganda war against the British Empire. "The cruel mismanagement in the East Indies" led her to connect imperial outrages from "the Ganges to the Mississippi" in a bold move that was shared by other American activists whose pamphlets and broadsides took aim at the coordination of monopoly and colonialism within the British world-system.[2]

In the early 1770s, East India popped up at all levels of the American printscape. Warren's frequent interlocutor John Adams warned in a pamphlet that Britain had one common "design upon America and Asia" that viewed each as cash cows to service the empire.[3] Striking a more proletarian stance, a Pennsylvania tradesman in 1776 penned an article alleging that unless the course of human events were soon reversed, the great "capital houses" of England "will have the whole wealth of the province in their hands" to bring Americans to "the condition that the East-India Company reduced the poor natives of Bengal."[4] These tendentious comparisons were calculated to play on orientalist fears of dependency and servility, as Warren did when she wondered whether Britain's goal was to "involve this Extensive Continent in the same Thralldom that Awaits the Miserable Asiatic."[5]

Addressing "Messieurs Printers," a correspondent to the *Boston Gazette* wondered if Americans were becoming "as compleat slaves as the inhabitants of Turkey or Japan" after a series of parliamentary measures had effectively made Governor Hutchinson, along with the judges of Massachusetts, unanswerable to the colonial legislature by paying their salaries directly from London.[6] Lumping together entire populations, these not uncommon analogies reveal how the promise of universal liberty remained conceptually a narrow idea, one restricted to those fortunate enough to be living at the westernmost edge of the *translatio imperii*. But the impulse to compare also suggests something of the opposite: a note of yearning within the printscape to broaden the scope of political critique in an effort to better understand the situation of the American colonies within a vast imperial system.

Language was pushed to extremes by comparisons that likened British North Americans to Asiatic slaves. From a geographic perspective, this rhetoric drew together the colonial antipodes while in political terms it nervously portended that the white inhabitants of the thirteen American colonies faced forms of drudgery, which, for the most part, hitherto had been reserved for darker peoples. This emotional charge seems a far cry from the measured pace of deliberative democracy associated with the formal proceedings, resolutions, and declarations that have been construed as integral to national formation in early America.[7] The hurly-burly world of print facilitated bluster and accusation, but it also had the capacity to generate a geopolitical critique that could not be made by other more rational and restrained means. The undisciplined communications of the printscape packed a potent conceptual analysis of how modern states, instead of providing security and stability for their subjects, exposed political life to the precariousness of a market empire.

Yet alarmist communications about British rule in Asia and America also traded on rumor and emotion in ways that recall how propaganda can manufacture and mobilize public opinion. Letters and pamphlets that revealed critical connections between the colonial systems of India and America are never too distant from more modern campaigns that distort "facts" and encourage outright lies. The last hundred years are rife with examples, beginning with the history of the Committee on Public Information (1917–19) and continuing but surely not ending with the false intelligence that fueled the U.S. hunt for weapons of mass destruction in Saddam Hussein's Iraq. Even though President Woodrow Wilson, who issued the directive to establish the committee, had campaigned on the pledge to keep the country out of a European war, this propaganda bureau enjoyed unparalleled success in selling the American public on the idea of entering World War I. Dismayed by this quick march of mass persuasion in the twentieth century, intellectuals such as John Dewey and Walter Lippmann each looked back to the eighteenth for models of rational debate and careful deliberation in search of an era free from the taint of propaganda. The retrospective of each was rooted in a fond backward glance at the American Revolution. The allure of Thomas Jefferson's ideal of a small settlement of independent farmers led Dewey to reflect on a time before "the local face-to-face community" was "invaded by forces so vast, so remote...so far-reaching in scope and so complexly indirect in operation" that today's corporate news and information monopolies seem right around the corner.[8] The emphasis on the immediacy of direct communication literally suggests a pristine sphere without media (*im + media*) as though eighteenth-century individuals could shut their eyes and ears to the declamations and ripostes of colonial printscape. Dewey's enlightened citizens inhabit only local settings and seem wholly unrelated to the early American propagandists who entertained imaginative affinities with colonials on the other side of the world.

Lippmann's position was perhaps more conflicted since he at first had signed on to work with the Committee on Public Information only to grow disgusted by the contempt for objectivity that the agency displayed. His *Public Opinion* (1922) hardly overflows with optimism in its exploration of the information distortions that warp democratic society. But this classic study of propaganda also turns a wistful eye on the "the pioneer democrats" of the eighteenth century who shaped national consciousness. Spared the sophistication of film, photography, and corporate journalism, Revolutionary writers did not have to hustle their message at the expense of "their illimitable faith in [the people's] dignity." The quaint backwardness of these early agitators constituted their virtue since modern communications had not yet introduced a gap between their practices and the democratic principles that had "prevailed for two thousand years" ever since Athens.[9] This view of propaganda as thoroughly modern intensified during the Cold War when Jacques Ellul claimed propaganda as the child of a technological society born at the start of World War I. Even more than Lippmann, Ellul argues for the distinctiveness of twentieth-century propaganda, which by the time of his

*Propaganda* (1962), was battle tested by two world wars and honed in the nuclear brinksmanship of the Soviet Union and the United States. To understand modern propaganda as continuous with the propaganda of the nineteenth or eighteenth century "is to cling [to] an obsolete concept of man and of the means to influence him."[10]

This image of the citizen during the age of Atlantic Revolutions as either a deliberative democrat or an earnest but unsophisticated publicity agent fails to account for the complex influence of the letters, pamphlets, and broadsides that compose Revolutionary-era propaganda. While scholars of early America would now dispute Lippmann's claim that "a reasoned righteousness welled up spontaneously out of the mass of men," Thomas Paine and other agitators saw the necessity of using print and other media to impel that mass to defy an empire.[11] The point is not that eighteenth-century propaganda is as modern as the creations of the Committee on Public Information of 1917–19 or as postmodern as the "multimillion dollar covert campaign" of 2004–2005 to foster an independent press in Iraq by seeding it with stories paid for by the Pentagon.[12] Rather than force such a convergence, this chapter argues that the association of early American literature with mass persuasion is productive because the resulting similarities—as well as the asymmetries—suggest how propaganda functioned as a circulatory mechanism that enabled such extreme comparisons as Mercy Otis Warren's pairing of the Ganges and the Mississippi to make perfect sense.

## Critical Media

The most significant propaganda is not the sort that screams for action in big red letters. Instead, Ellul prioritizes a form of mass communication that "did not exist before the twentieth century": integration propaganda.[13] The state requires this complex tool to weld individuals to the collective body of the state. Its allure is existential, proffering an end to modern alienation by incorporating isolated citizens into communities that affirm individual behaviors and attitudes. "*Propaganda is the true remedy for loneliness*," writes Ellul to explain why individuals crave a mind-set that subtly adjusts inner thoughts to social norms.[14] This deep-seated desire for belonging causes propaganda to flourish in democracies. Because the states of western Europe and North America, from Ellul's Cold War perspective, are buoyed by notions of implicit consent, hegemony can be secured only by presenting the state as being already in alignment with individual feelings and shared beliefs. Propaganda "makes the people demand what was decided beforehand," consolidating social and political order.[15] For modern democratic states whose legitimacy rests on consent of the governed, popular sovereignty and propaganda go hand in hand.

National integration was not the only possible outcome of the transformation of British North America into something else. American radicals did not set out with identical endpoints in mind— the nation—or even an end point at all. The process was not logical or measured, as though zealots like Sam Adams labored first to inflame the public sphere with agitation propaganda and then took up the matter of state stability. Unlike integration propaganda, agitation propaganda "unleashes an explosive moment" that seems too volatile to suit the purposes of a durable nationalism.[16] Yet the unsuitability of this propaganda for promoting long-lasting nationalism should not be read as a sign that American Revolutionaries had their sights set on a terrain that was somehow "less" than the state. Their willingness to reimagine the geopolitical landscape gave intermittent access to a sensibility more capacious than the American nationalism that eventually took its place. Too often, Revolutionary America has been identified simply as a forerunner of the United States, ignoring the extent to which colonial propagandists had in mind broader ideas about the Caribbean, Africa, and especially East India. The predominance of the state, not only in studies of propaganda but in narratives of American history that assume colonial resistance as a prologue to national formation, constitutes a myopia that prevents this larger sphere from coming into focus. More than seventy years ago, Philip Davidson, in what is still the most comprehensive study of American Revolutionary propaganda, took the implicit view that the rebellious tide of colonial newspapers inexorably flowed toward a democratic state. Assumptions about a national telos since then have remained largely unchallenged in the work of national historians and early Americanists who, in Jack Greene's words, "operate within the traditional view that colonial histories are subordinate to national histories and are useful principally for the light they shed on emergent national institutions and cultures."[17] A focus on propaganda helps to counter this default view by bringing into temporary focus a different set of geopolitical markers.

The gravitational suck of the nation-state on narratives of the Revolution lingers even though U.S. national history exists within a longer history of settler colonialism, one that extends from British subjects living in eighteenth-century America to U.S. citizens of the nineteenth century, who terrorized native peoples and expanded across the frontier like locusts.[18] This emphasis on the continuities— as opposed to the exceptions—of settler colonialism dethrones a nation-centered history, emphasizing other climes that knit together an empire. News appearing in the 1770s about the "poor natives of Bengal," the monopoly of the East India Company, and the atrocities committed by British troops all reflect an anxious but misplaced awareness of settler colonialism. Anxious because American propagandists exploited fears that colonists were about to share the fate of colonized people in India. Misplaced because this worry effectively blinded the settlers of British North America to their own roles in removing American Indians. Colonists do not simply reside in marginal units found along a periphery. They also inhabit a larger system of colonization that forces subjects to confront their location within a complex set of economic, political, and cultural relations, which, in the case of Revolutionary America, were potentially worldwide.

For American colonials qua patriots, it was difficult to shake the dawn of national independence free from the mercantilist shadow of empire. Even as propagandists were gearing up for national independence, they were also living prior to the establishment of an American state. As colonial inhabitants but not quite independent citizens, Americans during the decade of the 1770s became interstitial subjects, stuck in the strange position of being incompletely "after" the empire but still "before" the nation. Far from disabling, however, this odd temporality supplied tactical insight for those trying to understand their place at the edges of an imperial system. Within Revolutionary propaganda, an emergent nationalism became the vehicle for conveying an incipient geopolitical critique with anticolonial overtones. Paine's simultaneous devotion to nationalist cheerleading and denunciations of imperialism did not stop at the shores of North America but instead extended to other outposts in the hemisphere and beyond. His pamphlets and newspaper writings were part of a loose set of print materials that placed the extremes of America and East India along a shared axis of critique. Such propaganda functioned not as comparative literature but as literature that compares.[19]

The first task of the comparison was to suggest how colonials in one part of the British Empire (such as America) were never living only locally or regionally but were instead exposed to an economic and military system that likened them to colonials in other hemispheres. Such convergence provides the context of "'Asiatick'-America," as the next section of this chapter is titled. In making comparisons between East India and America, propagandists expanded the appeal to independence beyond national frameworks, locating their grievances well beyond state-centered contexts. This unconcern for the state represents an important strand—one that competes with national attachments—of Revolutionary propaganda. As later sections of this chapter will show, pamphleteers such as Paine and printers such as Isaiah Thomas of the *Massachusetts Spy* reaped the conceptual possibilities of this situation, using colonial newspapers and pamphlets to locate America within a different political geography. Propaganda in this vein presented an image of America as decidedly unexceptional, its imbrication in a colonial system of war and trade at once spelling a serious threat to liberty and providing knowledge of global contexts crucial to making strategic comparisons. In the 1770s, these aspects of propaganda supplied a basis for critical media.

By staging and disseminating a geopolitical analysis, the printscape of the Revolution offers a glimpse of what made it, at times, revolutionary: its seizure of past histories of the colonial system in India and elsewhere as points of comparison for projecting the future of America. Fusing together disjointed times, an expanded comparative history renders the recent past of one colonial space as the future of another. In this delayed simultaneity, the operations of the British Empire in India in the 1760s–1770s prefigure the peril thought to be facing American cities along the Atlantic seaboard circa fall 1773. Such simultaneity might even be drawn out still further to the point where that conjunction recalls the coordination of commercial and military empire today.

## "Asiatick" America

In October 1773, a Revolutionary broadside warned of threats against liberty and commerce by asking American subjects to compare themselves to "the helpless Asiaticks" of British India.[20] Along with several companion pieces, this piece was later bound into a pamphlet entitled *The Alarm* that exhumes Queen Elizabeth I's chartering of the East India Company, details the extent of its monopoly, compares its operations to the excesses of Spanish conquistadores in sixteenth-century Mexico, accuses it of creating a catastrophic famine in Bengal—all to provide a systemic critique of how the colonies were caught in a web of global mercantilism. Beware the schemes of Parliament and the Crown, the author of this leaflet cautions, or colonists will soon find themselves reduced to a state of exotic vassalage. Since Americans at this moment tended to be neither Asian nor passive, but were instead outraged by news that ships carrying the trade of the East India Company were bearing down on North American ports, perhaps the danger implicit in this comparison seemed rather distant, no doubt as far away as the Indian subcontinent. For colonists bold enough to entertain ideas of independence, the prospect of forging a new nationalism was so untested an idea that thinking about oppression on the other side of the globe might seem a luxury for another time, not what was needed at a moment of crisis when stirring up partisan feelings at home remained the most pressing task. Crisis is the ideal breeding ground for agitation propaganda, but, according to Ellul, its capacity to incite action is tempered by its transitory effects. Unable to sustain anything as profound as the state, the relative "weakness" of such propaganda also determines its "strength" in encouraging other-than-national connections. It is a fitting coincidence that Tom Paine a few years later launched a global critique through a series of propaganda articles known as *The American Crisis*.

India as well as other conflicted zones within the imperium served as revolutionary relays, linking Americans to histories of worldwide struggle. The appearance of a propaganda song in the pages of the *Virginia Gazette* celebrating the dumping of the tea—"into the deep descended / Cursed Weed of China's Coast"—provides evidence that this consciousness was more than a New England phenomenon.[21] Through the efforts of such popularizers and publicists as this anonymous songster, early American propaganda outlined an experimental political geography, one that sought to pinpoint the location of the North American colonies with respect to what was then the most powerful and sophisticated trading empire on earth. Never merely spatial, this assemblage demanded a revolutionary understanding of what a future history might look like. In contrast to conventional assumptions that have shaped understandings of early American literature, this vantage did not have its sights set on a national outcome or state stability but instead coolly appraised the British coordination of mercantile and military power to imagine wider ambits of space and time. Edmund Burke echoed this view of the British system by conjuring up the empire's "mighty and strangely diversified mass," which Parliament had bungled by assuming "that the natives of Hindostan and those of Virginia could be ordered in the same manner."[22] As with the Revolutionary broadside comparing Americans and "Asiaticks," Burke's April 1777 report to his constituents seeks to convey a lesson about comparative conditions on a global scale.

Thriving port cities such as Boston, New York, Philadelphia, and Charleston traded in much more than goods. Writing and print were exchanged with as much avidity as commodities—in no small part because novels, almanacs, pamphlets, and other artifacts of the printscape were commodities. Bundles of English newspapers along with the latest correspondence arrived on ships loaded with porcelain, silks, and, of course, tea. This "Atlantic newspaper system," to use William Warner's description, acted as "shareware" that could be "adopted and modified according to each paper's needs and interests."[23] The six-week ocean crossing to America also brought back letters from colonial agents, whose ranks included Franklin and Burke, that conveyed intelligence about Parliament's recent doings. The docks served as "vital networks of communications," which mobilized both people and ideas up and down the Atlantic seaboard, according to Benjamin Carp. These circulations supplied "a political awareness of imperial proportions" so that many American colonials, above all city dwellers, acquired something of a "global outlook" as they chafed against the policies of the British Empire.[24] Instead of simply promoting ideas of national independence— indeed such ideas were infrequent before 1775—propagandists seized on East India and other global signposts to frame the magnitude of their defiance. The patriots' talk about natural liberty ebbed and flowed in accord with the "planetary currents" of eighteenth-century revolt that Peter Linebaugh and Marcus Rediker see as part of the Atlantic circulation of labor and commodities.[25]

Yet this geography of critique never shed its provincial origins. Stuck at one end of the British Empire, British Americans were sensitive to Asian associations because the Tea Act of 1773, whose wording expressly promoted "the benefit and advantage...[of] merchants of England trading to the East Indies," had tied their fortunes to colonials at the other end.[26] For years, more than one white Creole of the Atlantic tried to compensate for this peripheral standing, as Franklin had in the 1750s–1760s, by so heartily identifying with the metropole as to "become a thoroughgoing imperialist and royalist," as Gordon Wood observes.[27] In practical terms alone, Asian commodities were never all that remote, and Franklin had wondered about the feasibility of transplanting silk production and crops from China to the American tropics. But tensions specific to the printscape of 1773 revealed that imperial associations might circulate in unpredictable ways. Starting in the fall of that year, Boston newspapers regularly ran short updates reporting that the tea had not been permitted to land in Philadelphia and New York, hinting that port cities in Massachusetts should be likewise defiant.

At the height of the crisis over tea, a pseudonymous contribution to the *Massachusetts Spy* that took up the entire first page of the December 16, 1773, issue laid out in acerbic detail the "Rules by Which a Great Empire May Be Reduced to a Small One." Its sarcastic suggestion that the colonies should be sent "prodigals who have ruined their fortunes, broken gamesters or stockjobbers...as *Governors* for they will probably be rapacious" echoed Mercy Otis Warren's casting of Hutchinson as Rapatio. So, too, the headnote that the enclosed item had been "presented privately to a *late minister*" and was "now first published" recalled the chain of circumstances that had exposed Hutchinson's private letters to public scrutiny—in the pages of this very newspaper. Despite these allusions to Massachusetts politics, the advice dispensed seems deliberately vague. America is never mentioned, and the general outlines of the satire make for universal recommendations that "however peaceably your colonies have submitted to your government...you are to suppose them always inclined to revolt and treat them accordingly."[28] The rules strive for broad applicability so that while the irony clearly draws on the situation of the American colonies, its outlines are loose enough that the entire geography of empire is in play. The author of "Rules by Which a Great Empire May Be Reduced to a Small One," cloaked by the pseudonym Q.E.D., positions Americanist critique within a wider frame.

Ben Franklin, of course, has long been known as the author of this hoax. Published first in the *Public Advertiser* of London in September

1773, Franklin's satire, by the time it turned up in the *Massachusetts Spy* four months later, had acquired more precise contours to bring its general reflections about colonies into a bit sharper focus, as British North America and East India entered the picture. The role of printscape in creating this comparison began with the transit of news and rumor from a London newspaper to Isaiah Thomas, whose *Spy* regularly reprinted items from the British press. It then became better defined by other notices in the December 16 issue of the newspaper, which included intelligence received by the Committee of Correspondence that the townspeople of Plymouth, among them Mercy's husband, James Warren, had signed a series of resolutions about "the dangerous nature and tendency of importing teas here…by the India company."[29] News that residents of the coastal village of Marblehead had drafted similar resolves also found place in this issue alongside Franklin's twenty rules for disaggregating an empire. Via the multiple spaces—London, India, Boston, and outlying towns—that converge in the newspaper, print set in motion a series of relays that make "common cause," to quote the language of the Plymouth resolutions, out of the interconnections of empire.[30] Without straining for causality, we might enumerate one more congruity: later that evening, hours after the last copies of the *Spy* containing Franklin's satire had sold, a band of men disguised as "Mohawks" descended on the waterfront and dumped forty-six tons of tea belonging to the East India Company into Boston harbor.

While imprecise and largely metaphoric, the linkages between Americans and "Asiaticks" suggest awareness of a vast, coordinated system of military and mercantile interests that positioned Americans within a global commercial empire. Invocations of the colonial antipodes across Revolutionary printscape represent something different than an early attempt at international history or even an incipient transnational literary culture. Rather than take some form of the nation as a reference point, more than a few American advocates for revolution framed their critique against an expansive backdrop that connected, however loosely, British India and British North America. For a brief but conceptually resonant moment, people thought about politics and culture in revolutionary ways that become virtually unimaginable after "1776" retroactively established the nation-state as a governing principle of literary and historical consciousness. Even though "national histories are part of global histories," as Thomas Bender writes, there remain other, alternative units of the global.[31]

These units may be "less" than the nation, but as in the case of colonial pamphleteers and propagandists whose critical fascination with Asia, the East India Company, and tea preceded national consciousness, less can often be more. That is, less nationalism is more comparison.[32]

The many venues provided by print—Franklin's hoax sent from London, circular letters transmitted by committees of correspondence, the latest dispatches from seaside towns, and the broadsides and pamphlets about the East India Company—created an unorthodox testing ground for comparative thinking of this sort. Despite the tendency to articulate the colonies' grievances within the context of British nationalism, by 1773 some Americans found the nation too narrow a conceptual entity for framing their political and economic protests. For such critics, the intensification of British nationalism in the decades before the Revolution had left Americans behind as second-class subjects in the bid to assume the mantle of historic British legal protections and equity. One alternative was to fire back with the discourse of natural rights because its vague, universalizing contours gave colonial ideologists room that was no longer found in the constricted discourse of British nationalism.[33] A significantly different alternative seized by agent provocateurs of Revolutionary printscape lay not in the universal but in the global.

As opposed to the philosophical abstractions of universalism, a geography of critique attuned to the dimensions of British rule obsessed on America's location within a world-system of trade and military expenditure. For Revolutionaries contending with the "global expansion of the capitalist world-economy" that characterized the late eighteenth century, the plight of colonies did not automatically flow into the tapered channels of protonational discourse.[34] After all, on the eve of the Revolution, of the nearly thirty-eight million subjects of the British Empire, only 8.4 percent lived in all of the Americas. Even with the British Isles added to the mix, the majority of the imperial population (58.1 percent) lived in East and South Asia. As Carole Shammas concludes from this data, "empires not states constituted the standard global political unit" for most eighteenth-century subjects.[35] To understand the size and scope of their enemy, to tackle the immensity of a system that encased their present desires and future aspirations, American agitators enlarged the scope of analysis, in effect, by converting patriotic zeal into an insurgent geopolitical discourse.

## East India and America

Even a commentator as astute as Hannah Arendt—her *On Revolution* is a comparative political study without rival—could write that the American Revolution "has remained an event of little more than local importance."[36] The War of Independence did not echo with world historical significance, despite the grandiose claims often made about a minor skirmish at Lexington Green between farmers and British regulars. That honor, for Arendt, instead lies with the French Revolution, which challenged the existence of social misery in ways that the thirteen colonies, financially dependent on and morally compromised by slavery, could not. *On Revolution* is a work of political theory that examines the philosophy of James Madison, Robespierre, and other eighteenth-century statesmen, unmindful of the view from below. This below, as Linebaugh and Rediker specify, can be located below decks: the working-class, multiethnic world of sailors and slaves that posed a sprawling, hydra-headed threat to European and American powers engaged in global traffic. "The American Revolution," they assert, "was neither an elite nor a national event, since its genesis, process, outcome, and influence all depended on the circulation of proletarian experience around the Atlantic."[37] Their perspective suggests that the American Revolution was not merely American but rather a transatlantic phenomenon driven by the unprecedented development of commercial capital on a world scale. Following the same routes as Bohea, Souchon, and Congou tea as well as other commodities, the oceanic compass of this protest pointed to colonial enterprises from the Americas to East India and China.

The colonial printscape facilitated a critical outlook that was as extensive as the British Empire itself. At the same time, though, this perspective remained circumscribed by the imperium, rarely exceeding the geography of Britain's commercial dominion. Whatever global thinking existed in the papers printed along the Atlantic seaboard came in reaction to British imperial policies. When Benjamin Rush in a letter headlined "On Patriotism" that appeared in the *Pennsylvania Journal* warned of "the machinations of the enemies of our country to enslave us by means of the East-India Company," he located civic virtue amid an empire of goods.[38] The inside pages of this issue of October 20, 1773, matched Rush's high-minded language about "the cause of liberty" with threatening specificity by urging that "a committee be immediately chosen to wait on those gent-leman" who have been "appointed by the East-India Company" to sell the inbound shipment of tea. Taking Rush's counsel "on patri-otism" as agitation propaganda, the committee was directed to gently remind anyone serving as a consignee for tea that he was "an enemy to his country" and would do well "immediately to resign their appointment."[39] Whether coordinated or not, this unsigned directive intensifies Rush's letter, displaying how print forces confrontations: feelings about *amor patriae* run up against the realities of East India commerce, a rousing article on patriotism is paired with a plan of intimidation, and groups of partisans pay visits to anyone who might disagree.

The overlapping of nationalist sentiment and imperial awareness found in these specimens from Massachusetts and Pennsylvania pa-pers represents a complex condition of simultaneity: because propa-ganda did not necessarily promote state integration, more than a few writers temporarily conceived of American identity not as some-thing separate or exceptional but as part of the same oceanic cur-rents that made Britain's commercial empire possible. Printscape in these contexts encouraged a somewhat different experience of si-multaneity than that described by Benedict Anderson in his account of print capitalism and the origins of national consciousness.[40] American writing about Asian commodities, for instance, reveals the coincidence of imperial belonging, patriotic identification, and incipient global awareness. These competing tensions, many of which would not be sorted out for generations, as the work of Kariann Yokota suggests, made the path to national consciousness fitful and episodic.[41] Certainly in 1773, many Americans, if not most, still thought of themselves as British. Appealing to historic English liberties while comparing their experience to colonials on the other side of the world, propagandists employed a geography of critique that entailed multiple locations.

Consider John Dickinson, who used a couple of platforms, first the newspaper letter and then the broadside, to explore what the import of East India tea meant for America. In his worry over reve-nue-grabbing policies in Ireland and fears that American colonists would soon bear the brunt of British designs on Florida and Nova Scotia, Dickinson in 1767 had stressed the importance of colonial unity in his letters to the *Pennsylvania Chronicle*, which were col-lected in pamphlet form the following year and published as *Letters*

*from a Farmer in Pennsylvania.* Sometimes viewed as a moderate—
Dickinson refused to sign the Declaration of Independence because
he thought reconciliation still a possibility—he articulated an analysis that identifies the dangers of what from our present perspective
looks like an early version of the military-industrial complex. In
case this label seems anachronistic, we might more appropriately
say that from an eighteenth-century perspective Dickinson was
confronting the military-mercantile complex. For economic historians of empire, this connection stresses the degree to which British
financial policies were organized around the production of war.
Spending on military operations and the resulting debt amounted
to a whopping 80–90 percent of the total governmental budget.[42]
The immensity of this coordinated commercial and military empire
comes across in a comparison to estimates from today's liberal blog-
osphere that anywhere from 30–50 percent of the U.S. national
budget is earmarked for the Pentagon.[43] Continuing war became
Britain's chief export. Perhaps most significant was not the colossal
nature of this war machine but the creative financing that allowed
Britain to "pay for large-scale war without bankrupting its citizens
and, thereby, sparking the internal unrest that frequently destabilized other ancien régime monarchies," T. H. Breen points out.[44]
Colonists like Dickinson, however, doubted that Parliament saw
colonials as full citizens: the pamphlets they churned out and the broadsides they printed on the cheap aroused suspicions that the transoce-
anic commercial interests uniting different ends of the empire directly
financed a permanent state of war.

In a November 1773 broadside signed "Rusticus," Dickinson takes
aim at the government outsourcing of war that creates violence and
famine in the East Indies. His concern is rather partisan than cosmopolitan, consumed with fears that the East India Company is planning to subject the American colonies to the same "Barbarities,
Extortions, and Monopolies," not to mention the "Indigence and
Ruin," which have destabilized British India. "Are we in like Manner
to be given up to the Disposal of the *East-India Company*," part of an
overall scheme for "enslaving *America*?" he asks.[45] Much more than
just a private trading corporation, the East India Company profited
from a symbiotic relationship to the state that invested heavily in
company shares, floated the company's debt, and borrowed from and
lent money to the company, all the while supporting those financial
interests by dispatching soldiers and weapons to India. As much as a

third of the revenue pouring into the British treasury came from customs duties paid by the East India Company. This coordination of
monopoly and governmental power helped pioneer development of a
fiscal-military state that exercised administrative control over populations brought under the sway of its commercial empire.[46] Such considerations animate Dickinson's letters on tea. Because his perspective
is not yet contracted to the national, "Rusticus" can trace the implications of imperial commerce, following the path from exclusive trading rights to monopoly, from total economic control to the erection of
puppet governments, and from political instability to war and famine.

Dickinson charges that 1.5 million people perished during the
Bengal famine of 1770 (modern geographers calculate that this estimate is wildly inaccurate, as roughly one-third of the population, or
10 million people, died from starvation and disease). In her commentary on the East India Company, Mercy Otis Warren estimated that
fourteen thousand people died each week in the province of Madras
alone.[47] Dickinson and Warren each understood that the famine was
not a natural calamity (starvation did not occur "because the Earth
denied its fruits") but rather the product of the East India Company's
disastrous revenue practices, which held food at inflated prices while
hoarding grain and other "Necessaries of Life" to heighten scarcity.[48]
When Parliament granted the East India Company a monopoly to
distribute tea in the American colonies, Dickinson worried that the
same chain reaction leading from unfair trading practices to famine,
a pattern he saw established by the recent history of British India,
was fast unfolding in America.

Tea was labeled a pernicious commodity that encapsulated the
designs of the fiscal-military state on America's liberties. At the least
this view typifies the position of the many writers who in fall 1773
issued broadsides, sent angry letters to newspapers, and spat out
rebuttals denouncing tea as the material embodiment of Parliament's
corrupt dealings with the East India Company. To stem the financial
hemorrhaging of the East India Company, Parliament contravened
the free-market faith of American merchants and consumers by
granting the corporation the exclusive right to ship, sell, and distribute tea in the colonies. The significance of this policy was not lost
on the colonists, especially after the passage of the Regulating Act
that summer giving Parliament increased control over the administrative affairs of India. In a one-page leaflet printed in Philadelphia, "A
Mechanic" described this agreement as a dangerous collusion of "the

Sword" and the commercial company that had decimated India.[49] So, too, another "Mechanic" in a New York broadside deplored this combination of economic and military power as "the Conduct of an Artful Assassin, who cunningly throws gold Dust into your Eyes, while he is slily endeavouring to cut your Throat, unperceived."[50] In this case, gold dust was the promise of East India tea at lower prices. Tea exposed colonists' vulnerability within "an empire of goods," its daily use among consumers prompting common identifications that conferred "national consciousness" on an otherwise scattered set of people.[51] This argument by Breen connecting commodity exchange to political solidarity, however, assumes the nation before fact, setting it up as a foregone conclusion, the only possible outcome of Revolutionary thinking. But the "mechanics" and other writers who kept colonial printers busy tell a different story: for a few months in 1773, as propagandists and pamphleteers warily watched "the most powerful Trading Company in the Universe," as newspaper readers and consumers alike fretted that they were soon to be rendered "the most miserable Slaves upon the Globe," ideas about a broader rhetorical geography were given sharper focus within the workings of printscape.[52]

As the epitome of a global economy, tea cultivated in India, put into exchange with slaves from Africa, and purchased with silver mined from South America provided a lesson that exceeded the rather restricted appeal of early American nationalism. Each phase of its circulation bespoke the nightmares of exploitation, famine, and slavery. One week after the destruction of the tea, the *Massachusetts Spy* printed the rumor that "the Tea Consignees, having sold their country, are about purchasing a number of negroes, and preparing to embark for the Bay of Honduras."[53] America seemed to be just another link—hardly an exceptional entity—in a system of hemispheric exploitation. Tea exposed the precarious position of the colonies within a commercial empire. Adding insult to injury, Parliament had mandated that Governor Hutchinson and his lieutenants be paid out of customs duties collected on tea. By taking the matter of officials' salaries out of the hands of the Massachusetts legislature, the British government seized control of what seemed the last bargaining chip that colonists had in negotiating with the administrators of empire.[54] The local loss of autonomy resonated with fears that America might be part of larger pattern of rapine. The fiery propaganda of the Revolutionary printscape tapped this anxiety, as writers as famous as Dickinson and Paine joined with those who only went by the name "A Mechanic" to frame American colonization, however briefly, as part of a world-system of empire administered by the regnant combination of British financial markets and military force.[55]

As Paine declared, "my country is the world."[56] Although Paine made this pronouncement twenty years after East India was front page news in fall 1773, global thinking had only a brief political life. Even within the short space of Dickinson's letters on tea, cosmopolitan sympathy fades before feelings of nationalist pride. After warning that the East India Company has its "Eyes on *America*, as a new Theater" now that India has been stripped of its resources, he supplies readers with a bit of hope by playing on ethnicity: "But thank GOD, we are not Sea Poys, nor Marrattas, but *British Subjects*, who are born to Liberty."[57] Retreating to narrow feelings inspired by ethnic difference, Dickinson here gives up on the conceptually adventurous and inclusive nature of this critique for a couple of reasons. First, he echoes the tradition of colonial polemicists who as early as the Stamp Act crisis of 1765 had contended that their opposition to Parliamentary measures amounted to nothing other than insistence on their rights as Englishmen. For Dickinson, this reminder could save citizens from rushing over the cliff of separation. Second, it seems safer to envision liberty from within a frame that is already national, making it hard to distinguish political virtues from commodities. After all, if one New York printer could attest that it was his duty as "a lover of my country, to prefer the English" tea to smuggled Dutch imports, a devotion to liberty could appear as not altogether different from brand loyalty.[58]

The competing loyalties expressed in Dickinson's letter, itself a reflection of heated attacks and counterattacks launched in the waning months of 1773, emerge from a deeper uncertainty about the frame of rights and liberty. What is the proper frame for life, liberty, and property and how do understandings of these terms change in accordance with geography? Nancy Fraser has asked this question with respect to justice, arguing that the facts and forces of globalization require a seismic shift to relocate justice from the province of nations to a more porous domain that runs between and across sovereign territorial states. "It has ceased to be axiomatic that the modern territorial state is the appropriate unit

for thinking about issues of justice," she writes, describing a geo-
politics that includes subjects who fall between the cracks of state
sovereignty or who have affiliations that override national impera-
tives. This process is already fast occurring via "global mass media
and cybertechnology," which support entities such as nongovern-
mental organizations and networks of transnational public
opinion.[59] In talking about eighteenth-century letter writers and a
twenty-first-century political theorist in the same breath, my purpose is to wonder how far removed are broadsides from cybertechnology. The question is not an idle one: although the broadside or
leafleted letter could not be zapped from colonial coffeehouse to
tavern, the circulation of these quickly printed and distributed
bits of ephemera prompted American colonials to stretch the borders of political community within the limits of existing media
technologies. The point is not that the eighteenth century looks
surprisingly a lot like the twenty-first or that an unchanging mon-
olithic capitalist world economy governs each. Rather, this historical doubling instead amplifies the conclusion that "what turns a
collection of people into fellow subjects ... is not geographical
proximity, but their co-imbrication in a common structural or in-
stitutional framework."[60] To put this ethos of expanded connection into the parlance of "Hampden" and other Revolutionary
American subjects, tea is a wicked commodity, "the Profit of which
is to support the Tyranny of ... the East, enslave the West, and pre-
pare us fit Victims for the Exercise of the horrid Inhumanity," the
same process as was perpetrated in India.[61]

As they kept up the pressure on the empire, print agitators necessarily enlarged their geographies of colonial identification. Sam
Adams, for one, dispatched circular letters to advise Boston's sister
cities to feel similarly endangered by Britain's reaction to the dumping of East India Company tea in Boston Harbor. Writers such as
"Hampden" took heed from the perilous fate of colonies other than
America, whose subjects saw resources and revenues "dragooned"
by the fiscal-military state.[62] And, finally, propagandists zeroed in on
British atrocities in India to warn how the combination of military
force and commerce put entire populations at risk. Awareness of
British dealings in India enabled American subjects to imagine their
political struggle, even if only momentarily or through conde-
scending comparisons to "helpless Asiaticks," in relation to events
and people on the other side of the globe.

## The "Universal Empire...of a Writer"

How long "grassroots globalization" will survive into the twenty-first century is not known, although observers such as Fraser predict that this is a trend still on the upswing.[63] It is hard to see this thinking in the eighteenth century lasting much beyond 1773; it surely must have been dead by 1776 when the colonies declared themselves free and independent states.

Yet concerns over the East India Company did not wane so quickly. In spring 1777, the Continental Congress warned that the British government had plans to transport captured soldiers to Gibraltar and turn them over to the East India Company, which would then ship the prisoners to its settlements in India. In effect, American Revolutionaries would be declared enemy combatants and detained in an offshore military garrison encircled by the sovereign territory of Spain. Echoes of what was Camp X-Ray and now Camp Delta at Guantánamo Bay, Cuba, are hard to ignore. Whereas the U.S. military and the White House have insisted on total control over detainees from the war on terror that has dominated foreign relations in the first decades of the twenty-first century, the British government in 1777 seemed eager to unload its prisoners on a private contractor, according to East India Company documents cited by delegates to the Continental Congress. In February of that year, John Adams relied on epistolary networks to forward a letter to Mercy Warren's husband that contained this alarming intelligence: "I believe you have not yet been apprised...that the British Government offered to deliver the Prisoners taken on Long Island to the East India Company, to be sent to their Settlements, if the Company would send for them to Gibralter [sic]," Adams's correspondent had written.[64] This news exposed like nothing else what it meant for American farmers, artisans, and tradesmen to be caught up in the web of commercial and military empire. Then again, the threat should not strike us as extraordinary. Swept up in the global war on terror that began after September 11, 2011, "taxi drivers, shepherds, shopkeepers, laborers, prostitutes" from Iraq and Afghanistan have been identified as suspected militants and transported to offshore U.S. facilities, known as "black sites," such as Abu Ghraib and Guantánamo Bay.[65]

While Dickinson and other Americans forcefully asserted a historic sense of English belonging to protest "the violation of the liberties of the people," their simultaneous identification as colonials led to increasing anxieties about a different manifestation of Englishness, namely, the empire's pursuit of war and commercial enterprise on a geographically vast scale.[66] Having battled on two fronts since the Seven Years' War, when royal soldiers were sent to India, Britain sent still more troops eastward during the American Revolution. The extent of these military operations encouraged the Continental Congress to search for cracks within the empire. Amid a report on British troop movements and reinforcements, delegate Samuel Johnston in 1781 paused over some intercepted communiqués, which "make it evident that the British have suffered very considerably in the East Indies under an Army of Asiaticks."[67] People once seen as "helpless" in 1773 now enter the conversation as something like equal partners. Officials in the British government shared the opinion that crises in India would further destabilize American affairs. Three days before colonists dumped 342 chests of tea in Boston harbor, Charles Jenkins, the first Earl of Liverpool, who at various times held the posts of lord of the Treasury and secretary at war (these phases of his career exemplify the connections between state-finance capitalism and military operations), worried that open investigation into the corruption of the East India Company would have "a bad influence on our American business."[68] Even though the Boston ruffians who ransacked the company's vessels disguised themselves as North American Indians, it is tempting to wonder if any thought ran through the mob that colonists were playing Indian in more ways than one.

In England, a director of the East India Company searched for solutions by comparing East and West theaters of overseas administration. Might it prove advantageous to "fix the government of the territories in India on a plan something similar to the American colonies," granting the population of India the protections of British subjects? The alternative was to render Indians "mere slaves of the Company."[69] Ultimately, he rejected such a solution as unfeasible. While the director took care to separate among different sorts of colonials, noting that "Indians are inured to oppression," these extreme parallels alarmed the white inhabitants of America.[70] Comparisons between British colonies in America and India not only created political and administrative problems for East India Company officials but have vexed historians into the twentieth century. Despite the conclusion in 1912 that the company "will always stand out in history as a monument to British enterprise and honour," reconciling the simultaneous history of American independence and British hegemony in India has not been easy.[71] Even if "the success" of the company "is largely due to the pre-eminent gift for government with which the Anglo-Saxon race is endowed...it will be necessary to explain away the loss of the American colonies at the very moment when the East India Company was consolidating its position in India."[72] How to explain the consolidation of mercantilist hegemony at one end of the antipodes and imperial disintegration at the other? This conundrum, in part, contains its own answer: measures taken to subdue India, in addition to the famine and war that ensued, sent tremors of concern halfway around the world. As "Rusticus" closed his letter on the tea tax, he recommended that in American cities and towns, "Watchmen be instructed as they go their Rounds, to call out every night, *past Twelve o'Clock, beware of the East-India Company.*"[73] The alarm was not just that the British were coming, as Longfellow later imagined it, but that the imperial state was rounding up troublemakers in an effort to tighten its hold on colonial subjects.

Longfellow's schoolroom standard hardly counts as significant evidence that the comparative sensibility of American propaganda outlasted its historical moment. Yet for participants in early American printscape such as "Humanus" and "Atlanticus"—two of Paine's pseudonyms—the imbrication of America and India offered a vital illustration of the need to keep the pressure on the military-fiscal state. Seeking to rally the flagging spirits of the Continental Army during the long winter, Paine laid bare America's connection not simply to the East Indies but also to the Caribbean and Africa. Although Paine's reputation largely rests on *Common Sense* (1776), a publication that issued "an unprecedented call to nationalism," it is by no means a foregone conclusion that the entire flow of his leveling rhetoric is absorbed into nationalist currents.[74] Instead Paine's varied activities in Revolutionary printscape promote world interest. In this respect, it is helpful to remember Arendt's observation that interest acts as a revolutionary faculty when it is understood as *inter-est*, that is, as a way of thinking about the world that highlights the concerns that unite people.[75] As Paine considers the fate of the colonies and global trade, he suggests that Americans, Asians, and, as we will see, New World Africans share such common interests.

Before publication of *Common Sense*, Paine wrote several pieces for Pennsylvania newspapers condemning British rule in the East

Indies. Perhaps his most creative is "Reflections on the Life and Death of Lord Clive," largely an interior monologue attributed to the British general who administered colonial policy in India in the 1750s and 1760s. Paine represents Robert Clive as suffering from posttraumatic stress disorder, his enjoyment of an elaborate London dinner pierced by flashbacks to the battlefields of Bengal. In Clive's traumatic consciousness, metropole and colonial outpost, two spatially distant sites, become temporally coincident. "Loud laughs" transmogrify into "groans of dying men," "the joyous toast" seems like "the sound of murder," and the "crimson colored port" resembles nothing so much as "blood." Elsewhere Paine charges that Clive oversaw a campaign of terror whose cruelties involved strapping Indians to the front of loaded cannons and blowing them to bits, an accusation confirmed by subsequent commentators. As Clive relives his actions in this minidrama, he mourns that "the scenes of India are all rehearsed, and no one sees the tragedy but myself." Unable to escape the past, Clive endures an isolation that makes him an object of pity in the eyes of poor and working-class observers. The former commander-in-chief of British India experiences a sharp pang on overhearing a "ragged wretch" say, "Ah, poor Lord Clive!" while he considers somewhat more humane ("more mercifully cruel," in Paine's words) the chimneysweep who curses him directly. Of the mass of humanity that Paine depicts reflecting on Clive's ignominy— orphans, widows, beggars, and nabobs—only this "sooty sweep" condescends to interact with the disgraced hero who, courtesy of the Battle of Plassey in 1757, seized Bengal for the East India Company. The chimneysweep represents the sole human contact for Clive now that he has returned from India with his bribe taking exposed and his stake in world interest (or *inter-est* in Arendt's sense) retracted to working-class scorn. For the man whose influence once took a global dimension and whose actions determined the fate of thousands, severe isolation eventuates in suicide. In light of this irony, Paine wonders about a fitting memorial for this tragic figure: "let his monument be a globe," but this nod to global significance quickly fades, as it becomes clear that Paine cleverly insists not on *the* globe but on *a* globe, that is, "a bubble" in which fame and renown are only temporary illusions.[76]

Paine sharpened the edge of colonial critique by explicitly connecting it to American contexts a few months later. His meditation on America's interpolation within a spider's web of commercial and military expansion segues from an examination of the "horrid cruel-ties exercised by Britain in the East Indies" into a consideration of the "most horrid of all traffics, that of human flesh." The juxtaposi-tion of these two crimes—the "artificial famine" created in Bengal and the transatlantic slave trade—impelled Paine to look for ways of extricating geographically disparate peoples from a global empire.[77] A nation-state seems too puny an entity for this task. By confronting America's place within a world-system governed by the coordination of trade and might, such propaganda stresses the urgency of a colo-nial separation in which independence will not automatically re-quire the scaled-back perspective known as nationalism. Paine hopes that the first act of this new sovereign entity will be hemispheric in scope, namely, a ban on the slave trade and eventual emancipation for Africans in the New World. The subsequent decoupling of these contexts and the ascension of national interest is, of course, a fa-miliar story, but Paine's devotion to a propaganda of extremes reveals a possible alternative trajectory for critique before it hardened into nationalist narrative.

Although the Boston Tea Party was soon eclipsed by more mo-mentous events, Paine's zeal for pamphlet culture ensured that the context of East India kept its prominent place in Revolutionary print-scape. In the series of sixteen articles written from 1776 to 1783 that make up *The American Crisis*, he repeatedly accused Britain of barba-rism, trapping Americans in a world-system of injustice that included India, Africa, and the Caribbean. The stirring rhetoric of these essays, as scholars have noted, served to stoke the patriotic fires, a purpose dramatically realized with General Washington's order that the first issue ("These are the times that try men's souls") be read to troops preparing to cross the Delaware. But global sensibility was also simul-taneous with nationalist sentiment: *The American Crisis* refuses to re-linquish the excessive geography of anti-imperial critique. Construed as propaganda, this exemplar of Revolutionary literature lacks an element deemed essential to twentieth-century propaganda: a thor-oughgoing commitment to the state. The flip side of this lack is a tem-porary fullness, a cosmopolitan flicker that frees critique from a national lens so that a comparative vantage becomes possible. But this alternative perspective is rarely adopted. Because readers of Paine concentrate on "the book" to the exclusion of pamphlet culture, an emphasis on state formation and national origins often obscures the extent to which early American literature qua propaganda does not orbit the state. Focusing on *Common Sense* as an iconic manifesto rather than as one item of propaganda among the many of its day, scholars have heralded Paine as the "first to recognize the absolute priority of a national argument in revolutionary America."[78] This assessment amounts to a dubious honor: the canonicity of one "stand-alone" book should not determine the critical horizon for a range of pamphleteering and other propaganda activities that intermittently afforded an other-than-national perspective. Even as Paine proclaimed that the United States soon "will sound as pompously in the world" as Britain, he expresses uneasiness about the place of this sovereign state in the world and whether such pomposity need also sound the death knell of an incipient cosmopolitan sensibility.[79]

Thus in the same issue of *The American Crisis* that touts the nation's budding status, Paine reserves highest grandeur for the republic of letters, specifically because this literary terrain exceeds national jurisdiction. "Universal empire is the prerogative of a writer," boasts Paine, absorbing "all mankind" into his audience and concern (1:58). Pitting the republic of letters against monarchy, he shifts "empire" from geopolitical to ethical ground, claiming that the universal domain of literature—as opposed to the global designs of the fiscal-military state—embodies a "far higher character in the world" than the questionable integrity of lords and kings (1:58). Paine's "prerogative" includes subjecting imperial actors to the vicissitudes of the printscape. Clive, in Paine's mock soliloquy, blames "the newspapers, fatal enemies to ill-gotten wealth" for his tumble down the ladder of respectability and virtue. His undoing comes at the hands of fortune, which "publish[es] me in folio to the world." Clive, in effect, becomes a text, bandied about in public discourse by an audience whose interests dwarf those of state-run commerce. Clive reflects, "Lord Clive is himself a treatise upon vanity, printed in golden type." His conversion into print is total; he has become subject to the medium of propaganda. Clive now circulates much like a lurid pamphlet that anyone, "even the most unlettered clown," can get his hands on and then scribble in its margins by leaving "explanatory notes thereon." As proof of how readers become writers by participating in printscape, the marginalia from the pen of the semiliterate offsets the titles of nobility that military men like Colonel Clive were able to buy. Paine's "Reflections" models this engagement since his own text is peppered with footnotes that provide "explanatory notes" about how Clive amassed his wealth in India. Paine as author merges with the "unlettered" reader because they share a vested interest in dissemination: just as the common reader writes comments all over Clive's text so that he can convey his ideas to "his children," Paine compiles footnotes for this exposé of the famous and the dead.[80]

If Paine spared no venom in converting Clive into a public text, he had no problem enacting a similar transformation on his own person, making himself into a text, giving his identity over to print so completely that he signed issues of *The American Crisis* with the pseudonym "Common Sense." Authorship is totally submerged to the printscape, and it is this submersion that gives writing a horizon that is other than national. As a reflection of "universalizing norms of public print discourse" that Michael Warner has identified as a crucial component of the republic of letters, Paine's tactics resonate with far more than either state sovereignty or the realm of an abstract public sphere; "universal empire" also evokes the precise coordinates of the eighteenth-century world-system.[81]

Still, the propagandist's location was worlds apart from the actualities of empire. Nothing illustrated this gulf more than the offer of amnesty that Richard Viscount Howe issued in the fall of 1776. Newspapers such as *The Continental Journal* and the *New York Gazette and Weekly Mercury* published the full text of Lord Howe's proclamation promising "full and free Pardon of all Treasons" to colonists who had taken up arms against the king.[82] Addressing himself to Lord Howe, Paine seemed bemused that "your lordship...has now commenced author." Had relations between the parent country and the colonies deteriorated to such a degree that titled nobles would now condescend to enter the public realm of print? Paine's response uses the second issue of *The American Crisis*, which surveys the expanse of the writer's "universal empire," to assess Howe's offer. Despite this vastness, Paine declared that there was not enough room for both Howe's proclamation and his rebuttal, and that one must necessarily eclipse the other. Howe has "published a proclamation; I have published a *Crisis*. As they stand, they are the antipodes of each other." This imaginative cartography of the printscape overlays a real map of world power where Britain's hegemony extends to opposite ends of the earth, from North America to East India. But these same global forces allow Paine to take heart: "so quick is the revolution" of the earth that Howe's proclamation is vanishing over "the edge of the political horizon" while patriot propaganda is rising with the dawn of a new day (*American Crisis* 1:59).

When it comes to the military-mercantile complex that united Britain and the East India Company, Paine speaks of several worlds, distinguishing geopolitical events from spiritual affairs. He cuts this distinction with a vengeance, asserting that while sin and retribution are "reserved to *another* world," Britain's sins of ravaging other lands invite a "punishment" that "can only be inflicted in *this* world" (*American Crisis* 1:66). And for Paine, the geography of this world requires gruesome specificity, as he accuses Britain, via the East India Company in particular and its trading empire in general, as having "the blood of India," "the wretchedness of Africa," and the "butcherly destruction of the Caribbs of St. Vincent's" on its hands (1:66). Published in January 1777, this installment of *The American Crisis* asks colonists to consider Britain's history on three continents before accepting Howe's offer and seeking the Crown's mercy. The colonial Revolution in America, he argues, cannot be conceptualized apart from the workings of empire.

Paine sought to prove that the public had gotten this message about the importance of translating the abstractions of liberal universalism into the specifics of geopolitical critique. Quoting a petition drafted by a Revolutionary citizens' committee, he argues that pleas for peace and reconciliation are too localized and shortsighted for Americans and other imperial subjects. As the committee charged, British policy "has filled India with carnage and famine, Africa with slavery, and tampered with Indians and negroes to cut the throats of the freemen of America" (*American Crisis* 1:93). While Paine expressed more nuanced views, especially on the issue of slavery, the citizens' petition echoes his conviction that war is not altogether distasteful to those who profit from the operations of the military-mercantile complex. Far from it: Tories are "*happy*" to live under a government that is "never better pleased" than when violence flares up in Asia or Africa (1:93). In this light, hopes for reconciliation are nothing other than a devious plot orchestrated by Parliament to encourage rebellion so that private holdings in America can be seized and confiscated, the spoils of war flowing into the coffers of the fiscal-military state. The trajectory of this critique explains why Paine persists in labeling destabilization around the world a set of "national cruelties" (*American Crisis* 1:66). Even though these atrocities take place within a global theater, they remain motivated by interests that, in comparison to the "universal empire" of republican letters, appear self-serving and constricted.

The expanse of the eighteenth-century world-system—its reliance on the fiscal-military state, its detention of enemy combatants via a network of extranational jurisdiction, its commercial traffic in war and slavery—made it difficult to conceptualize, let alone critique, a geopolitical apparatus whose intricacy and seeming totality defy comprehension. To expose the immensity of this system and, particularly, America's place within it, Paine returned to the routes of commodity circulation. Tea, once a sure sign of British hegemony, now signified less securely, connecting America to East India in ways that spelled the unraveling of that hegemony. "It is remarkable that the produce of that ruined country [India], transported to America, should there kindle up a war to punish the destroyer," Paine writes. His amazement at this improbable linkage is exceeded only by his sense of poetic justice that colonial oppression perpetrated in the antipodes reappears as colonial insurgency at the other extreme. This irony both pinpoints and simplifies the conjunction of East and West under commercial empire: with the resources of East India depleted through government corruption, America appears as the next tantalizing "market for plunder" (*American Crisis* 1:142–44). It is a threat whose magnitude reveals America's imbrication within a sweeping geography of trade and war.

## Moveable Types

Ultimately, though, this geopolitical concern to map America's position within an imperial system could not keep pace with the enthusiasm for commerce and world trade. To take one prominent example, *Common Sense* peddles corn and other commodities as the relays of a new world culture ushered in by independence. Paine, it seems, believed that American corn was an ideologically different species of commodity from tea. As Immanuel Wallerstein reminds us, the Revolution conformed to the general pattern of settler decolonization in the Americas by having no "revolutionary effects" on the world capitalist system.[83] The eclipse of other-than-national critique was unavoidable, and today its traces exist largely in broadsides and other artifacts of the Revolutionary printscape that the Library of Congress catalogues as "ephemera," hardly the stuff of a lasting critical tradition.

Paine tried to dispel notions that provincial interests motivated his partisan pamphleteering. "Perhaps it may be said that I live in

America," he began in defense against those who might pigeonhole his efforts as merely national. In an issue of *The American Crisis* addressed "to the People of England," he proclaims that "my attachment is to all the world, and not to any particular part" (1:146). This declaration asserts that critique must do more than focus on any one part of empire by remaining vigilant about the transit of commodities, people, and print across the entirety of the world-system.

The passage of the Boston Port Bill in 1774, the first in a series of measures that would become known as the Intolerable Acts, justified this watchfulness. Drafted by Parliament in retaliation for the destruction of the tea, the port act closed Boston Harbor to all maritime traffic, although exceptions were allowed to provision British soldiers quartered in the city. It seemed, however, that rumor could still travel unchecked when the *Massachusetts Spy* reproduced an extract from a London letter describing the British government's plans to line the pockets of printers willing to propagate information favorable to the Crown. According to an unnamed source, thirteen letters, one to each colony, had been dispatched to printers willing to do their "utmost to influence and cajole the ignorant, to deceive and mislead the wise." In light of this information, colonists had to be careful readers—"watch your News-Papers and be prudent"—lest they swallow the government line.[84] Where Parliament had been unable to unload surplus tea from the East India Company on America, it was now trying to seed the hinterlands with misinformation.

By that time, however, the *Spy* itself had already become mobile. Its proprietor and publisher, Isaiah Thomas, had earlier opened a printing house in Newburyport and would soon relocate press operations to Worcester after British regiments landed in Boston. Revolutionary upheavals demanded that printers be just as itinerant as their products. Thomas made a point of noting that he "removed my Printing Utensils" from Boston on April 19, 1775, the same day as the skirmishes at Lexington and Concord.[85] After a brief hiatus, the paper resumed on May 3, and one of the surviving copies of that issue bears Thomas's inscription: "This News-paper is the first Thing ever printed in Worcester."[86] It would not be the last.

# Epistolary Propaganda

## COUNTERFEITS, STOLEN LETTERS, AND TRANSATLANTIC REVOLUTIONS

In a letter dated June 12, 1776, General George Washington confided feelings to his cousin and plantation manager, which, had they been made public, might well have sounded heretical to his fellow Revolutionaries. "We have overshot our mark," he wrote of the colonies' bid for independence. "We have grasped at things beyond our reach: it is impossible that we should succeed; and I cannot with truth, say that I am sorry for it; because I am far from being sure that we deserve to succeed."[1] But the letter did not remain confidential: having supposedly fallen into British hands, it appeared in newspapers on both sides of the Atlantic and was bound together with six other letters and printed first in London in 1777 and then in New York in 1778 as a Loyalist pamphlet, *Letters from General Washington to Several of His Friends in the Year 1776*.[2] Independence did not put an end to the embarrassment that the letters created for Washington. As late as the 1790s, these pirated epistles continued to circulate to the chagrin of the general become president. Why did these letters, which were widely discredited upon their appearance, remain available in the printscape for much of the late eighteenth century?

This set of seven letters is not a factual document, but rather the work of a creative propagandist seeking to sow doubts about the American Revolution by purportedly revealing Washington's secret misgivings. The ruse rested on the conceit that Washington's mulatto slave had been captured while carrying a packet of letters addressed to his wife, adopted son, and cousin. The fabrication contains a lot of truth: Washington did own a mulatto slave who was taken prisoner in 1776; he did write his family to express reservations about independence; some of his letters had in fact been intercepted by the British. Revisiting this episode in 1788, Washington acknowledged that the forger had done more than a passable job in sprinkling the letters with just enough detail to lend "the greater appearance of probability to the fiction."[3] In admitting the plausibility of the counterfeit, Washington's remarks offer insight about the interconnections between literary convention and political propaganda.

Forged, stolen, and intercepted letters are all stock features of the epistolary novel that migrate to the world of popular politics.[4] As a forgotten bit of eighteenth-century intrigue, the Washington counterfeit of 1776, especially in its reappearances and recirculation during the 1790s, illustrates how the movement of private letters across the printscape constituted a political activity in its own right. Appearing not long after Hutchinson's stolen letters added to the turbulence of colonial affairs, these documents supposedly seized from Washington's slave courier sought to return the favor by nettling Whig leaders. As cleverly devised as any of the epistolary fictions of its day, this bit of propaganda done up as a series of letters attained notoriety for its capacity to circulate apart from any considerations about authenticity. Indeed, it often seemed that the more unauthorized a letter or document was, the more widely and easily it could be disseminated. While matters of fact or fiction were not inconsequential, the overriding concern wrapped up in these suspect communiqués was that public access to private or secret information remain unrestricted.

While motivated by blatant partisan purposes, the letters constitute a genteel sort of propaganda. Starting with the Stamp Act in 1765 and through the 1770s, when the transatlantic press parodied colonial rulers and pilloried rebels, this forgery is notable for its restraint and decorum, presenting a leader who is neither venal nor dishonorable, perhaps to enhance its air of believability. Although Washington's nineteenth-century biographer sniffs that these "insidious" epistles depict the general "expressing sentiments totally at variance with his conduct," the forgery is neither outrageous nor slanderous.[5] "Washington" in these documents appears as a man of integrity and candor who is merely unburdening himself to his closest friends. The fake Washington's confession that it was "sorely against my will...to accept of the command of this army" hardly seems an indecorous lie in light of Washington's actual disclosure in November 1775, "Could I have foreseen what I have, and am likely to experience, no consideration on earth could have induced me to accept this command."[6] Replete with tidbits about hemp production and

Washington's personal life (years after the Revolution the president surmised that the letters "were evidently written by some person exceedingly well acquainted with my domestic and general concerns"), the forgery smacked of enough authenticity that Washington himself understood why many would believe him as its author.[7] Blending an aura of private feeling and partial truths about domestic intimacy, epistolary propaganda functioned as a sort of cottage industry in the manufacture of public opinion.

## "Propaganda Is to Democracy…"

Public opinion is of course often manufactured, and the petitions, rallies, newspapers, and pamphlets of the late eighteenth century indicate that early America had no shortage of media devoted not simply to reflecting but also creating popular sovereignty. Small-scale operations for taking—and accelerating—the people's pulse swelled to over one hundred papers by 1790, making it plain that public opinion was not a preexisting entity but rather something shifting and up for grabs.[8] Walter Lippmann famously described this process as "the manufacture of consent," referring to modern methods of persuasion and manipulation, which, in his view, made a self-willing citizenry a thing of the past.[9]

Republican printers of the eighteenth century behaved more like artisans than modern manufacturers of public opinion, and yet their transatlantic interests, as we will see in the example of Benjamin Franklin's grandson, were just as capacious.[10] As printer and publisher of the Philadelphia *Aurora General Advertiser*, Benjamin Franklin Bache used the knowhow, education, and European connections cultivated by his grandfather to champion French and American republicanism simultaneously. Virtually every issue of the *Aurora* from 1794–95 conveyed the latest intelligence from Revolutionary France while keeping its readers up to date about the Democrat-Republican societies of the United States. The gambit was to widen the geography of republicanism. As with the critical attention that Paine and other Revolutionaries paid to the imperial contexts of trade and monopoly in their newspaper writings, printer-propagandists such as Bache rarely confined themselves to narrowly domestic interests. Public opinion in the post-Revolutionary era, as Jason Frank suggests, often acquired an international dimension that made "the dissemination of political knowledge" a key resource for that mutable entity known as "the people."[11]

The need to create consent has been around for a long time, but as Lippmann's stress on a process associated with modern industrial society—manufacturing—implies, the twentieth century required new and improved methods for removing unpredictability and spontaneity from political life. The manufacture of consent, for Noam Chomsky, has muzzled genuine dissent so thoroughly that among U.S. citizens opposition to American military aggression in places such as Vietnam, Nicaragua, and El Salvador is reduced to quibbling over tactics rather than systemic critique. "Propaganda is to democracy what violence is to totalitarianism," quips Chomsky, equating modern media in democracy with the brute force of repressive regimes insofar as each produces the forcible impression that the people must consent to what their government does.[12] While Chomsky invests propaganda with a more sinister bent than Lippmann does in *Public Opinion*, each identifies consent as a hegemonic operation that pawns off a sorely constricted range of perspectives as true democratic debate. Lippmann goes so far as to declare that the modern blitz of propaganda makes it impossible "to believe in the original dogma of democracy," but the Washington counterfeit tells a different story, holding out the possibility that propaganda could be integral to democratic practice.[13]

Not many have sought to tell a story in which the propagation of information—as well as misinformation—enhances public debate, open access, or other aspects of democracy. Exploring the significance of propaganda to democratic politics is a fraught enterprise, a risky undertaking to pursue in light of the often-irreparable damage done by distortions and even outright lies. Yet propaganda remains unavoidable. "Any modern state, even a democratic one, is burdened with the task of acting through propaganda. It cannot act otherwise," writes Jacques Ellul.[14] Propaganda often functions as gentle coercion that makes people tractable to being governed because they have, after all, been cajoled, urged, pressured, and convinced to give their consent. Without this "engineering of consent," to recall an idea developed by Bernays, inefficiency and disorder can paralyze even the most liberal and open-minded citizenry.[15] Technocratic optimism is the flip side of Ellul's despair: the language of advanced mechanization common to Lippmann and Bernays resounds with the hope that a professional class of social managers can streamline the messiness of public opinion into coherent, unambiguous social policy. From this perspective, propaganda offers a safeguard against political entropy.

Intended to slow the dissolution of the colonial system that erupted with full force in 1775, the Washington letters would seem to confirm propaganda as a stratagem employed by elite interests to manage public opinion. The associations between propaganda and social governance extends back to 1622 when Pope Gregory XV convened the Congregatio de Propaganda Fide, a group of cardinals entrusted with the mission of spreading the Catholic faith among infidels, which at the time included the many lambs who had been led astray by the Protestant Reformation. Propaganda radiated in one direction, outward from the Vatican to the rest of the world, as part of a concerted effort to reestablish the religious authority of Rome that seemed everywhere disintegrating but also everywhere expanding as the prospect of converting New World populations suggested. The idea, it might be said, was to create a "world literature," not in Goethe's sense of learning from the globe's multiple literary traditions, but in terms of disseminating texts about the one true faith across the face of the earth. There could be no message without infrastructure: to facilitate its pastoral undertaking, the conclave of cardinals decreed that the Vatican Post Office would not require any levies for documents sent out under the auspices of the congregatio.[16] The circulation of doctrine is as crucial as the doctrine itself. But it is almost always circulation with tight controls: one-way communication is typically a defining feature of propaganda that emanates from a technocratic set, church, colonial administration, or other institution.

This understanding of propaganda as a type of social engineering would have been recognizable to more than one eighteenth-century American at the receiving end of pulpit oratory or statehouse displays, but the historical matter of the printscape also suggests that many persons approached dissemination and propagation as virtuous public activity. Claiming his grandfather's mantle as an Enlightenment printer, Benjamin Franklin Bache began publishing the *General Advertiser, Political, Commercial, Agricultural and Literary Journal* on October 1, 1790, in order "to diffuse among the mass of men knowledge of this kind," namely, news and intelligence that would enhance the public good. Opening "channels of correspondence in London, Paris, and the West-Indies" was the first step toward this lofty goal.[17]

FIGURE 4.1 *Masthead of the* Aurora General Advertiser. *The motto "Surgo ut Prosim" translates as "I rise to be useful." Courtesy of the American Antiquarian Society.*

Four years, later when this undertaking evolved into the first issue of the *Aurora General Advertiser*, Bache made a similar promise to the public that the paper "shall diffuse light within the sphere of its influence"[18] (fig. 4.1). Not everyone believed that the editor's interest in diffusion was so pure or disinterested. Rivals at the *Gazette of the United States* took stock of Bache's venture and concluded, "There is in each of our large towns, at least one newspaper constantly employed to expose our own government…to the contempt and hatred of our own people."[19] The *Aurora* swiftly turned this attack inside out to decry the Federalist press as a rubber stamp of consent: "There is in each of our large towns, at least one newspaper constantly employed in representing the officers of government, who are but men, as infallible, in attempting to impress a belief that administration can do no wrong."[20] In contrast, then, to twentieth-century views of propaganda as a collection of managerial tactics enacted on behalf of the state, evidence from the early Republic suggests a more complicated picture: even as some press organs rallied around the federal government, other institutions of the printscape diffused an ethos of democratic vigilance that encouraged suspicion of elected officials in place of customary deference.

Far from circumscribing communication within prescribed limits, as Lippmann or Bernays might propose, eighteenth-century propaganda exposed public opinion to oppositional and often unruly crosscurrents. In contrast to contemporary views of propaganda as unified around the state and the corporate interests that it supports, the spurious Washington letters open a window onto a moment when propaganda appears less villainous, less the tool of public relations practiced by governments and corporations spreading misinformation or lies, and more a set of practices for disseminating heterodox truths. As we will see, the Washington counterfeit in its metamorphosis from a Loyalist ploy discrediting Revolutionary leaders to an item in the republican print arsenal suggests that propaganda does not always remain under the control of well-heeled elites. In their transit from nonexistent handwritten missives to broadside to pamphlet to a reissued edition twenty years later, the letters in their mobility show that propaganda can have unintended effects beyond the control of both producers and receivers.[21]

Letters, even faked ones, bear the imprint of exchange and circulation. Colonial American correspondence, according to William Warner, can best be described as a "communication network" that complicated the flow of information so that it evolved into something more than a hierarchical system for people to send their petitions and opinions *up* the chain of command to ministry officials.[22] Unlike traditional appeals that moved from the people to the sovereign, epistolary discourse such as the documents generated by the Boston Committee of Correspondence in the 1770s traveled outward along multiple paths. "It is this change in direction of address—from up to out, from the King in Parliament to the people—that carries revolutionary potential," writes Warner.[23] Even a famously conservative correspondent during the era of eighteenth-century revolutions, Edmund Burke, recognized that letters and print allowed for the horizontal, uncontrolled spread of information. In *Reflections on the Revolution in France* (1790), Burke repeatedly warned of "propagators" who were spreading radical ideas across Europe, unhinging the public mind not only in Paris but also potentially in places like Prussia and England. Burke, who had been sitting in the Cockpit during the Privy Council's attack on Franklin for his role in publicizing Hutchinson's letters, readily grasped the connections between communications and revolution. Originating in "a correspondence between the Author and a very young gentleman at Paris," Burke's *Reflections* claimed "the freedom of epistolary intercourse" in weighing in on the excesses of the French Revolution.[24] Burke thought that he controlled the flow of information; after all, he sent hundreds of pages *to* a French aristocrat about liberty become license. But as *Reflections* recounted the activities of "propagators" both in England and France, alarming details emerged about correspondence among radical intellectuals, conspirators, and foreign governments. As much a part of transnational print circuits as the dangerous writings that Burke himself abhorred, *Reflections* was enmeshed in the very communication networks that fueled fanaticism.

Mercy Otis Warren underscored Burke's susceptibility to revolutionary propagation. In her view, this prolix opponent of the French

Revolution became—despite his avowed intentions—an unsuspecting conduit for radical ideas. When her friend and confidante the British radical Catharine Macaulay countered Burke's panicky assessment of social and political turmoil in her *Observations on the Reflections of the Right Hon. Edmund Burke, on the Revolution in France* (1790), Warren affixed a letter of recommendation to a Boston edition of the tract. As she celebrated the republication of Macaulay's work, Warren savored how Burke had become an unintended relay for retransmitting the spirit of republicanism back across the Atlantic to America. "Whatever convulsions may yet be occasioned by the revolution in France, it will doubtless be favourable to general liberty, and Mr. Burke may undesignedly be an instrument of its promotion, by agitating questions which . . . have been almost forgotten, or *artfully disguised,* in America," wrote Warren with characteristic appreciation of the irony that found a reactionary publication sparking discussions about liberty in Britain, France, and the United States.[25] Burke, in effect, had become an inadvertent propagandist for the cause he viewed with such alarm.

Print was not inherently revolutionary, however. Rather, it was the circulations of the printscape—publication and republication, interception and theft, invention and forgery—that imbued information as well as rumor with a radical and at times unpredictable charge. For Warren and other Democrat-Republicans, the principles of diffusion, to use a word favored by Bache, fostered a robust civic demeanor that prized curiosity, questioning, and openness. Their opponents saw matters differently, warning that the distribution of information without regard to the authenticity or value of the content posed a threat to public tranquility. This spreading outward, this "propagation of tenets," as Burke called it, carried an anarchic charge that raised the possibility of creating and deploying propaganda for democratic purposes.

When Jacques Ellul wondered, "Is it possible to make democratic propaganda?," he was less than optimistic that the content could correct for abuses of the form.[26] While propaganda frequently puts a spin on events and skews information, it always comprises more than content. The content of propaganda cannot be separated from the dynamics of its distribution. When propaganda diffuses outward, when it flows along transatlantic currents, when its direction becomes multiple, its political value and potential change correspondingly. Or in terms specific to the late eighteenth century: when talk of revolution bounces among France, England, and America, as it did in the epistolary networks favored by Warren and Macaulay, and when potentially embarrassing episodes from the Revolutionary past are dredged up, as they were in Bache's print shop, the connections between propaganda and order theorized by twentieth-century observers such as Bernays suddenly seem a lot less secure.

In Burke's phrasing, the "propagators of novelties" gave "rise to new and unlooked-for strokes in politics and morals."[27] Or in Mercy Warren's view, anyone was liable to become "undesignedly" a propagator since mobility and circulation were inseparable from the content of transatlantic communications. Unwelcome political strokes and unplanned changes in public morality that Burke did not want to see burst into view amid the back-and-forth transit, the crisscrossing, the exchanges, which like a series of letters characterized correspondence and print networks in the Revolutionary Atlantic world. As we will see with the transmission and recirculation of *Letters from General Washington*, propaganda at times served as a focal point for radical republican sentiments that exceeded the initial design of the counterfeit and spread beyond national boundaries.

## "Propagators of Novelties"

"Understanding the American Revolution is a literary pursuit," writes Robert Ferguson.[28] As helpful as this statement is in describing the aesthetics of colonial insurgency, it also clouds the issue by dislocating writing from a charged transatlantic atmosphere in which writing is also propaganda. According to Ferguson, Americans invested literature with a generally conservative function designed to guide citizens toward shared conclusions and thereby produce accord. Such "consensual literature" depends on an Enlightenment faith in rationality that all people—with the proper aesthetic encouragement—can be induced to discern fundamental truths.[29] But literature may also be propaganda, intended to divide, conquer, vilify. Even after the successful creation of an independent nation, these highly partisan aims remained very much part of American literary pursuits; twenty years after the British were defeated, new editions of the spurious Washington letters continued to appear. The reasons behind the forgery's circulation in the 1770s and again in the 1790s lay not simply in local national circumstances but in larger cataclysms of the Atlantic

world, particularly the French and Haitian Revolutions as well as the
Anglo-American counterreaction to these leveling events. The forgery found its widest audience not during the American Revolution
but twenty years later among citizen-readers dissatisfied with the
Federalist consensus. In its strange career, *Letters from General
Washington* transformed from pro-British propaganda to a dissenting register of public opinion. The document's fictionality accorded it
a flexibility useful for getting at the truth in ways other than those
circumscribed by Enlightenment rationality or national consensus.
Instead, epistolary propaganda combined a false show of private feeling with the ferment of transatlantic republicanism to widen political
discourse beyond either the strictly empirical or official public
opinion. Such amplitude facilitated the spread of oppositional discourse by challenging standards of authenticity, evidence, and truth
located in the narrowness of national letters.

But first the context of the forgery's initial appearance in 1777: the
propagandist's hope in fabricating Washington's letters likely was to
employ fictional techniques associated with the epistolary novel to
publicize the general's private sentiments. The epistolary novel had
special currency in Revolutionary America, where tales of seduction
and infidelity found ready ears among colonials worried about turn-
coats, shifting loyalties, and sexual betrayal. Even as letters were received as "genuine expressions of some kind of authentic self," the
unverifiable nature of their claims and sketchy provenance rendered
epistolary communication "a powerful tool for artifice and emotional
counterfeiting," writes Elizabeth Hewitt.[30] *Clarissa* and other novels of
seduction were popular, as Jay Fliegelman argues, because "they spoke
to the large preoccupation not only with deception, but more specifically with the seductive power of the potent word to convince others
to surrender themselves freely to one's will."[31] In the world of Anglo-
American pamphleteering and bookselling, the faked letters easily fit
the literary marketplace and were advertised alongside *Pamela* and
*The Mysteries of Udolpho*.

The forgery proffers a private glimpse for those wishing to un-
mask Washington's true feelings about the colonists' cause. In addition to expressing qualms over the rush to independence, the general
voices secret contempt for Patrick Henry, Thomas Paine, and his
military subalterns. A handwritten inscription in a copy of *Epistles
Domestic, Confidential, and Official from General Washington* (the
forgery circulated with more than one title) attributes the entire

scheme to "a Mr. V—then a young Episcopal Clergyman, who came from New York in order to make his fortune *here* in the character of a loyalist."[32] But the gambit did not succeed, and *Letters from General Washington to Several of His Friends*, the most common title given to the pamphlet, failed to make much of a splash. A few London papers reprinted some of the letters, hardly encouragement for provincial newspapers to give space to the supposedly private epistles. When the forgery arrived in the insurgent colonies, Loyalist newspapers printed a few of the letters, and George's letter to Martha lamenting his and his compatriots' "future to be deemed traitors to so good a King!" circulated as a broadside.[33]

So might the story of the spurious letters of Washington end here. The creation of a forgery for partisan political purposes never achieved the popularity of the epistolary novel whose form it mimicked. But because *Letters from General Washington* enjoyed a second life that was more popular and fractious than its first incarnation, its longevity stands as a lingering symptom of the uncertain relationship between foreign sympathies and domestic public opinion. Should citizens take an interest in European radicalism that appeared to some as the next phase of revolution, or should Americans cultivate more local attachments to the fledging union? In the early Republic, consent needed to be secured at a national level, but the high tide of popular political sentiments often spilled over domestic borders and ran toward transatlantic contexts, especially those of Revolutionary France. What if consent were at odds with a broader range of public opinion? Could citizens at once feel national and express loyalty to wider currents of hemispheric republicanism? *Letters from General Washington* hardly answered these questions; instead, the purpose of this epistolary propaganda was to pick at this suture, making it still more raw and irresolvable.

During Washington's second term as president, mulitple printings in new editions of the counterfeit appeared. On the surface, the reprinting seems intended merely to satisfy antiquarian curiosity by delivering "an INTERESTING view of AMERICAN POLITICS" to supplement "the official letters of General Washington" that had been recently published first in London and then Boston.[34] But antiquarianism may harbor motives other than those of the disinterested scholar: as a companion to official documents, *Letters from General Washington* forms a critical supplement, which on its republication in 1795, two decades after the letters' original appearance, joined a larger partisan battle over the manufacture of consent. Epistolary propaganda drove a wedge between public opinion and consent, exploiting the gap in an effort to address readers whose republican sympathies overran strictly national attachments. In an attempt to sow doubts about the Revolution of 1776, the original propagandist gave voice to Washington's supposed apprehension concerning divided loyalties, his own included. The general laments that all Americans do not share the same principles and confides to Martha that "our young Virginia men...dislike their northern allies."[35] This schismatic account of public opinion acquired new vitality when *Letters from General Washington* was republished in the last decade of the eighteenth century as the divisiveness between Federalists and Democratic-Republicans reached its height. The pamphlet's reappearance registers how the president fell prey to changing public opinion, unable to depend on the national patriotic contexts that had made his reputation sacrosanct. Propaganda attacks on Washington's character throughout the summer of 1796 pulled public opinion away from a strictly American orbit toward potentially more extranational feelings. These feelings ran toward Revolutionary France and the cause of transatlantic republicanism. While the Washington administration tried to achieve consensus around its rapprochement with Britain, Americans in the streets of Philadelphia and elsewhere were greeting one another as "citizen" and toasting the French Revolution.

Despite the president's attempts to distance himself from French republicans like Citizen Genêt, *Letters from General Washington* pulled him into the maelstroms of transatlantic revolution. After being wrenched from its original context of the American Revolution, the forgery resurfaced alongside advertisements for primers on radical republicanism such as Maximilien Robespierre's *Report on the Principles of Political Morality*, Revolutionary calendars and songbooks, and popular histories memorializing key events in the overthrow of the French aristocracy. In the pages of the *Aurora*, the forgery sold for twenty-five cents along with translations of various French Revolutionary texts (fig. 4.2-4.4), including *The Morality of the Sans Culottes of Every Age, Sex, Country, Condition; or, The Republican Gospel*, a pamphlet whose title alone is enough to conjure up the specter of working-class radicalism gone global. Translations of Robespierre's addresses, printed and distributed by the same press that reissued the scandalous Washington letters, fanned the flames

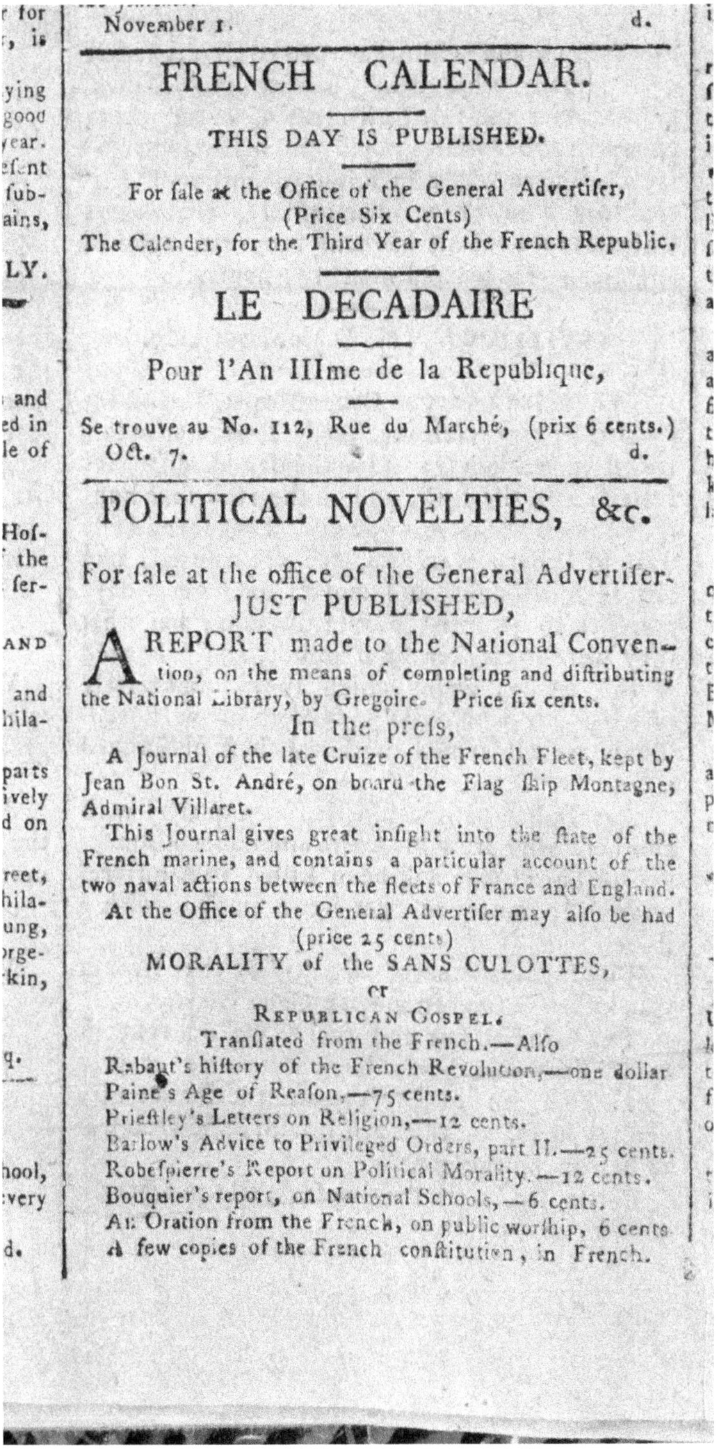

# FRENCH CALENDAR.

### THIS DAY IS PUBLISHED.

For fale at the Office of the General Advertifer,
(Price Six Cents)
The Calender, for the Third Year of the French Republic,

# LE DECADAIRE

### Pour l'An IIIme de la Republique,

Se trouve au No. 112, Rue du Marché, (prix 6 cents.)
Oct. 7.                                           d.

# POLITICAL NOVELTIES, &c.

For fale at the office of the General Advertifer.
### JUST PUBLISHED,

A REPORT made to the National Convention, on the means of completing and diftributing
the National Library, by Gregoire. Price fix cents.
### In the prefs,

A Journal of the late Cruize of the French Fleet, kept by
Jean Bon St. André, on board the Flag fhip Montagne,
Admiral Villaret.

This Journal gives great infight into the ftate of the
French marine, and contains a particular account of the
two naval actions between the fleets of France and England.

At the Office of the General Advertifer may alfo be had
(price 25 cents)
### MORALITY of the SANS CULOTTES,
or
REPUBLICAN GOSPEL.
Tranflated from the French.—Alfo
Rabaut's hiftory of the French Revolution,—one dollar
Paine's Age of Reafon.—75 cents.
Prieftley's Letters on Religion,—12 cents.
Barlow's Advice to Privileged Orders, part II.—25 cents.
Robefpierre's Report on Political Morality.—12 cents.
Bouquier's report, on National Schools,—6 cents.
An Oration from the French, on public worfhip, 6 cents
A few copies of the French conftitution, in French.

FIGURE 4.2 *Bache and the* Aurora *offered a steady stream of Revolutionary texts,
including titles by Paine and Robespierre advertised here. Figs. 4.2–4.4 courtesy of
the American Antiquarian Society.*

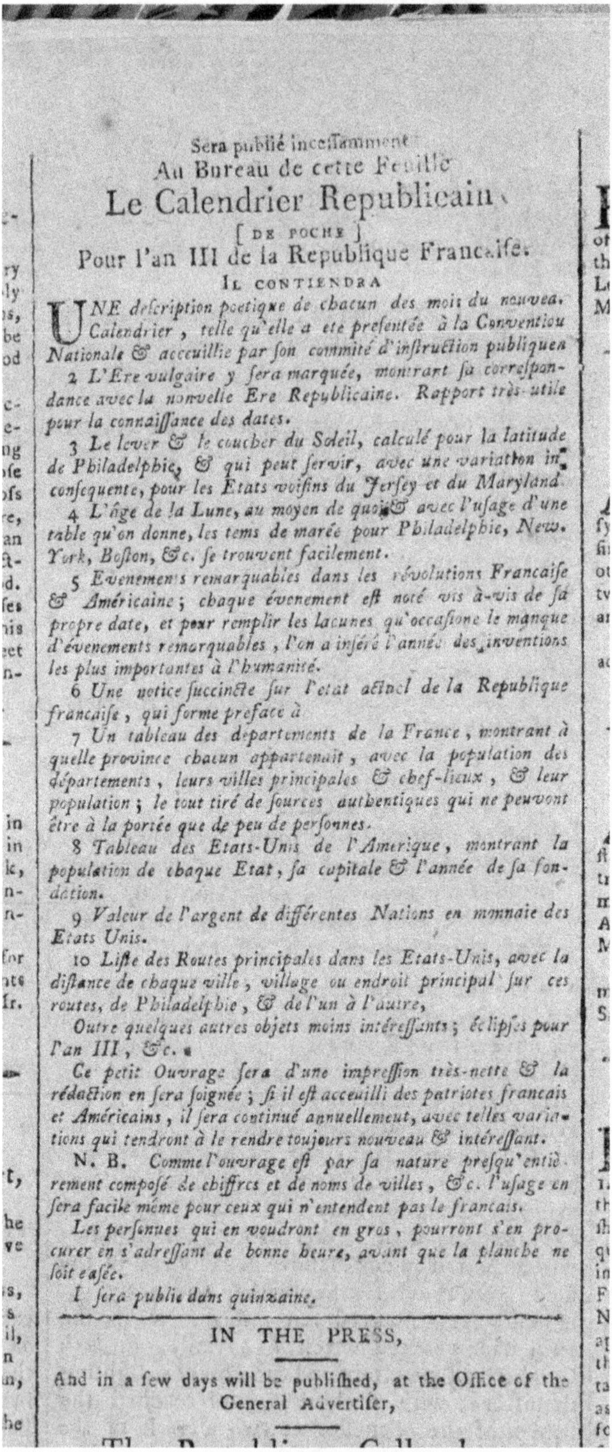

Sera publié inceſſamment

Au Bureau de cette Feuille

# Le Calendrier Republicain

[ DE POCHE ]

Pour l'an III de la Republique Françaiſe.

IL CONTIENDRA

UNE deſcription poetique de chacun des mois du nouveau Calendrier, telle qu'elle a eté preſentée à la Convention Nationale & accueillie par ſon comité d'inſtruction publiquea.

2 L'Ere vulgaire y ſera marquée, montrant ſa correſpondance avec la nouvelle Ere Republicaine. Rapport très-utile pour la connaiſſance des dates.

3 Le lever & le coucher du Soleil, calculé pour la latitude de Philadelphie, & qui peut ſervir, avec une variation in, conſequente, pour les Etats voiſins du Jerſey et du Maryland.

4 L'âge de la Lune, au moyen de quoi & avec l'uſage d'une table qu'on donne, les tems de marée pour Philadelphie, New-York, Boſton, &c. ſe trouvent facilement.

5 Evenemens remarquables dans les révolutions Françaiſe & Américaine; chaque evenement eſt noté vis à-vis de ſa propre date, et pour remplir les lacunes qu'occaſione le manque d'évenements remarquables, l'on a inſéré l'année des inventions les plus importantes à l'humanité.

6 Une notice ſuccinéte ſur l'etat actuel de la Republique françaiſe, qui forme preface à

7 Un tableau des départements de la France, montrant à quelle province chacun appartenait, avec la population des départements, leurs villes principales & chef-lieux, & leur population; le tout tiré de ſources authentiques qui ne peuvent être à la portée que de peu de perſonnes.

8 Tableau des Etats-Unis de l'Amérique, montrant la population de chaque Etat, ſa capitale & l'année de ſa fondation.

9 Valeur de l'argent de différentes Nations en monnaie des Etats Unis.

10 Liſte des Routes principales dans les Etats-Unis, avec la diſtance de chaque ville, village ou endroit principal ſur ces routes, de Philadelphie, & de l'un à l'autre,

Outre quelques autres objets moins intéreſſants; éclipſes pour l'an III, &c.

Ce petit Ouvrage ſera d'une impreſſion très-nette & la rédaction en ſera ſoignée; ſi il eſt accueilli des patriotes francais et Américains, il ſera continué annuellemeut, avec telles variations qui tendront à le rendre toujours nouveau & intéreſſant.

N. B. Comme l'ouvrage eſt par ſa nature preſqu'entiérement compoſé de chiffres et de noms de villes, &c. l'uſage en ſera facile même pour ceux qui n'entendent pas le francais.

Les perſonnes qui en voudront en gros, pourront s'en procurer en s'adreſſant de bonne heure, avant que la planche ne ſoit eaſée.

I ſera publie dans quinzaine.

---

IN THE PRESS,

And in a few days will be publiſhed, at the Office of the General Advertiſer,

FIGURE 4.3 *Notices for French Revolutionary texts from the* Aurora *printed in French.*

*soit easée.*
*I sera publie dans quinzaine.*

## IN THE PRESS,

And in a few days will be published, at the Office of the General Advertiser,

## The Republican Callendar;

[FRENCH POCKET ALMANAC]

For the III year of the French Republic.

CONTAINING:

1. A POETICAL definition of each of the months of the new French Callendar; such as presented to the National Convention and approved by their committee of public instruction.

2. The vulgar Æra will be noted, shewing its relation to the new Republican era; an arrangement which will facilitate the knowledge of French dates.

3. The rising and setting of the sun; calculated for the latitude of Philadelphia, and will serve with an immaterial error for the neighbouring states.

4. The age of the moon; with which and the use of a table given the time of tide for Philadelphia, New-York, Boston, &c. can easily be found.

5 Remarkable events in the American and French Revolutions; Each event is marked opposite its proper date, and to fill up the chasms occuring by the want of remarkable events, the years of useful inventions has been set down.

6 A concise sketch of the present state of France; which is an introduction to

7 A table of the departments of France; shewing to what province each formerly belonged, with the population of each department, the principal cities and capitals, with the population of these; the whole taken from authentic sources, in the hands of but few persons.

8 A table of the United States of America; shewing the population of each state and its capital, as well the year of its first settlement.

9 Value of different coins in federal money.

10 List of principal roads in the United States; with the distance of each town, village or remarkable place on those roads from Philadelphia and from one another.

Besides other articles less interesting, Eclipses &c.

This little work will be neatly and correctly printed. If it meets a favourably reception it shall be continued yearly, with such variations as will render it always new and interesting.

N. B. This work though in French, from its nature, being composed chiefly of figures and names of places, can easily be used by persons who do not understand that language.

Those who purchase by the quantity shall have the usual allowance. Such are requested to apply early, while the form is kept standing.

It will be published within a fortnight.

☞ Printers in this and the neighbouring states will oblige the Editor of the General Advertiser by giving the above in whole or in part a place, for a few times, in their respective papers. If it is convenient to republish any account of the contents and they find it too prolix as it stands above they can shorten each article by closing the period where the semicolon cuts the sentence.

November 1.                                    d.

## FRENCH CALENDAR.

FIGURE 4.4 *English version of advertisement from the* Aurora *for French Revolutionary materials.*

by arguing for the continuing necessity of terror in revolutionary society. "Terror is only justice prompt, severe and inflexible; it is then an emanation of virtue," wrote the French firebrand on the 18th Pluviose in the second year of the republic, that is, five months before he was guillotined in July 1794, confirming the unyielding nature of his own dictum.[36] To the consternation of social conservatives in the United States, the terror was not overseas in France but close at home among the working-class white males, white women, and blacks who lent their support to demonstrations celebrating America's new sister republic. Issue after issue of the *Aurora* printed the resolutions of stateside Democratic-Republican societies alongside lengthy proceedings from Revolutionary councils in Paris and reports from Cap François, Haiti. In this way, Bache's emphasis on diffusion was also a bid to foster broad international sympathies that would connect revolutionary states across the Atlantic.

Alarm only increased, even among Democrat-Republicans like Jefferson, when revolutionary developments spread from France to the island of Saint-Domingue. Slave revolt was well past the limit for pushing republicanism beyond a national geography. Might Jacobins—including the black Jacobins described by C. L. R. James— represent the latest incarnation of the American Revolution? Might the French and Haitian Revolutions rekindle the flames of their American prototype, engulfing proletarians and the racially oppressed at home? The *Republican Calendar* advertised in the *Aurora* correlated the "remarkable events in the American and French Revolutions," in effect, plotting the two events on a single, coincident timeline.[37] As William Appelman Williams wrote, "It seemed, at least for a time, that there might be a third American revolution more influenced by events in France than developments in France were guided by the American example."[38] Since this pronouncement, historians such as Alfred Young, David Waldstreicher, Simon Newman, David Brion Davis, and Joyce Appleby have documented how the hundreds of festivals, parades, and other celebrations staged in support of the French Revolution gave radical republicanism an energetic public presence in the United States. A partisan edge sharpened the tone and spirit of these popular gatherings, as "the Republicans made remarkable use of the French Revolution to drive home their criticisms of a nascent aristocracy."[39] Not to be outdone, Federalist orators sought to shore up post-Revolutionary society against this tide, and followed Edmund Burke by painting the confluence of French and American republicanism as a dangerous conspiracy. Paranoia had its uses: by 1798 the Federalists had successfully implemented the Alien and Sedition Acts to muzzle their partisan opponents.

The reappearance of Washington's counterfeit letters amplified the transatlantic scope of their original publication to include notions of popular democracy associated with French Jacobinism. Loyalist propaganda was revamped in a second performance intended to deepen American sympathies with French Revolutionaries. *Letters from General Washington* insinuated that revolution was not exceptional to the United States but rather a shared legacy that united citizens with *citoyens* across the Atlantic. Back in 1776, the image of Washington second-guessing his rebellion against the king had been calculated to help put the brakes on American Revolutionary nationalism. "I do not really wish for independence," the counterfeit general admitted in a private letter.[40] By 1795 the landscape had changed: "evidence" of Washington's lingering affection for Britain revealed in the letters was now construed as an obstacle to the Revolutionary sentiment that viewed Jacobin France as the next installment of 1776. Yet in the eyes of Washington's detractors the landscape had not changed much at all: Washington was still being seduced by Britain, this time preferring the interests of Anglo-American trade to the republican values of France. Republication of the Washington imposture carries the charge that the Federalist consensus is based on an overidentification with British aristocracy at odds with the popular enthusiasm that aligned the post-Revolutionary United States and Revolutionary France. According to this radical outlook, the United States might not be post-Revolutionary but still Revolutionary.

The forgery relocates national prospects within a comparative framework. Are Americans better off with a king or a band of self-doubting rebels? When *Letters from General Washington* asked this question in 1777, "Washington" provided the answer by regretting his precipitous break with a kind monarch. But by the 1790s both the question and answer had become more complex than the choice between colony and nation. Added to the mix were considerations that opened out on to the lure of radical republicanism in France, slave revolt in the West Indies, and the profits of oceanic trade. This literary imposture, especially as it was framed and advertised by the Democrat-Republican press, in particular Bache's *Aurora*, encouraged an idea of America not as an exceptional nation but as a nexus of comparison.

The importance of French colonial possessions in the Caribbean cannot be underestimated, as ports in Martinique and Saint-Domingue provided American shipping interests with ready access to slaves and sugar. With the outbreak of the Haitian Revolution, American merchants were able to buy at fire sale prices the goods of West Indian planters and ship them to France or to merchants in New England. When war erupted between France and Britain, U.S. crews carrying French commerce soon found themselves under the guns of the British navy. After the slave revolt on Saint-Domingue, American vessels sought to enter a temporary trade vacuum and seize the bulk of the transatlantic commerce running among the United States, France, and Haiti. The British cabinet reacted with an order in council authorizing the Royal Navy to board any vessels trading with Martinique and other French colonies, and hundreds of American ships were caught in the net.[41] In response to British predations, Washington urged appropriations for improving naval defenses. Federalists in Congress supported their president and voted to increase the excise tax on distilled spirits to raise the necessary revenues. The result, as students of American history know, was the Whiskey Rebellion, but what often gets glossed over is that this episode of domestic unrest began in no small part with French, British, and American reactions to the Haitian Revolution.

The West Indian context quickly worked its way back to the president. In contrast to the thoroughly national ring of "father of his country," the forgery renewed insinuations that excessive Anglophilia tempered Washington's nationalism. Over the twenty-year lifetime of the counterfeit, the letters inscribed Washington as an Atlantic subject. In 1777 the letters disclosed a Creole nationalist confessing that he is actually a fallen British colonial; in 1795, the confession was recontextualized by the Napoleonic Wars and the economic importance of the West Indies. The pro-British sentiments of "Washington" now confirmed the president's alignment with reactionary forces battling the spread of French republicanism. The propagandist has Washington experience the strain of "being perpetually obliged to act a part foreign to our true feeling."[42] This admission of feeling "foreign" would take on different meanings over the years, but what remains consistent is the charge that Washington wears a false countenance, pretending to support liberty, whether it is American liberty in 1776 or the more radical French variant in 1795, while harboring affection for aristocracy. Epistolary propaganda sought to change not just what people thought about Washington but, more broadly, the geography of public opinion. Was popular feeling another term for national patriotic sentiment, or was it potentially a more diffuse category of sympathy for Atlantic republicanism? In the context of such questions, *Letters from General Washington* revived scurrilous rumors that Washington remained smitten with British authority, ready at any moment to turn his back on France and the broader cause of transatlantic liberty.

The biggest blow to Washington's popularity was yet to come. British seizures of American vessels had nearly "brought the U.S. and England to the brink of war," and in 1794 relations between the two countries remained fragile.[43] To meet the crisis, Washington dispatched John Jay to England, at which point the president's troubles really began. Jay's mission and the treaty that he eventually secured touched off a bitter propaganda war in which Federalists and Democrat-Republicans fought over "the legality of popular participation in politics."[44] Until Jay returned from England to meet accusations that he had sold out the transatlantic spirit of equality to British financial interests, Washington's reputation had been encircled by a political halo (fig. 4.5). This aura dissolved under charges that the agreement negotiated by Jay was perfidious on several counts: for opponents, the treaty forced the United States to turn its back on France, its ally during the Revolution; it privileged commercial interests over political principles; it safeguarded the importation of luxury goods from England, creating a culture at odds with a republican ethos; it seemingly embroiled Washington and his administration in backroom deals that ran counter to notions of democratic openness and transparency. From the beginning, Jay's appointment as special envoy to England aroused suspicion since his sympathies were assumed to lie with British aristocrats and not French Revolutionaries. Assessing Jay's reception at the British court, an *Aurora* correspondent by the name of "Philo-Republicanus" expressed dismay that the deferential posture adopted by the American minister did not measure up to the standard established twenty years earlier by the "manly behaviour of Franklin when examined before the British Privy Council" during the scandal over the leaked Hutchinson letters.[45] Instead, rumors about Jay's observance of courtly customs imagined him as all too ready to "fawn, flatter, and cajole" in ways

BURNING JAY'S EFFIGY.

FIGURE 4.5  *John Jay being hung and burnt in effigy, as imagined by a nineteenth-century artist in* The Youth's History of the United States *(1887).*

hardly befitting the representative of a free people.[46] The diplomatic accord he brought back to the United States intensified those suspicions, not because of any specific provision, but because its contents were kept secret for months by Washington and the Senate. Public opinion fed on rumor, and the debate over the treaty, in Washington's words, became "enveloped in mist and false representation."[47]

Even though the treaty was highly unpopular, it became one of the best-selling items put out by Bache, who printed it as a pamphlet after its contents were leaked to him by a disgruntled Republican member of the Senate. The ploy hinged on the idea that a confidential document—like the private letters of a general to his wife—was now available to the public. While the *Aurora's* editor traveled to New England to sell copies of the treaty, his wife reported that not long after sunrise crowds had formed outside the printing house to buy the treaty along with the day's edition of the *Aurora*.[48] Publication of the once-secret treaty was perhaps not so much a propaganda tactic as an exercise in public information. Then again, it is the spread—the propagation—of knowledge as well as innuendo that makes information into propaganda.

Bache's activities in leaking sensitive government information did not go unchallenged. The Federalist poet Lemuel Hopkins fired back in verse via a mock epic entitled *The Democratiad* (1795), which takes a dim view of the links among popularity, print culture, and public opinion. Hopkins distorts Bache's concern for openness into the image of an unhinged Jacobin spewing sedition and whipping people's feelings into a frenzy. Beginning with a satiric dedication to Bache, the poem employs rhymed couplets to savage the editor and his Democrat-Republican cronies: "Now wretched Type runs raving round the streets, / Accosting every Democrat he meets."[49] Hopkins was one of the Connecticut Wits, and the witticism here is the pun on "Type," which conflates Bache with the product of his profession—printing type—so that it is not just his person that is let loose in public, but more dangerously, the swill he prints at his Philadelphia offices, including pirated copies of the Jay treaty and forged Washington letters.

The "streets" of the early Republic covered far more than local ground. According to Simon Newman, "The French Revolution...dominated the politics of the street during Washington's presidency."[50] As Bache ran about the public thoroughfares, he fulminated against the treaty on grounds that its ratification would undercut popular sovereignty. The

*Democratiad* imagined the newspaper editor saying, "I'll bet my ears and eyes, / It [the Jay Treaty] will the people all *unpopularize*."[51] Hopkins's neologism associated popularity with misinformed public opinion and the unregulated spread of print. Unpopularizing the people, from Hopkins's perspective, was not such a bad thing and may even have provided a necessary check on the propaganda that sought to pull people into the wider currents of transatlantic revolution. Bache fired back with a neologism of his own when he printed a pamphlet that asked if his fellow citizens "had sufficiently *un-monarchized* their ideas and habits" to wake up to the fact that presidential power merely continued the excesses of kingship.[52] Letters—this time authentic ones—played a part in the pamphlet's appendix, where Bache printed extracts from Washington's official correspondence but interspersed snarky comments in brackets that disparaged the president's courtly style and fawning expressions of Anglomania. To counter what he saw as the sacrifice of the people's will to presidential authority, Bache exercised the prerogative of a printer.

Bache was exactly the sort of "propagator" that made Edmund Burke nervous. What Bache printed was not so much cause for concern as the fact that he traveled the Eastern Seaboard selling his pamphlets, that his newspaper communicated with other presses, that the *Aurora* provided foreign news, in a word, that he propagated. Brought to France and Switzerland for an education among philosophes by his famous grandfather, Bache cultivated contacts that later lent an impressive international flavor to the *Aurora*, a paper considered by historians of print culture as one of the best sources of European news in the early United States. Even the printing supplies that Bache had at his disposal had a Continental flavor since his matrices (molds for casting letters) had been imported for him from France by someone who knew his way around a print shop: Benjamin Franklin.[53] Dubbed "Young Lightning Rod" by his detractors, Bache used the *Aurora* to charge public opinion with oppositional energy.

But as Bache's reprinting of the treaty showed, it was not necessarily the content of what he printed that proved scandalous.[54] The worry rather was that he printed at all. He did so without following any protocol, dumping issues of the *Aurora* as well as the treaty pamphlet on the public indiscriminately. He tapped the democratic potential of propaganda by recognizing its tendency to spread laterally across public spaces. The Jay Treaty may have been under control in the Senate, but its public dissemination became the stuff of popular ferment, one of the "unlooked-for strokes" that Burke's *Reflections on the Revolution in France* sees residing in the unchecked circulation of information.

The spread of popular resentment over the proposed treaty had its source in political affection for the French people, a sense of loyalty owed to the European power that had thrown its weight behind the thirteen colonies' Revolution and that was now experiencing its own Revolution. Democrat-Republicans charged that "the wretched negociator," as "Scipio" referred to Jay in the pages of the *Aurora*, did not have the interests of their sister republic at heart and instead cared more about the pocketbooks of the merchant class.[55] Historians have often given credence to these suspicions, concluding that Jay did not press his hand when dealing with Lord George Grenville, though it remains a matter of debate how much leverage the U.S. envoy had in securing an accord to protect American shipping while addressing unresolved issues from the American Revolution, such as Britain's control of the Great Lakes forts. At a gut level, however, Jay and other Federalists most certainly sided with Anglo-American business interests over transatlantic republicanism. In this diplomatic and political context, *Letters from General Washington* reappeared, reviving insinuations that Washington had too much feeling for the British. As epistolary propaganda, the counterfeit implied that the American general's unguarded political sentiments in the past gave evidence of the president's danger of once again being seduced by the British.

## "True History"

Fake did not necessarily mean untrue. According to this logic, epistolary propaganda could disclose the true colors of a false patriot. This casual disregard for facts corresponds to theories and practices of fiction emerging in the eighteenth century. As Catherine Gallagher argues, under "the rise of fictionality," novelistic narrative prioritizes truth over fact, not in spite of but because its invented particulars are readily taken to suggest general facets of the human condition. If "fiction somehow suspends, deflects, or otherwise disables normal referential truth claims about the world," then it also enables irregular truth claims founded in plausibility, innuendo, or other unverifiable assertions.[56]

In the case of the Washington counterfeit, letters privately exchanged are put into public circulation in a process best associated with epistolary fiction. As the preface to a 1795 edition put it, the epistles offer a view of the famous man in his "real character" gleaned from "private reflection and domestic concerns" that vies with official reputation.[57] Their truth-value inheres in the belief that intimate correspondence, despite the layers of untrustworthy statements, disguise, and even forgery, nonetheless provides a reliable index of where loyalties actually lie. The American commander inhabits a world of false appearance, confessing that he "wear[s] a countenance dressed in the calm serenity of perfect confidence, whilst my heart is corroded with infinite apprehensions."[58] "Washington" extends the deception beyond his private self by claiming that a fiction underwrites the entirety of the colonists' cause: "It has been our policy...to hold out false lights to the world. There are not an hundred men in America that know our true situation; three-fourths of the Congress itself are ignorant of it."[59] The truth of Washington's forged letters is that the general tells lies. Even as fiction goes to great lengths to establish its historical verisimilitude, "early novelistic narrative... also partook of a standard of truth-telling alternative to the empirical," as Michael McKeon writes.[60] Secret loyalties, covert allegiances, masked sympathies, unstated agendas—all of which resist empirical proof—are political truths ferreted out by the inventions of propaganda.

It is perhaps the British radical William Godwin who in 1797 first assessed the political import of such inventions. In what amounts to an early theory of fiction, he suggests that exaggeration, fable, romance, and letters often communicate a deeper, truer truth than fact-driven history. As though Godwin had *Letters from General Washington* in mind, he writes that in order to gain real knowledge of any individual, "I would see the friend and the father...as well as the patriot."[61] This pursuit leads beyond public persona, creating a demand for access to private and perhaps hidden materials—"I would read his works and his letters, if any remain to us"—that supplement official, state-sanctioned knowledge about political actors. The turn away from the empirical toward what Godwin called "the operation of the human passions" entails more than the substitution of psychological impressions for tangible bits of evidence. His concern lies instead with fiction's pedagogical functions, its ability to explain as well as motivate action. Godwin, who wrote his own novels and biographies (including a candid memoir of his wife, Mary Wollstonecraft) about dark secrets, presented fiction as an investigative tool. Such disregard for standard measures of ascertaining veracity leads to a dethroning of history and the elevation of a discourse "which bears the stamp of invention." For Godwin, the impact of literary "invention" can exceed any factual basis, in effect, becoming one of the "unlooked-for stroke[s]" from the pens of propagators that so worried Burke in his history of the French Revolution.

Godwin's indifference to the study of history and impatience with empirical standards produce a significant recalibration: "I ask, not as a principal point, whether it be true of false? My first enquiry is, 'Can I derive instruction from it? Is it a genuine praxis upon the nature of man? Is it pregnant with the most generous motives and examples? If so, I had rather be profoundly versed in this fable, than in all the genuine histories that ever existed.'" These are the criteria not of Enlightenment rationality but of propaganda. As opposed to unhelpful distinctions between truth and falsity, Godwin introduces "genuine praxis" as an alternative benchmark. While it is tempting to understand *praxis* here as practical thinking that offers a springboard for social and political action, as in contemporary usage influenced by Marxist thought, more likely Godwin's sense of the term originates with the now obsolete meaning of a "collection of examples to serve for practice or exercise in a subject" (*OED*), that is, a working model whose pedagogical function provides repeated opportunities for practice. A praxis is a material artifact of seventeenth- and eighteenth-century print culture that could be regularly consulted for gaining proficiency in linguistic areas such as syntax and grammar. Insofar as the inventions of fiction and propaganda constitute a praxis, their pedagogical function lies in providing insight into human motivations. More than a collection of names and dates about what happened and when, fictionality as a praxis corrects for an inert array of facts by accounting for the hidden motives and unspoken affects that inspire human beings to act.

Godwin's method for distinguishing factual accounts from fictive history bristles with undisciplined energies. Like Burke, he surveys the French Revolution, but his perspective is far more buoyant. Suppose the task is to understand the events leading from the fall of the Bastille to the execution of Louis XVI. To aver that a mob on July 14, 1789, stormed a prison tells us nothing just as knowing that the

French monarch was guillotined at the Place de la Concorde hardly begins to explain momentous political and social convulsions. Facts supply only "the mere skeleton of history. The muscles, the articulations, every thing in which the life emphatically resides, is absent." The contrast is both instructive and chilling: history can be received in forms as impersonal and as inert as Louis XVI's headless body or it can be experienced as a realm of motive power. Sticking to facts (the mere bones of history) leaves praxis as but a dead possibility. Muscles instead allow for movement and action, but as Godwin no doubt knew (perhaps in anticipation of the gruesome body that his daughter, Mary Shelley, would imagine in *Frankenstein*) soft tissue decomposes more quickly than bone. What remains is the skeleton of history, an evidentiary trace, which, like a ruin that can be visited or a date that can be verified, cannot move as it hardens into fact. To revivify history, Godwin recommends the insight provided by fable, romance, and story, implying that fiction and invention can breathe life back into character, sentiment, and morality. Not only does the skeleton of history begin at this point to move; more importantly, it begins to move us.

Ideas and impressions conveyed by a novel or other fiction augment an otherwise impassive chronicle of fact with scenes of emotion. A feeling for what Godwin calls "the empire of motives," a region not on any map, provides a praxis for gauging human behavior. The pedagogical qualities of "instructive inventions" reside precisely in their inventive attributes. Knowledge of sympathies, loyalties, and other affective attachments constitute the connective tissue that make a fictive history both kinetic and edifying, in other words, truer, than any onslaught of facts. As Godwin put it, "true history consists in a delineation of consistent, human character, in a display of the manner in which such a character acts under successive circumstances." One might say that "true history" is necessarily fictive and, in extreme cases, perhaps as fake as a series of forged letters that nonetheless purport to reveal the truth by offering a coherent portrait of a subject's private motives. Consider that when *Letters from General Washington* first appeared, the falsified documents were said to shed true light on Washington's character even by those who saw through the sham. A British journal scoffed that "we cannot look upon these letters as genuine," but in the next breath the editors nonetheless maintained that "they would do great honour to General Washington, could his claim to them be indisputably established."[62] The verisimilitude of the forgery rested on its claim to represent a private view of the man even if that perspective was not based strictly on facts. The real Washington resembles his invented counterpart.

Such consistency of character underwrites the most vilifying charge leveled by the fake letters. How to explain why a lover of liberty in 1776 would twenty years later side with an aristocratic order over a republican one? How to account for a leader who would disregard an accord with France, its ally during the American Revolution, to broker a treaty with its former enemy? A "true history" in Godwin's sense, *Letters from General Washington* offered answers by inventing a paper trail that showed how the father of his country had always harbored pro-British sentiments. Not public facts, but imagined private disclosures and unverifiable confessions discovered in secret correspondence provided an instructive narrative of political character. Much as private letters revealed the general's abiding Anglophilia, now the president seemed to be conducting public politics in private by insisting that the specifics of the Jay Treaty remain out of sight, its contents shielded by the locked doors of the Senate.[63] Behind false fronts and secret government proceedings, so the slander implied, lies the truth of Washington's duplicitous nature. At the very least, the manner in which Washington kept the treaty under wraps reinforced suspicions both that anti-French sentiments were guiding foreign policy and that the whole scheme showed disdain for transparency. When a copy of the treaty that Jay had negotiated at last completed the Atlantic crossing (previous copies had been tossed overboard when a French privateer closed in on the ship carrying the diplomatic papers), the Senate already had adjourned while the president, citing executive privilege, saw no reason to make the contents of the document public.

During the recess, the print war between factions intensified, and, by the time the Senate reconvened, charges about Democrat-Republicans as godless Jacobins and countercharges about neotyrannical Federalists were flying fast and furious. Although the Federalists eventually won the battle, passing the treaty by the slimmest of margins, they lost the larger ideological war by appealing to public opinion in ways "that helped to hasten the acceptance of a more open, democratic culture espoused by the Republicans."[64] In opposition to the public debate waged in newspaper columns, the Senate conducted its discussions of the treaty behind closed doors. When the House of Representatives protested the lack of transparency, the president laid out his case in a March 1796 letter informing congressmen that he would not buckle to their demands because in his view "the nature of foreign negotiations...must often depend on secrecy." He then proceeded to school Congress on the extent of executive authority, asserting that treaty-making powers lay with the president "with the advice and consent of the Senate."[65] After all, as Washington reminded the representatives, he was there when the Constitution was written and this particular point established. The upshot was that the House had no say in passing treaties. Because the decision to side with the British Crown over French republicans had been made in secret, without public discussion, and with no input from the people's representatives, the insult rankled that much more keenly. Viewed as a counterforce to the Senate's elite and restrictive nature, the House, many of its Republican members felt, had been cut out of the governing process.

Although few citizens had actually read the treaty until it was leaked to the press, everything about the document from its drafting to its ratification seemed to confirm Democrat-Republican suspicions over the government's antidemocratic tendencies. Its genesis lay in a counterrevolutionary impulse hostile to French liberty. Its passage bespoke a shift toward a unitary concentration of power. And its implementation gave depressing proof that the people's representatives had been made auxiliary. "Jay's Treaty of surrender," to use Paine's inimitable phrase, was unpopular in the truest sense of the word: for Bache at the *Aurora* and his fellow Democrat-Republicans, there was nothing *populāris* about the matter; the treaty hardly seemed to be belonging to the people as a whole.[66] These struggles over the meaning of the popular breathed new life into the propaganda of the faked Washington letters.

For weeks in spring 1796, the Philadelphia *Aurora* ran notices for a new edition of *Letters from General Washington* published by the Federal Press (fig. 4.6). The advertisements neglected to mention that the Federal Press was in actuality Bache's printing house, but it would have been clear to any reader that the *Aurora* was in the thick of the fracas.[67] The conflict over the Jay Treaty had given the *Aurora* the first major scoop of the Republic when Bache broke the seal on its secret contents after a copy had been smuggled out of the Senate. This move displayed not so much an eagerness to profit on the sensation of what everyone was talking about (although profit would will permit. On the merit of the performance, not a word need be said: the writer is well known to every friend to literature; and it is enough to mention, that the work now offered has never before been, in whole or in part, published.

The price of subscription is one-sixth of a dollar for each weekly number. To non-subscribers the price will be advanced. The price of three numbers to be paid on delivery of the first, and the same sum on the delivery of each third number thereafter.

The number of the edition is necessarily limited. Those, therefore, who wish to be possessed of this valuable novelty (which is also a beautiful specimen of typography) will early avail themselves of this opportunity by setting down their names.

Dec. 13. d.

THIS DAY IS PUBLISHED,
And to be had at the Office of the AURORA, and of all the principal booksellers.
(PRICE 25 CENTS.)

Letters from Gen. Washington

To several of his friends in June and Ju 1776, in which is set forth an INTERESTING VIEW of AMERICAN POLITICS, at that all-important period.

PREFACE to this new EDITION.

The following Letters are, at this time, republished from a Boston Edition now out of print, as furnishing an interesting appendix to the official Letters of General Washington which have lately made their appearance. d

ADDRESS
From the WORKING CABINET-MAKERS, Of PHILADELPHIA, To their Mechanical Fellow-Citizens.

CITIZENS,

IN addressing you on a subject of such importance as that of Society, we feel much satisfaction in knowing that we do not stand particular from the greater part of our Mechanical Brethren as to the necessity of so important an object. But as rapid advances have been made to introduce into this FREE COUNTRY, that system of oppression and disorganization which European mechanics labour under, from the intolerable avarice of their employers, we would think ourselves highly criminal, if we did not, at this important period, step forward, in order to preserve that independence which as active and industrious citizens we ought to possess. For the more speedy and effectual accomplishment of this object, we hope and intreat, that an union of the respective MECHANICAL BRANCHES in this City, and throughout

THIS DAY IS PUBLISHED,
At the OFFICE of the AURORA,
And to be had of the BOOKSELLERS;
[Price One Eighth of a Dollar.]

Thomas Paine's latest Work,
A DISSERTATION ON FIRST PRINCIPLES OF GOVERNMENT.
To which is added his LAST SPEECH to the CONVENTION on the same subject.

A LARGE EDITION of this WORK, which the EDITOR of the AURORA has just received from the AUTHOR in PARIS, is now opened for Sale. The usual allowance will be made to BOOKSELLERS, and POLITICAL WORKS taken in exchange.

The design and nature of this small tract may be collected, by the following extract of a letter from the WRITER on the subject:

" It is intended to bring what I have already said upon that subject [THE FIRST PRINCIPLES OF GOVERNMENT] into a small compass, and into a direct point of view."

PUBLIE ADJOURDHUI,
Au BUREAU de l'AURORA,
Et chez les LIBRAIRES,
[Prix un huitieme de gourde]

Le Dernier Ouvrage de
Thomas Paine,
UNE DISSERTATION SUR LES PREMIERS PRINCIPES DE GOUVERNEMENT.

L'EDITEUR de l'AURORA vient de recevoir de l'AUTEUR a PARIS une EDITION EN FRANCAIS de cet ouvrage. Les LIBRAIRES pourront s'en procurer. Il prendra en echange des livres sur la politique.

La nature de ce petit ouvrage s'explique dans l'extrait qui suit, d'une lettre de l'AUTEUR :

" Mon intention en ecrivant cette dissertation a été de condenser et concentrer mes idées sur ce sujet" [LES PREMIERS PRINCIPES DU GOUVERNEMENT.]

Nov. 19. d

THE First Physicians, terrified with the ravages of the VENEREAL DISEASE, and alarmed by the insufficiency and danger of the remedies commonly applied, have constantly wished for a medicine free from the inconveniencies of MERCURY, and a real specific against that cruel disease.

M. LAFFECTEUR, in the year 1777, came

FIGURE 4.6 *Notice from the* Aurora *for a new edition of the counterfeit Washington letters alongside French and English advertisements for Thomas Paine's works. Courtesy of the American Antiquarian Society.*

have been welcome to this printer whose republican sympathies discouraged would-be advertisers) but rather an activist commitment to democratic openness and the virtues of an informed citizenry. The new preface tacked on to *Letters from General Washington* also traded on the idea of propaganda as publicity by "furnishing an interesting appendix to the Official Letters" written by Washington as military commander.[68] Exactly what amounted to "interesting" may have been open to interpretation, but as a matter of propaganda, the gist was clear: in a climate where the official government seemed to operate behind a veil of secrecy, unofficial documents provided the only legitimately popular source for forming public opinion.

Whether stolen by the British during the American Revolution (as the "Washington" letters supposedly were) or smuggled out of Congress (as the treaty was), the disclosure of private letters and papers helped to "diffuse," as Bache had put it in his notices for starting a newspaper, popular knowledge. The epistolary novel's penchant for turning private matters into public ones set the stage for propaganda in the early Republic to circulate, one might say, as a rogue version of the Freedom of Information Act *avant la lettre*. In the world of epistolary politics, forgery might prove an effective means for getting at the truth. Taking a page from the novel of letters, Bache, it is tempting to surmise, believed that fake letters accurately portrayed the true state of Washington's British sympathies. "Much has been done by the executive administration toward recolonizing us a new [sic]," the *Aurora* charged, identifying Washington's aristocratic pretensions and mercantile loyalties as the most pressing threat to republicanism.[69] Bache's newspaper made this allegation on July 4, 1796, a full six months after the Jay Treaty went into effect, suggesting that the time had come for a second American revolution. The anxiety that the neocolonialism of a merchant class was taking root in the United States prompted printer-activists associated with the *Aurora* to report on the nation as foreign to itself, estranged from the core principles of republicanism. For Bache and the émigré writers who flocked to the *Aurora*, the frequent correspondence that the paper received from Paris and London in conjunction with the counterfeits, exposés, and unauthorized editions of the printscape together formed a connective tissue for circulating ideas about comparative revolutions in America, France, and, to a lesser extent, Saint-Domingue.


## "War! War!! War!!!"

As World War I had confirmed for Lippmann and as the history of secret wars in Central America suggests to Chomsky, propaganda provides little public enlightenment. But in the propaganda of 1776 and its retransmissions during the 1790s, we witness an alternative practice that links fiction and forgery to the dissemination of information. Such information need not be accurate or factual to be true.

Instead, truth inheres in its propagation. If information is repeated and spread widely enough, it can attain the sort of consistency that Godwin saw as essential to the invention of "true history." So, too, while Burke recognized that the fanaticism of the French Revolution was easily demystified, he seemed less assured about combating "a multitude of writings dispersed with incredible assiduity and expense."[70] The sophisticated networks of print alluded to here in Burke's *Reflections on the Revolution in France* are a variation on earlier episodes of dissemination such as the unauthorized circulation of Governor Hutchinson's personal letters or the strategies of replication found in Mercy Otis Warren's correspondence and dramatic satires. The propagandist's forged letters of George Washington were consistent in playing up the intrigue over correspondence, but what made them remarkable was their return to printing shops long after the moment of their initial appearance in 1777. Throughout their life in print, the counterfeit epistles revealed not a private truth about Washington but a public truth that heterodox communication and dissenting reports could be circulated.

In the midst of pushing a new edition of *Letters from General Washington*, the *Aurora* publicly advertised for the production and circulation of more propaganda. The appeal was laced with sarcasm and irony. An "Advertisement Extraordinary" in the *Aurora* solicited fabrications that could be used to legitimize the Jay Treaty. Offering $1,000 for a "plausible story" that would rally public opinion around ratification, the paper advised that the distribution of fictional inventions best engineered not consent but opposition. "The bugbear of war is likely to prove most efficacious" in making people back governmental actions that run counter to popular interests.[71] Only by stirring up fears that military conflict with Britain was imminent could Federalists foist their fraud on the public. Back in 1787, writing as Publius in *The Federalist*, Jay had concluded "that there are *pretended* as well as just causes of war."[72] Whether or not Bache was remembering this point from the debates over the Constitution, the *Aurora* now took this logic to its satirical extreme by inviting manufactured news reports that would provide just cause for the Jay Treaty.

Two weeks after this "advertisement" in the *Aurora*, just as Washington was reminding Congress of its place with respect to treaty negotiations, a contributor (most likely Bache or one of his staff) claimed the prize. The winning entry took the hint about "the bugbear of war" by ominously forecasting that the United States would be besieged on all sides by enemies if the House of Representatives blocked the Jay Treaty. Threatening "War! War!! War!!!" in its headline, this piece spun a far-fetched scenario in which "no less than five different wars" will be "declared against us immediately" if the ire of Britain is provoked. Joining the alliance against the United States would be Tippo Saib of India, who had been resisting British forces led by Lord Charles Cornwallis (then currently reviving his career after Yorktown by fighting a different set of colonials). A recent pact between the sultan and the British would bring an invading Eastern force to the shores of America "to avenge the insult offered to his puissant ally" in the event that the British treaty is rejected. From the North "all the Indian nations are ready at a single war whoop" to stream over the Canadian border while from the Southern Hemisphere prison ships loaded with convicts from Botany Bay will be pointed to America in order to enforce the monarch's will and tame the "jacobinic crew" opposing the president and his plans for rapprochement with England.[73] A version of this accusation echoed with the republication of *Letters from General Washington*, which the paper had been steadily promoting in the preceding weeks: a dangerous mixture of fear and love caused many at the highest levels of American government to overidentify with the British Crown.

Was the American public to be cowed by a pro-British faction that sided with an imperial power whose "forces [are] triumphant in every quarter of the globe," or would people's sympathies remain with its sister nation that in 1789 had continued the republican fight to do away with aristocratic social distinctions?[74] The battle waged across the printscape by Bache and the *Aurora* was to defy not England but American Anglophiles. This stand implied extending the American Revolution of 1776 into the present, a task best accomplished if revolution were viewed not as an exclusive American monopoly but as an experienced shared by other transatlantic locales. Bache's opposition also meant that he would soon be jailed under the Alien and Sedition Acts signed into law by Washington's successor, John Adams. In this hostile environment, propaganda contrivances such as "War! War!! War!!!" sought to keep popular support for transatlantic republicanism in focus even as it was becoming eclipsed by scenes of French Revolutionary terror, the specter of Haitian slave revolt, and charges of sedition at home. Before Bache could stand trial, he contracted yellow fever and was dead at age twenty-nine.

Although Bache's efforts to turn the tide against a growing Federalist consensus were cut short, it is uncertain that these ironic installments would have had much sway in shifting the course of public opinion. The shortcoming lay not in the merit of the message but in the mode of address: the bite of satire does not persuade as readily as propaganda that seeks to gain assent. By manufacturing not consent but dissent in his printing shop, Bache ultimately found himself working at cross-purposes from his goal of broader dissemination. Like his namesake who in 1773 had facilitated the transmission of Hutchinson's stolen letters, Benjamin Franklin Bache saw the political value of reprinting Washington's stolen letters even if the whole scheme was a known ruse. And like Mercy Otis Warren before him, Bache discovered that his labors to diffuse fact and fiction in an effort to "keep pace with the public curiosity," as he claimed to be doing by printing resolutions that the president surrender all secret documents relating to the treaty, narrowed his audience to a faction.[75]

Notwithstanding the differences in scale between an eighteenth-century newspaper named the *Aurora* and modern media conglomerates, Bache's failure provides a still relevant lesson. Then, as now, the free flow of communication provoked scaremongers. By May 1796, the *Aurora* reported that its stories and dispatches had been denounced as "a link of the chain of terrorism by the alarmists."[76] Yet no one was expected to take the *Aurora*'s extraordinary fiction as fact. Neither India nor Sardinia with "100,000 picked troops" (one more power that would supposedly rally to Britain's side) was set to invade America. The writer admitted, "I have invented lies enough to terrify all the old women in the Union."[77] The obviousness of the satire calls attention to the role that fabrication and forgery play in creating public opinion. Its subtlety, however, lies in pointing out how consent never is formed purely inside domestic settings but is instead a product of more global contexts. The lesson—and it is not confined only to this one case—is that supposed secret intelligence about war needs to be framed by the contexts of propagation in which fake histories and heterodox truths circulate.

# Aftermath

## THE POETRY OF THE POST-REVOLUTION

Bits of communications about global empire and radical republi-canism examined in the preceding chapters surfaced once more in the inaugural issue of an obscure newspaper begun by Philip Freneau, the so-called Poet of the American Revolution. More than twenty years after the Revolution itself, the first installment of *The Time Piece and Literary Companion* of March 13, 1797, greeted the public by stressing the continuing need for "disseminating useful knowl-edge" if the prospects for public enlightenment and social happiness were to stand a chance in America. The concern for information scatter, a practice that had proved so critical to correspondence net-works of the 1770s (see chapter 1), motivated this publication venture despite the fact that Freneau already had left a string of failed news-papers in his wake. The first issue featured a long column on East India (discussed in chapter 3), informing readers about Lord Cornwallis's role in leveling the temples of Pondicherry, India, and asking them to consider the luck of American cities in escaping a similar fate. The "propagators of novelties" who caused such conster-nation in *Reflections on the Revolution in France* (see chapter 4) reap-pear in an article on Edmund Burke's *Letters on a Regicide Peace* (1796), which, according to this New York paper, played up reac-tionary fears that "atheism, jacobinism, and regicide...[would] be disseminated among other nations" if Britain entered into negotia-tions with Revolutionary France. Days later, the second issue of the *Time Piece* returned to the affair of Washington's counterfeit epistles (also chapter 4) by printing a testimonial from the former president that sought to put to rest the embarrassment created by "a base for-gery" that he "never saw or heard of...until [it] appeared in print."[1]

Freneau made a case for this latest journalistic undertaking by highlighting the connections between dissemination and popular politics in an address "to the Public" on page one. Emphasizing the matter of dissemination with metaphors of seeds and propagation, Freneau observed that widely sown knowledge would be "within the reach of every man who will but take up a spade or a mattock for the purpose of attaining it."[2] Such simple agricultural virtue resonated with the republican lifestyle of the sort that Mercy Otis Warren and her husband (see chapter 2) imagined for themselves as the new owners of a farm—really Thomas Hutchinson's confiscated country estate—in Milton, Massachusetts. For diehard republicans like Freneau and Warren, knowledge and information should not follow the same course as wealth in the new Republic where land and other economic resources were fast becoming the subject of rampant speculation and consolidated into fewer hands. In drawing these battle lines, the opening column in the *Time Piece* reacted to the pervasive tensions between republican values and liberal interests that historians see as endemic to post-Revolutionary society.[3]

What is noteworthy is the rebroadcast of this public address in poetic form just three pages later. A "Poetic Address" from the editor celebrates this latest publishing venture by claiming in decasyllabic rhyme that "wherever our pages may chance to be read," then surely their message will be "spread."[4] The paper's layout illustrates how these "public" and "poetic" expressions mirrored one another. Printed on both sides of a single sheet and then folded to create four pages, the *Time Piece* places the "Poetic Address" on the back page in the same relative position as the page-one announcement of the newspaper's public mission. This visual overlapping of prose and poetry raises questions about the relationship between literary media and continuing revolution. Do prose and verse move at different speeds across printscape? How does attention to literary genre, so often studied in terms of formal properties, enhance our understanding of propaganda as preeminently a kinetic form that entails public distribution and circulation? Such questions are at core a media matter that concerns the uncertain relevance and viability of Revolutionary communications in post-Revolutionary society.

## Poetry in "the Ocean of News"

Poems and ballads have always been found in the quivers of American propagandists. Paine's "Liberty Tree," after its initial appearance in the *Pennsylvania Magazine* of July 1775, surfaced in at least five news-papers. Mercy Otis Warren had less success when she made the Boston Tea Party the subject of a mock epic, likely because the thick layer of poetic allusions in her "The Squabble of the Sea Nymphs" lacked the rousing feel of Paine's composition. Further to the south, an anonymous song printed in the *Virginia Gazette* in early 1774 (mentioned in chapter 3) set its lines about the "Cursed Weed of China's Coast" to the tune of a familiar melody in a bid to popularize the dumping of the tea.[5] While averring that "no one can gauge the influence of this musical propaganda," Arthur Schlesinger looks at the broadsides and news sheets from the time of the Stamp Act to the onset of the Revolution to surmise that it constituted a lively addi-tion to the patriots' rhetorical arsenal.[6] In the migration of popular poetry and song to the common spaces of public inns and taverns, the artifacts of printscape soon diffused and dissolved into oral cul-ture as well.[7] Poetry rarely achieved the rarefied status that it is some-times seen as having today; it was always embedded within the rude bustle of printscape, appearing without much fanfare in penny sheets and handbills.

Philip Freneau's poetry—like the bulk of the verse produced and published in his day—never escaped the creases and smudges that were an everyday feature of print shops. In several poems about printers and printing that Freneau wrote, he often acknowledged that poetry fails to transcend the materiality of its own inked exist-ence. Lyrical offerings, "wet from press" and hastily folded and placed in the post rider's bag, to quote from Freneau's "The Country Printer," had a decidedly homespun aura.[8] The visible traces of hur-ried production suggested an urgent politics that made this printer "the patriot of the town" who "with press and ink attack'd the royal side."[9] This candid portrait of the condition of poetry was itself des-tined for the printed and folded sheets of the *National Gazette*, the Philadelphia newspaper that Freneau edited from 1791 to 1793. Although collections of Freneau's poetry feature "The Country Printer" as a single coherent piece, it initially appeared in four install-ments over the course of several nonconsecutive issues. Readers had to wait many days and skip more than one issue in order to string together the installments of the poem. This hiatus dramatized how poetry, despite its pretension to formal polish and unity, was often rendered episodic and discontinuous. No wonder that Freneau's poem about a newspaper that was itself published in a newspaper dwells on the infelicities of printing—the "inverted letters," the "Colons derang'd," the "commas out of place"—that together make for "wretched proofs."[10]

In short, the situation of poetry was not pretty. Critics have not been much kinder than printers, often deeming such newspaper verse as workmanlike, too suited for the exigencies of the hour to attain lasting significance. Starting with the comments of George Washington, who famously expressed annoyance with Freneau, the poet's stature has frequently been tainted by the accusation that his writing was too partisan to qualify as poetic or dignified. As Thomas Jefferson recalled the occasion of Washington's outburst, columns in Freneau's *National Gazette* crossed the line of decorum and truth by "charging him with wanting to be a King." The president then used a phrase—"that *rascal Freneau*"—that left an indelible blot on his reputation. Washington was not merely complaining about content, although reading about his supposed grand plot to become emperor of America must have nettled this reluctant statesman who wanted only to return to his plantation at Mount Vernon. The president was just as irked by the matter of circulation: Freneau insisted on sending "him three of his papers every day, as if he thought he [Washington] would become the distributor of his papers."[11] The father of his country was no paperboy, but in inveighing against distribution he identified a crucial concern of post-Revolutionary media. Surely, nothing mattered more than the substance of political ideas, but how much did notions of the public good require their circulation, especially when much of what was being disseminated was characterized by personal attack, invective, and, as some alleged, sedition? This uncertainty became a source of deep division within Washington's administration, fueling rancorous disputes between Federalists and Democrat-Republicans that fractured the public sphere in the early Republic. In this context, the communication of political beliefs came to matter as much as the beliefs themselves.

Jefferson recognized this fact perhaps better than anyone when he undertook to establish a press organ that would be sympathetic to the viewpoints of Democrat-Republicans and compete with the newspaper aligned with Alexander Hamilton and the Federalists, John Fenno's *Gazette of the United States*. He first approached Benjamin Franklin Bache, who had already begun editing a paper at his Philadelphia printing house. When Bache declined, he turned to Freneau, whose fame as a poet lent more than a little refinement to the enterprise. Had Bache accepted, it is likely the that the project would have had a different look, since the inaugural issue of Bache's *General Advertiser* (later to become the *Aurora General Advertiser*) had straightaway announced that while the paper would from time to time feature "poetical performances," the editor just as soon preferred that his paper "should be without a poetical sprig."[12] Under Freneau's direction, issues featuring a hodgepodge of poetry, invented dialogues, meteorological charts, governmental reports, and letters from Saint-Domingue formed something like an experiment in mixed media.

Since the profitability of newspapers was always a risky proposition, Jefferson secured Freneau a post as a translator at the State Department at a salary of $250 a year, which left him plenty of time to devote to running a national newspaper for the opposition. Beginning October 31, 1791, the *National Gazette* "by PHILIP FRENEAU," as the masthead proclaimed twice a week for the next two years, set out with the goal of reaching subscribers not just in Philadelphia and other urban centers but also in the outlying areas of the states. As Freneau put it in a poem typeset for the first issue, since the public is "launch'd ... on the ocean of news," readers would do well to subscribe to a paper that promised to follow Dutch, French, and British publications. Frequent intelligence printed about the Revolution in France, the tumult in Saint-Domingue, and the military campaigns by the federal government against the Creeks and other tribes reflected the paper's diplomatic ties to Jefferson in his position as secretary of state. As Freneau's poem laid out a somewhat desultory justification for the paper, "Revolutions must happen, and printers must live," so why not give this new venture in publishing a try?[13]

When Hamilton, Jefferson's rival at the Treasury Department, got wind of the fact that Freneau was in the State Department's employ, the line of attack against the *National Gazette* and Freneau became obvious. Should an officer of the government be in the business of subsidizing a newspaper editor in a country that valued an independent press? Was it not a conflict of interest for Jefferson to be allied with a paper that was critical of Washington's administration when he himself was a member of the president's cabinet? To Hamilton, it seemed that Freneau was receiving a government salary "to oppose the measures of government, and, by false insinuations, to disturb the public peace."[14] The charge was not too far off the mark: as an ardent republican, Freneau was by definition a member of the loyal opposition.

As part of the fallout from this newspaper war, Jefferson resigned his cabinet post, and when the yellow fever epidemic hit Philadelphia, Freneau's paper closed its doors without ever reopening despite the editor's promise to readers "to resume the publication of this newspaper in short time" with a new and improved look courtesy of the latest "elegant printing types from Europe."[15] The feud between Jefferson and Hamilton is well known, and historians have discussed the part that the respective newspapers, the *National Gazette* and the *Gazette of the United States*, allied with each played in inflaming partisan divisions.[16] Less studied is how Freneau's poetry became a casualty of this internecine strife. Among the historians and literary critics first to return to Freneau were Progressive-era scholars whose studies were inevitably framed by the sobering revelations about the role that propaganda had played in shaping public opinion during World War I. "The poet of the American Revolution," Vernon Parrington wrote in 1927, "came to be regarded as the hireling mouthpiece of Jefferson, a writer of wretched and insolent doggerel."[17] More than the matter of Freneau's reputation is at stake: the larger issue is how the embattled situation of poetry illuminates deep, unresolved tensions within early American propaganda that sought to disperse information that would enlighten citizens while simultaneously using half-truths and emotional appeals to persuade them. Or as Freneau's country printer at his "ink-bespangled press" neatly encapsulated these contradictions, "if he prints some lies, his lies excuse" because the important consideration, indeed perhaps the final consideration, was not veracity but dissemination.[18]

When poetry rallies people to a cause or exerts other types of rhetorical influence, in the eyes of many it has already ceased to be poetic and has become propaganda. Freneau ran afoul of this attitude when a rival newspaper editor classed him among the "propagators of calumny" who threatened public tranquility.[19] This accusation from the pages of John Fenno's *Gazette of the United States* draws on the biblical injunction (Exodus 23:1) against spreading false reports and echoes Edmund Burke's warnings that the recent revolution in France had spawned "propagators of novelties" who were threatening the stability of Europe. Fenno's barb stuck, and critics have almost universally decided that Freneau's literary talents were sacrificed to political causes, much in the same way that modern readers have sometimes regretted that Mercy Otis Warren's aesthetic sensibilities were commandeered by the Revolution. Even before his association with Jefferson and the *National Gazette*, Freneau put his talents to use by penning poems to counter specific legislative acts such as a New York City ordinance of June 10, 1790, that would have required the cutting down of all trees in the city.[20] In case any poetic ambiguity exists over the poem's purpose, Freneau attached a prefatory sentence and footnotes to make the matter explicit. Such blatant messaging speaks to a sense of political exigency—there's no doubt in the poet's mind that it would be reckless to chop down every single tree in the city simply because some view them as a nuisance—but the more perplexing question is why this viewpoint should be communicated in a poem. For Freneau, who spent much his adult life working for one newspaper or another despite the fact he did not possess a printer's training or skills, the answer lay in the contrasting capacities of poetry and prose for communicating dissident political ideas and beliefs.

Aesthetic choices are always political choices: opting for either poetry or prose constitutes a commentary on the social world and its attendant conventions and forms. Of course, it would seem that in some situations there is no choice at all. Opinions on negotiations with Britain, taxes, or the treatment of prison inmates demand everyday expression associated with prose. Yet as a poet, Freneau did not give into these demands, and such verses as his "Mr. Jay's Treaty," "Occasioned by a Legislation Bill Proposing a Taxation upon Newspapers," and "On a Legislative Act Prohibiting the Use of Spirituous Liquors to Prisons in Certain Jails of the United States" would seem to test not only the distinctions between poetry and prose but also the assumptions about the politics conveyed by each mode. While titles such as "The Wild Honey Suckle" or "To a Caty-Did" reveal that Freneau composed verses on traditional lyric subjects, he also wrote poems on a range of nonpoetic subjects in order to express political views beyond the limits of prosaic wisdom. To be sure, Freneau appears in most anthologies of American literature, but he does so only as a poet. The effect of ignoring his prose is significant, not because his essays and newspaper articles have any special significance themselves, but because Freneau's ability to work in both genres, in tandem with his lifelong indecision about, changing attitudes toward, and strategic deployments of literary expression, suggests something about the nimbleness that political engagement requires. His occasional reflections on genre—What does it mean to frame an appeal in verse? Is prose somehow more democratic than poetry? In the world of public opinion, is poetry an inherently oppositional form? Is prose an accommodation to the world as it is?—reveal that the choice between poetry and prose is also a choice about the most effective means of propagation.

Examining the work of this Revolutionary-era writer and "lost" American poet enables reflections about the preferred mode of disseminating alternative viewpoints that have fallen out of fashion. Or as Freneau rhymed near the end of his life, "A poet where there is no king / Is but a disregarded thing," bemoaning that the oppositional worldview that is often inherent to poetic creativity has no place in an American society where consensus, not kings, reigns supreme.[21] His lament remains an instructive provocation to examine how aesthetic considerations—such as the choice of poetry or prose—are a media matter that is bound up with the meaning of politics at a vital level. In his devotion first to anti-British and then republican propaganda, Freneau discovered the extent to which the form of communication is always saturated with political content.

## "Deadborn" Poetry

Before I undertake this examination, a few remarks are necessary to set some parameters about the terms *poetry* and *politics*, especially in their relationship to one another. As has sometimes been the case in this book, a glance back to Progressive-era assessments of propaganda can prove instructive. It is a relationship that has interested not only literary critics but also the pioneers of public relations. The place of literary genre with respect to politics weighed heavily on George Creel, the consummate propagandist who directed the campaign that drew the United States into World War I. For Creel, it was a point of pride that the various media disseminated by the Committee on Public Information should outperform the propaganda efforts of other nations in creating patriotic support for the war. The quick turn in which citizens moved from consuming propaganda to producing it suggested success: many Americans, thinking that "the Germans could be overwhelmed with printer's ink," inundated the Creel committee with waves of poems, sermons, and stories.[22] Creel took time to reassure one washerwoman, who submitted a poem to support and honor her two sons in the army, that his team of public relations men "appreciated poetry by other standards than those of the Browning circle."[23] Poetry, in other words, could be put to prosaic uses. But then did it still remain poetry?

Such doubts inevitably arise whenever literature seems given over to a specific cause or ideological agenda. This attitude created all sorts of problems for Freneau, who was not simply the poet of the American Revolution but also its publicist. His post-Revolutionary work, he believed, had been damned in the public eye because it contained a few stanzas in honor of Tom Paine, whose name had become a synonym for terror and apostasy ever since the *Age of Reason* averred that all established religion was nothing but a plot to "enslave mankind."[24] So fraught was the political landscape for Freneau that he wondered why people did not object to "the Politics of the Paper-Maker" so that they could condemn his poems on that score as well.[25] Writing nearly a half century after 1776, Freneau complained, "my little two volumes [of poetry] seemed to have fallen nearly deadborn from the Press."[26] It seemed that Freneau—like the poetry he now published—had outlived the Revolutionary moment. Compare his report of "deadborn" compositions with the poetry serialized in the *National Gazette* amid the pitched battles of the Federalists and Democrat-Republicans. "The Country Printer" describes a lively network of townspeople, distant correspondents, and post riders brought together by a workman whose "press / Gives to the world its children" so that they can circulate. Some papers perish quickly while some, like "the Almanack...his longest-living brat," move easily among a community of readers.[27] In contrast, the verses that Freneau published near the end of his life had no real vitality because their political substance, it often seemed, had become an impediment to circulation.

Freneau nonetheless remained a self-appointed spokesperson for popular sovereignty long after it had ceased to be an accepted principle of democratic governance. "A democrat is a leveller, a destroyer of all order, a lover of the French, who wishes to overthrow all order, sacred and human—a democrat delights in blood, murder, and rapine," he wrote satirically under the persona of a stocking weaver named Robert Slender.[28] Freneau may have been an unrepentant democrat, but what sort of poet was he—indeed, was he a poet at all—if patriotic concerns circa 1776 and then later the interests of political faction trumped more finely tuned poetic sensibilities?

These doubts created an impression of Freneau as "a vulgar demo-crat, a disseminator of insubordination and infidelity," in Parrington's overview of the paranoid portraits of the *National Gazette*'s editor.[29] Literary criticism soon dismissed Freneau as a poet-propagandist who became the victim of his own zealous propagandizing. But per-haps this judgment is too harsh for a maker of quaint verses whose aesthetic tendencies disqualified his contributions to the public po-litical sphere at the outset. "Let us look a little into his merits. Is he a great politician.... No!—but he is a *Poet*," a Federalist adherent wrote dismissively of Freneau.[30] Either politics disqualifies the poet or a poetic tendency disqualifies the poet from having a political say. The fairest take on this conundrum about the relationship between po-etry and politics is that Freneau himself was never sure: he often preferred prose as a popular mode only to return time and again to poetry as he searched for an oppositional literary form.

Poetry exists as more than a crude delivery system for an author's political objectives. The choice of form is paramount not just in con-veying content but also in shaping it. To return to the example of Freneau: Why not write in prose since it seems an inherently com-monsense mode appropriate to democracy? Then again, why not favor poetry as a medium for expressing viewpoints that do not readily align with the prevailing consensus? Any effort to correlate literary modes with political content must recognize the initial ten-sion that surrounds the unavoidable use of a particular form. Literature necessarily begins with this gesture, which, however, is not the same thing as saying that literature lacks form until it takes shape as a sestina, sonnet, or short story. As Fredric Jameson points out, "the essential characteristic of literary raw material or latent content is precisely that it never really is initially formless." Instead of being purely organic, the building blocks of literature—sounds, words, images—spring from social considerations shot through with history and concrete material reality. Literary raw materials are "meaningful from the outset, being neither more nor less than the very components of our concrete social life itself."[31] Whether ex-pression congeals as a poem, newspaper column, or other form entails any number of considerations: the circulation of styles and conventions; the availability of prior models, the literary historical status of genres; the institutions of print; patterns of reception; the specifics of the occasion; popular tastes; and so on. These aesthetic concerns could be augmented with broader factors stemming from general economic conditions or the social pressures of historical epochs. Since each of these considerations is likely in flux, conventions or tastes are never fixed or static.

From Mercy Warren's anonymous pamphlet in opposition to the Constitution to Benjamin Franklin Bache's skewering of anyone associated with the Jay Treaty, partisan politics became acute in the war over public opinion waged by Federalists and Democrat-Republicans in the 1790s. Despite this visibility, scholars rarely treat politics in this era as encompassing matters of literary mode. Literary and generic considerations were unavoidable for writers of the post-Revolution who confronted propaganda as a formal system on at least two levels. First, there was the issue of which literary form—prose satire, dialogue, anonymous letters, or poem—was suited to the specifics of any particular urgency. Resistance to Washington's administration took shape in all these forms. Second, print provided an array of material options, including the pamphlet, the one-page broadside, and the folded sheets of the newspaper. As the title of Freneau's wartime satirical verse "Copy of an Intercepted Letter from a New-York Tory, to His Friend in Philadelphia, 1781" suggests with its implicit references to print reproduction and public disclosure, literary modes were always intertwined with the evidence of typeset materiality.

The dual understanding of form as both aesthetic shape and the materiality of print expands the range of what counts as political. To speak about form and politics, as Jameson does, is not to suggest that literature can become more recognizable in terms of traditional notions of the political as something that involves candidates, parties, and elections. Jameson is not angling for literature to be classed with more empirically minded disciplines; the goal is not to change the look and feel of literature so that it can appear as social science. Rather, the goal here is to shift definitions of politics so that matters like choosing to express one's thoughts via a poem or a pamphlet are themselves seen as a commentary on social content.

In other words, settling on a form is neither a matter of stylistic idiosyncrasy nor a purely aesthetic determination but is instead a political act par excellence. Jameson underscores this point by reversing conventional wisdom about form and content. As opposed to viewing form as something that sets the initial pattern to be filled by content as, say, when wine is decanted into a Grecian urn or words arranged into the fourteen lines of a sonnet, we should see what happens if we consider form "as that with which we end up, as but the final articulation of the deeper logic of the content itself."[32] One might go farther still: form is a dynamic process, an ongoing adjustment to and engagement with social institutions and historical content. Freneau's "Copy of an Intercepted Letter" can illustrate. Imagining the private thoughts of an unreconstructed Loyalist is an obvious gesture replete with obvious political content. At a more fundamental level, however, the decision to communicate and spread this content via a poem represents a political decision of a different magnitude. As a formal conceit, a poem pretending to be a stolen letter implies all sorts of movement: an envelope seized in transit, a supposedly handwritten document translated into type, a single original become many copies, a prose epistle set to the rhythms of verse, a personal expression published on the front page of the September 5, 1781, issue of the *Freeman's Journal* for all to see. No wonder that the Tory implores his correspondent, "Dear Sir, I am so anxious to hear of your health, / I beg you would send me a letter by stealth."[33] Later bound as part of Freneau's *Poems on Various Subjects, but Being Chiefly Illustrative of the Events and Actors of the American War of Independence* (1785), it can mistakenly seem to acquire a static aura. But like the clouds in a landscape painting, the interaction of various elements within the canvas as whole reveals movement. The interplay of private handwriting, political verse, and newspaper type suggests a dynamic printscape. Poetry, in this terrain and context, acts as public medium because it registers how words and information are always in motion.

## A "Literary Minute-Man"

In his work on the sociology of literary forms, Franco Moretti has endeavored to understand the relationship between political position and literary genre by posing a question so simple and fundamental that it is often left unasked: "Why are novels in prose?"[34] Like Jameson, Moretti is not focusing on politics at the level of legislation or other specific issues. Instead, he reads for the politics of form, which in the case of poetry, guided by repeatable pattern and symmetry, seems to line up with social interests that have a high stake in maintaining fixity and order. "Symmetry always suggests permanence, that's why monuments are symmetrical," he writes.[35] The architectural comparison is telling, as it suggests that whatever order is implied by poetry, it is a triumphalist one. Verse is retrogressive, its pattern and symmetry always returning expression back to the formal properties with which it began. Prose, in contrast, is progressive because of its indifference to symmetry. Prose is thus antimonumental: at a formal level, the progression of novelistic narrative has a political edge that enlists prose on the side of "im-permanence and irreversibility" with an orientation that is "forward-looking."[36] If verse and prose were electoral candidates, verse would be the incumbent and prose would be the voice of change and new ideas.

What to make of this political standoff between literary forms in light of the fact that Freneau was dubbed both the "father of American poetry" and the "father of American prose"?[37] Although these sobriquets date from the 1920s, they still have resonance in making us wonder how contrasting forms, each with a different political valence, could be engendered by the same writer. While people often act from ambivalent motives, the formal tensions within Freneau's work are especially germane because his output, both as an essayist and as a poet, is so strongly identified with Revolutionary politics. Acclaimed in his own day as the "Poet of the Revolution," he has since been called a "literary Minute-man" for his readiness to lend his creative talents first to the cause of independence in 1776 and then later to radical republicanism, a crusade he championed until his death in 1832.[38] Did Freneau's political attachments fluctuate with the formal decisions that he made, as he selected from an arsenal that included, on the one hand, satires in rhyme, Horatian odes, elegies, and newspaper verse and, on the other, prose pieces that ran the range from vituperation to essays voiced in popular vernacular? To what extent did his politics dictate certain generic choices and how did his use of poetry or prose commit him to certain political positions? Such questions resonate beyond Freneau and his eighteenth-century moment.

Rather than looking for one-way traffic in which a set of already established political beliefs determines the form of expression, the tougher challenge is to develop a more interactive account of how literary genre and political perspective converge, from different directions, around issues of propagation. The pressure to disseminate political ideas and viewpoints requires attention to literary form as a matter of movement. Even so, the political content of literature, as Freneau learned from writing poems about godless Tom Paine, frequently affects its mobility and circulation. In simplest terms, does an anti-elitist democrat such as Freneau communicate politics via a poem or prose? Does a poet necessarily engage the world from a specific political perspective in advance because he or she writes about that world in verse? Though Freneau's reputation, in Robert Pinsky's overview, has degenerated from a literary freedom fighter in the eighteenth century to that of "a disreputable hack" in the nineteenth century and to "an obscure footnote" in the late twentieth and now twenty-first centuries, the political battles he fought and the literary decisions he faced have renewed significance for at least two reasons.[39] First, the reaction and response to Freneau, given his avuncular but neglected status, illuminates how American literary history has been shaped by distinguishing literature from propaganda—a line that Freneau repeatedly crossed. Second, and more broadly, Freneau offers fresh insight by encouraging us to think of literary form as a matter of public relations.

At first glance, the measured traditions of eighteenth-century poetry seem out of step with the tempestuous demonstrations, impassioned crowds, and newspaper tirades that were a feature of early American democracy. This irresolvable tension between the medium of European court refinement and popular political culture inspired Freneau to comment directly on the formal inadequacies of poetry for representing the swirls and upheavals of democratic passions. As the story goes, Freneau simply accepted the defeat of his poetic ideals and redirected his energies toward prose by editing a string of unsuccessful newspapers. To keep the Revolutionary fires burning, he began editing the *Freeman's Journal* in 1781, and moved on to the *National Gazette* in 1791, which quickly "became the common clearing house for democratic propaganda" and was just as quickly denounced by Federalists as a Jacobin rag advocating lawless republicanism.[40] Other ventures included editing and contributing to the *Daily Advertiser*, the *Jersey Chronicle*, and the *Time-Piece and Literary Companion*, but no matter the venue his reputation as a partisan tool had been sealed by Federalists, who never missed the opportunity of attacking him—and, to be fair, Freneau regularly invited these attacks—as a rabble-rouser and second-rate maker of verses. "As a journalist engaged in propaganda, Freneau deliberately turned his back on literary aspiration," writes his biographer, Lewis Leary, who, as the subtitle of his book makes clear, considers Freneau's career a "failure."[41] The identification of Freneau as a propagandist relies on assumptions about the political content of his formal choices: had he followed his instincts and not wasted his talents on party politics and newspaper verse, he might have become America's first Romantic poet, an honor that literary critics usually bestow on William Cullen Bryant, instead of a merely "useful poet," as he was dismissed in eighteenth century, or as a producer of "applied poetry" as he was judged in the twentieth.[42]

To say that Freneau churned out propaganda is not to allege that he gave no thought to form. Rather, it is to say that he gave too much thought to matters of form as media, specifically, which means of expression would best spread a republican gospel of popular political rule while warning against the rise of aristocratic social pretensions in the infant nation. According to Jefferson, Freneau best accomplished this mission by editing the *National Gazette* since "his paper has saved our constitution, which was galloping fast into monarchy."[43] But according to the Romantic ideal of the writer, an ideal that would not emerge until the last decades of Freneau's life, a better, a more intuitive poet would not have concerned himself with addressing the masses or adjusting expression to popular tastes. A more accomplished poet would not have wasted precious creative energy considering how verse could be made useful or how poetry could be applied to social and political situations. Only someone with the temperament of an apparatchik and the meager talents of a hack would have devoted so much thought to form in an effort to produce prose and poetry that amounted to a veritable bargain basement of items from verses critical of George Washington to invented satirical speeches spoken by kings to bits of homespun vernacular calculated to appeal to less genteel audiences. And so it is that Freneau's work often seems calculating, formulated with an eye to what will prove most efficacious in promoting republican virtue in the hope that Americans of all ranks and classes would join him in asking: "Should we, just heaven, our blood and labour spent, / Be slaves and minions to a parliament?"[44]

Written for partisan purposes and laden with rather blatant messages, such verse borders on propaganda or, more exactly, renders the distinction between poetry and propaganda inconsequential. As Freneau put it in the "Advertisement" that prefaced the 1809 edition of his work, "These poems were intended...to expose vice and treason their own hideous deformity" while promoting "honour and patriotism in their native beauty," and it is not hard to see how lines contrasting brave American military commanders with feckless British generals fulfilled this stated purpose.[45] Attention to genre enabled Freneau to think about spreading this message so that *popular* (in the political sense of issues relating to the public) matters would be made popular (in the cultural sense of art and expression that appeal to the tastes of ordinary people). The desire for popularity, in an echo of Benjamin Franklin Bache at the *Aurora* (a paper that Freneau briefly helped Bache's widow to edit), suggested the notion of *populāris* as a deeply political sense of belonging to the people collectively. For the propagandist, if not the poet, the task is to spread information and opinion in ways that would be truly popular.

It is common to conceive of propaganda in terms of content, but Freneau's labors demonstrate that propaganda just as importantly involves the strategies used to propel content across social landscapes. Not unlike the public relations expert who drums up interest in a product or personality, the eighteenth-century poet, if he believes in republicanism as both a political movement and a cultural ethos as fervently as Freneau did, is charged with the mission of thinking about the respective virtues of verse and prose for mobilizing ideas. How best to get a message "out there" before the public so that it will be truly popular? In taking up this challenge, Freneau discovered that the form of expression proved as significant as anything he might have to say. If we recall the insight that form is not some pre-given pattern with which the artist starts but rather a dynamic engagement with social content, we see that Freneau's work often takes shape as a metacommentary on the possibilities and limitations of poetry and prose. Literary form, in these terms, is never merely a formal consideration but rather the historical articulation of a longing to engage people as widely and as fully as possible.

Freneau balanced his activities as a poet-propagandist with those of a prose writer who adopted various literary personae, including a hermit, an American Indian named Tommo Cheeki, a farmer's wife, and a craftsman who signed his articles "O.S.M." or "One of the Swinish Multitude," all in attempt to align literary form and expression around popular idioms. This fictive identity of "O.S.M." struck a jab at Burke's *Reflections on the Revolution in France*, which deplored that civilization was being "trodden down under the hoofs of the swinish multitude."[46] Freneau converted the insult into a badge of honor: after all, in his view, if anyone was guilty of piggish behavior, it was a commercial class of speculators and merchants who were busy adjusting the hype of the Revolution to the realities of a market economy. Not surprisingly, it is this same class that "swallows up all ideas of poetry, or refuses any attention to poetical productions, further than what is calculated for the fly market stalls."[47] In this jaundiced reflection about the fate of letters in a commercial society, Freneau wondered if poetry in the young Republic had become a secondhand good to be picked over by the populace. Even though the indifferent fate of his volumes of poetry seemed to confirm this suspicion, Freneau denied that the values of liberal capitalism were truly popular. He "became a spokesman for the poor and oppressed and aimed many of his works at the least sophisticated readers," writes Emory Elliott.[48] This aspect of Freneau's career has often been regretted by critics, leading to the conclusion that the turn to prose assured the defeat of more refined literary aspirations. But the standards important to an eighteenth-century propagandist are not the same as those upheld by modern readers. Freneau's criteria may today seem quaint and out of date, vestiges of a time when urgent political choices overruled concerns for aesthetic niceties. What a more thorough view reveals, however, is that aesthetic form is a political choice relevant to democracy, not simply as a belief that the people should govern but as a practice of spreading that belief widely across diverse social strata.

Writing about a different revolutionary moment than Freneau's, Kenneth Burke in 1935 described the propagandist as a "*spreader* of doctrine" whose central concern should be choosing symbols, vocabulary, and values that will popularize a cause. In "Revolutionary Symbolism in America," Burke seeks proletarian forms of expression that will extend the writer's "recruiting into ever widening areas"; the literary artist necessarily becomes a propagandist because he or she propagates ideas and information. When the task is to make political beliefs align with "cultural awareness in the large," the writer's duty is to employ language that promotes broad support for and identification with a particular viewpoint.[49] As an example, Burke believes that because the designation *worker* is too unromantic and constricted—who, after all, wants to work in the industrial machine?—it needs to be replaced by *the people*, a term that gives off a more inclusive aura. In contemplating which forms would enable the propagation of democratic values and create "cultural awareness in the large," Freneau often found that the most inclusive aura lay in an odor of the vernacular, as when, in a rebuke to the Loyalist printer of the *Royal Gazette*, he rhymed "despot" with "pisspot."[50] His wit ran toward New World accents, as when he imagined King George raging like "Xantippe" in reaction to British "losses along Mississippi."[51] No matter how clever, these "jingling rhymes," like "the monotony of metre" and other poetic "trifles," appeared to Freneau as remnants of a dying aristocratic cultural order.[52] But it was also the case that the emergence of powerful commercial interests seemed to be giving aristocratic values a second and more robust life within the early Republic.

The audience at the American Writers' Congress of 1935 gave Burke's "Revolutionary Symbolism in America" harsh treatment, sensing a grave misstep in the move to push the category of "worker" into the wings and replace it with "the people." Listeners responded that this elevation of "the people" unintentionally echoed Hitler's strategy of appealing to the *volk* and smoothed over "the actual living antagonism between the social classes."[53] Freneau avoided this complication by continually testing the links between genre, public media, and class inequality. He charged that the ability to propagate and disseminate had become restricted to "the advocates of aristocracy." Backing moneyed interests, the supporters of a new elitism were pushing "an opinion...to be propagated...that public affairs should only be discussed by 'men of property.'"[54] In case there were any doubts as to the identity of the *National Gazette*'s targets in this accusation, a thinly veiled reference to the nabob at Braintree made it clear that John Adams was squarely in the editor's sights. What Freneau most resented was not Adams's relative wealth but the fact that the vice president's station freed him from having to publish propaganda himself. For that task, John Fenno, Freneau's rival editor at the *Gazette of the United States*, already served a convenient purpose.

Amid the daily skirmishes of this newspaper war, poetic forms frequently struck Freneau as too thoroughly steeped in rituals of polite submission and servility to supply the basis for a republican ethos. He worried that the aesthetic forms of the Anglo-American world were good only for trumpeting pomp and circumstance as opposed to making a case for the simple virtues of citizenship. Based on his reading of literary history, Freneau predicted that poetry would be used to reinstall a culture of monarchical deference. After the Revolution when, as Freneau saw matters, a newly independent

merchant class was consolidating its authority and financial speculators were maximizing their opportunities for profit, poets who spent
their time composing birthday verses for Washington and extolling
government officials were unequal to the task of safeguarding the
public's interests. After all, composing verses for the king's birthday
had been the practice of British court poets. Why were Americans
aping poetic performances tainted by associations of courtly
deference?

Creative expression lagged behind the quick pace of revolution. "A
political and a literary independence," wrote Freneau, are "two very
different things."[55] He called for a literary protectionism of sorts: if
luxury goods imported from England paid heavy customs duties,
should not the works of British authors also be deemed luxuries and
taxed at a similar rate? In the context of the Jay Treaty and the trade
wars that vexed the early Republic, cultural independence was a
hard-fought battle without decisive victories. Political independence
may have been achieved in a mere seven years, but changing the
beliefs and attitudes of a people accustomed to an internalized sense
of creole inferiority seemed less certain. Freneau was not optimistic
and predicted that it would take hundreds of years to achieve sovereignty in aesthetic affairs. Would poetry help spread this new doctrine or would it remain mired in an older sensibility? In terms of
Kenneth Burke's focus on rhetoric and propaganda, the question
might be rephrased: could poetry communicate revolutionary symbolism or did the formal qualities intrinsic to the genre prevent the
development of a republican vocabulary to be used by the people?

In a mock advertisement addressed "To the Noblesse and Courtiers
of the United States," Freneau invited applications for persons of poetic skill willing to sell their talents to the government. Duties included composing verses praising "officers of the government," but
care should be taken since the comparison of the president or anyone in his administration to "any thing on this earth, would be an
anti-hyperbole, unsuited to the *majesty* of the subject." Behind the
irony lies Freneau's disillusionment with poetry as an antidemocratic
genre. Hopeful lackeys and aspiring bootlickers wishing to increase
their chances at becoming poet laureate would do well to bone up on
"the causes of decline of all the republics which have preceded us" so
as to be ready to rejoice in the appearance of any signs portending
the end of American democracy. Poems are needed to exemplify
how hierarchy and "certain *monarchical prettinessses*" such as state

receptions, court functions, and official titles augur favorably for "American prosperity" conceived not in terms of political virtue but as a crudely financial calculus.[56] The content of poetry seems incapable of overcoming the retrogressive nature of its form: in a world where amateur versifiers find work as professional flatterers, poetry fulfills an antipopular function in a double sense, first by being poised against the interests of the people and, second, by appealing to themes over their heads. The entire January 5, 1793, issue of *National Gazette* seems resigned to this fact: unlike the bulk of the other issues that contained at least one and sometimes two poems, not a line of verse appears. It was as if Freneau no longer had any use for rhyme.

This notice ran at the start of 1793 and by August of that year Freneau was writing poetry's obituary as a "declining art" now that panegyrists and other flatterers were no longer in demand. Then, sounding a more hopeful note, he predicted that "real poetry... will one day have its resurrection; but its professors will no longer be court sycophants."[57] This turnabout led the *National Gazette* to feature specimens of popular verse on this same page, including toasts offered and songs sung in honor of 1776. Perhaps the poetry of the future was not too far off, after all. This reinvigorated poetry would be guided by "republican virtues," initiating changes in content, tone, and form. If poetry were ever again to enjoy popularity, its producers had best remember that Americans are a people of "too much cool reflection to be amused" or swayed by poetic baubles dedicated to praising kings and other "crowned murderers."[58] In short, the problem with poetry was no different than what Freneau that same year decried as the royal trappings of the American theater: just as poetry seeks to amuse rather than to instruct or educate, the stage proffers "*alluring amusements*, in order to prevent *the people* from thinking."[59] By way of a broad social critique, these reflections on poetry and theater stressed the importance of popular culture in crafting hegemony. In its ability both to justify a political order and to forestall criticism or dissent, popular culture regularly served as a stabilizing mechanism, in effect, giving the people bread and circuses in the shape of verse and drama, deflecting their legitimate political concerns into pleasing but empty forms. Freneau, it might be said, scorned dramatic entertainment and popular verse as features of an eighteenth-century "culture industry" that offered popular deception in the place of the people's enlightenment. Although

Max Horkheimer and Theodor Adorno famously invoked the "culture industry" to describe the total alignment of film and radio to capitalist individualism in the post–World War II era and although the United States in the 1790s certainly lacked the mass media that created a "relentless unity" of politics and culture without alternatives or dissent, the comparison remains useful in spelling the scale of the counterrevolutionary threat that Freneau thought he faced from the very poetic forms he had once employed as the poet of the Revolution.[60]

If verse could not be purged of its courtly entitlement, was prose the medium of a republican future? During the days of 1776, Freneau had kept his rhymes at the ready to encourage resistance to British forces, but by the 1790s he saw a different foe—a rising tide of speculators, merchants, and bankers who were threatening to dilute the social and political significance of the Revolution. The contrast seemed almost as stark as the choice between prose or poetry: Americans could either pledge themselves to a notion of the common good and public harmony or they could surrender to the competitive self-interests of a market economy. In reality, however, the choices were not so simple. Republicanism requires unemployment and ease so that citizens, freed from time-consuming drudgery, can cultivate the virtues of civic life. "Republicanism is historically an ideology of leisure," while eighteenth-century liberalism emphasizes a worldview where is success is dependent only on hard work.[61] The divisions between civic virtue and liberalism were likely never as clear-cut as both Freneau and latter-day proponents of "the republican synthesis" in American historiography have believed.[62] Republicanism intertwined with liberalism since ideas about political rights and independence supplied bourgeois pursuits with emancipatory aspirations. For all those such as Mercy Warren and her husband who believed themselves to be uncompromised by liberal capitalism in America, the intricacies of the market told a different story. "Yeoman farmers operated very much in the capitalist marketplace and had highly developed commercial networks," writes Isaac Kramnick.[63] For Freneau, prose seemed the best way of untangling this ideological mess.

Unlike poetry that bewitched citizens, prose at moments seemed imbued with an instructive and edifying potential crucial to sustaining republicanism. To this end, Freneau toyed with a civic primer that would help readers navigate the fancy speech and palaver of the day. Thus *banking* is defined as "the real art of hocus pocus" and *genius* can best be understood as "money-catching," while *antifederalist*, a negative appellation that shows the extent to which Federalists had succeeded in framing the debate on their terms, should be revalorized as "a republican of seventeen hundred and seventy-six."[64] Likewise *patriotism* requires a new definition since it has been distorted by a culture of financial speculation into a justification for concentrating wealth into fewer and fewer hands. Prose facilitates popular knowledge, spreading colloquial definitions that enlighten instead of amuse. Freneau came nowhere close to compiling a lexicon on the scale of *Samuel Johnson's Dictionary*, but a few months later he did reflect in abstract terms that "as the world advances towards universal republicanism the ideas of mankind have become prosaic."[65]

## "Poetic Raptures"

The only complication to this story of republican prose is that Freneau repeatedly voiced regret that poetry lacked popularity in his post-Revolutionary world. As far as propaganda went, verse often seemed to him a poor dispersal mechanism. Ambivalence resounds in his statement about the "prosaic" nature of republicanism since the commentary comes laden with the imputation that political ideas expressed in this manner are dull and unimaginative. Counterbalancing the death of poetry that Freneau predicted in his prose writings, his verse often laments the ascendancy of prose that had pushed rhyme to the edges of the democratic public sphere.

The most obvious barrier to poetry as public political expression extends beyond its formal properties to the limitations of an audience, which, in Freneau's view, seems intent on employing its newly achieved independence to pursue only narrowly commercial interests that leave neither time nor inclination for more ennobling artistic endeavors. Rhyme automatically dissents from the thinking that aligns the pursuit of gain with the "pursuit of happiness"; the fact that Freneau is on the losing side in this broader ideological war is an injury that he cherishes, since the slights and wounds to his aesthetic sensibility allowed him to cultivate the air of a tragic and misunderstood visionary. His poetic persona often seems on the verge of giving up:

> An age employ'd in pointing steel
>> Can no poetic raptures feel
>
> ....
>
>> The *Muse of Love* in no request.
> I'll try my fortune with the rest,
>> Which of the Nine shall I engage
> To suit the humor of the age [?] (*Poems* 2:334)[66]

In a day when Erato, the muse of lyric poetry, has no followers and there are no muses specifically devoted to the prosaic business of trade, the poet realizes that his only option is to beseech Melpomene for assistance in producing tragedy and melancholy. For the tragic poet, poetry is itself the source of melancholia. In this new world, poetry lacks creative or instructive power; it appears more as a passive genre shaped by the current climate than as a force that can shape the priorities and beliefs of citizens. Still, such self-reflexive content reveals how poetry in and of itself registers social action. Poetry, by the sheer nature of its form, is a declaration of opposition to the prevailing consensus that prizes commercialism and limits the imagination to financial speculation. The growing irrelevance of the muses, the threatened obsolescence of verse, and careless regard for lyricism in the early Republic combined to make the use of poetic form a historical protest, somewhere between a sign of surrender and act of desperation, against a prosaic age.

Poetry counters—which is precisely why it counts. This insight, advanced by Freneau when he stood at the beginning of a tradition that would later be called American literature, has found echo in the work of contemporary poets. As Rosemarie Waldrop reflects, "I love the way verse refuses to fill up all the available space of the page so that each line acknowledges what is *not*."[67] While an entire history of experimentation lies between Freneau and Waldrop, there exists a sort of convergence around the idea of poetry as an oppositional counterforce. By its form alone, poetry invites negation: the "*not*" uttered by poetry downplays content and engages the substance of earthly affairs only to resist it. The poet or propagandist—for Freneau the difference between the two was negligible—has to do more than attend to the content of a message since particular modes of communication come already laden with meaning. The initial aesthetic codes of poetry and prose can be rewritten, and Freneau's quickness in reacting to the changing exigencies of print speaks to his inventiveness.

Still, a specific genre such as eighteenth-century poetry often shaped from the outset the messages that could be sent and received in ways that made the engagement with form an overriding, although not deterministic, concern.

For a writer like Freneau who was equally skilled in poetry and prose, the choice of one medium over another, especially a form such as poetry that seemingly was becoming rapidly antiquated, constituted a self-conscious political decision. In his view, poetry potentially had an imaginative power that invigorated the public political realm by elevating citizens' aspirations while widening the ambit of public discourse. The genre, owing to its utter uselessness, kept republican virtue from flowing into the narrow channels of profit and commercialism. The paradox is that poetry, unlike prose, was no longer a popular form, but this obsolescence was precisely what made poetry oppositional and especially conducive to minority viewpoints. With prose in ascendancy, poetry, by virtue of its form, was especially suited to the losing side.

Freneau had long done battle in verse. As part of a print war with Eleazer Oswald, editor of the *Independent Gazetteer*, he fired off a series of poems addressed to "the concealed Royalist." Belittling his opponent's poetic skills for cribbing lines from another author, Freneau counseled him to "No more your range in plundered verse repeat / Sink into prose—even there no safe retreat." Four years later he sharpened this final quip into an overall condemnation of prosaic expression by rewriting this line as "Sneak into prose—the dunce's last retreat."[68] At a practical level, the couplet found its mark, as Oswald became so incensed as to challenge Freneau to a duel. At a formal level, the target seemed harder to pin down, as Freneau sought to revalue the political significance of poetry so that it would shed its courtly associations and become realigned with democratic expression. It was with dismay, then, that Freneau noted how one of the most renowned writers of the day, Washington Irving, had sailed to Britain to "with the glittering nobles mix / Forgetting *times* of seventy-six." Back home, however, the yearnings for literary independence did little to bolster poetry's appeal. Americans of new wealth now qualified as "the homemade *nobles* of our times / Who hate the bard, and spurn his rhymes."[69] Whence this antipathy to verse? Because of its form, poetry necessarily dissented from the prevailing economic order that privileged commercial utility above all else. Prose ruled the day, rendering the place of the poet at best irrelevant and nearly forgotten.

One feature of the new poetic climate was, however, certain: writers were still making a mockery of their gifts by penning birthday odes for American dignitaries as had been the custom for British poets seeking, spaniel-like, to curry the favor of their monarch. Even though Freneau was not always consistent and had composed birthday verses for Washington in the past, he found this particular form of poetry exasperating for a supposedly democratic polity. Poetic praises lavished on the father of his country tended toward such exaggeration as to harm the idea of a rational public. Newspapers that should inform citizens and "spread the news" instead wasted time and space by elevating Washington to unbelievable heights, comparing him to stars and celestial entities.[70] In place of paeans and hosannas, Freneau urged expressions of plebeian forthrightness that represented Washington as a man, not a god. A true estimation of the founding father would resist the aggrandizing comparisons that imbued poetry with a lofty, antipopular tinge: "exalt it, if you can, / He was the upright Honest Man."[71] Freneau made this argument most fully in "Stanzas Occasioned by Certain Absurd Extravagant, and Even Blasphemous Panegyrics and Encomiums on the Character of the Late Gen. Washington, That Appeared in Several Pamphlets, Journals and Other Periodical Publications, in January, 1800," a work whose lengthy title aptly suggests how the building blocks of poetry—"stanzas"—could serve as material for constructing an oppositional viewpoint to the hagiography of Federalist leaders. The overt reference to January 1800 and a new century suggest a desire to slough off outdated conventions. Yet the poet could not overcome the ready availability of fawning verse, which enjoyed media saturation across the array of print platforms. Everywhere Freneau looked, from pamphlets to magazines, the signs of obsequiousness were "several." Poetic form, as the title of this composition so dramatically underscores, is not the starting point of literary expression but its end point. Form, to recall Jameson, represents the "final articulation of the deeper logic" of social forces. And Freneau's melancholy was that this adulatory genre might be the last word in the debate over what public communication should look like.

In his more hopeful moments, Freneau believed that his country would produce distinctly democratic verse—even if this development eluded Freneau himself, emerging perhaps not until Walt Whitman's *Leaves of Grass*. In a 1797 work later recycled as the introduction to the second volume of his *Poems* (1809), he expressed the sentiment that the United States would one day encourage topics "such...as no courtly poet ever saw." Here at last lay the promise for genre to match political function, but this prospect for public poetical discourse faded fast in a landscape more suited to the language of business and practicality:

> The coming age will be an age of prose:
> When sordid cares will break the muses' dream,
> And Common Sense be ranked in seat supreme.[72]

Embedded in this familiar rant against an economic calculus lies an unexpected allusion to Paine, who, after 1776, adopted his pamphlet's title as his pseudonym in newspaper pieces attacking the British during the Revolution. In terms of political sympathies, Freneau and Paine were very much on the same side and each became the subject of vitriolic attacks after finding fault with the Federalist consensus. On literary grounds, however, the two had long gone their separate ways. In Freneau's estimation, Paine's success as a prose pamphleteer belies a deeper failure: while the Revolutionary politics of "Common Sense" are beyond reproach, its form is susceptible to hierarchies in which business sensibilities are king. An oppositional politics requires an oppositional genre—and that genre in a society prioritizing trade and commerce is poetry, a mode of expression destined not only to be on the margin but also to speak to the interests of those on the margin.

Even though the situation of American literary study now seems far removed from the poetry and prose in Freneau's day, the decades after 1776 have much to teach us about the political and aesthetic significances of propaganda as a formal system. A focus on the media forms used to disseminate opinions and disperse information suggests the extent to which the expression of a political viewpoint is just as meaningful as, indeed, is inseparable from, the substance of the viewpoint itself. As Freneau's career-long engagement with print institutions and newspaper editing shows, the point where writers and readers opt for poetry, prose, or mixed media is also the point where politics begins.

# Coda

"You will please to excuse the Inaccuracies of this which is wrote in a hurry," James Warren importuned Sam Adams in a letter of November 8, 1772, sent from Plymouth to Boston. Like so much of the American correspondence of the day, Warren's letter was a hodgepodge of personal communication, political strategy, and philosophizing. Invoking "the free circulation" of "the Body Natural," he described efforts to take the "Pulse" of the "Body Politic." He happily reported that its fast beating indicated healthy "Resentment" to British colonial policies.[1] Warren's admission of haste suggests that his pulse was also quickened. The legibility of the handwriting in the original seems sacrificed to speed. To modern eyes, the lack of logical connections between Warren's sentences can suggest that syntax was a casualty of time considerations as well. After more two hundred years, the letter still gives off the impression that writing in Mercy and James's household was rarely a scene of languid reflection and instead was a hot spot for reacting to the social and political volatility of the moment. This tempo evidences the degree to which the exigencies of the printscape jarred with the leisured lifestyle associated with the Warrens' patrician understanding of republicanism.

Mercy's husband was moved to dash off this response to Adams because his interlocutor just days before had sent him news about a plan to "open a free Communication with every town" by which the latest intelligence would be "transmitted to each Town."[2] Adams's short message underscores how the growing unrest in the colonies had become inseparable from matters of transmission. "Each" and "every" inhabited spot on the map would soon be sending and receiving information. In the next letter that Warren sent, he enclosed a petition signed by the people of Plymouth. He did not take time to say who was being petitioned or what was at issue. Getting the document to Boston was the primary concern so that it "may be Inserted in the Papers...even if it gives you the Trouble of seeing it done."[3] Far more than an instance of simple transmission, Warren's forwarding of the petition and request that it be prepared for publication exemplified how diffusion heightened the political significance of correspondence and other texts. The conversion of handwriting into print was a necessary stage in the rush to propagate information and emotion (or "Spirit," to use Warren's term) but hardly the final one. Nor was it a one-way process. Print regularly became the occasion for more handwriting. Reports appearing in the colonial press often sparked additional commentary, as Mercy Warren's handwritten correspondence with her epistolary network shows.

James Warren could have written more to explain why transmission, like the circulation of blood in the human body, proved indispensable to the vitality of the body politic. But he had no time to reflect. "I am in great haste," he told Adams, expressing a feeling of urgency that was becoming widespread as the colonial crisis intensified.[4] Still, the pressure to disseminate the townspeople's petition had already illuminated the extent to which the meaning of popular expression could not be divorced form its propagation.

Creatures of the eighteenth century, Adams and Warren considered these communication practices essential to republicanism. Indeed, for many Whigs, propaganda was integral to liberty: despite their differences in social class, education, and gender, Mercy Otis Warren, Tom Paine, Philip Freneau, and Ben Franklin and his grandson, along with the many others who entered the printscape only to disappear soon after, all believed that the propagation of information and opinion across the various media of eighteenth-century printscapes would help speed new ideas about the connection between communication and political power. Although they likely would have shied away from using "democracy," a word that throughout the eighteenth century was tainted by connotations of anarchy and mob rule, these thinkers and activists contended that the movement of secrets and other information supplied a serious challenge to monarchical privilege and colonial rule. During the 1790s when reports of French Revolutionary terror stoked fears about American Jacobinism, the speed and spread of propaganda continued to play a vital role in fueling democratic vigilance about power grabs and inside deals reputed to be taking place among the elected officials of the early Republic.

Just as James Warren did not slow down when composing his letters to Adams, other letter writers and pamphleteers frequently did not pause to examine whether the material they were relaying was authentic or if it rested on a sketchy foundation of rumor and invention. Instead, their activities contributed to an ungovernable flow of information that did not always align with established protocols of communication. At times their objectives echoed Enlightenment optimism that the transparent presentation of knowledge could make people more virtuous. At other times, the realities were more complex: citizens created, doctored, and reacted to public opinion, not by looking at facts or exercising reason but by trading in half-truths and stolen confidences. In a world where private letters were commandeered out of public interest, where forgery got at the truth in roundabout ways, and where the elliptical language of poetry could seem the most candid form of confrontation, political behavior expanded well beyond an empirical register. The steady stream of propaganda in the late eighteenth and early nineteenth centuries suggested that a good deal of communication and intelligence did not take shape as a self-evident truth.

Although propaganda typically has a pejorative connotation that dates back to the flag-waving and jingoism surrounding U.S. participation in World War I, this book has provided a longer history of the concept in an effort to grasp the importance of media communications during the American Revolution and its aftermath. Once a fuller genealogy of propaganda comes into focus and the concept is no longer cast in simplistic terms as intentionally misleading or dishonest, its potential for helping us understand the importance of dissemination to democracy begins to make sense. Once propaganda is no longer treated reductively as a top-down phenomenon and is instead viewed as a more horizontal form of communication, it illuminates multiple points in a discursive environment where people can consume and produce texts, broadcast and ignore opinions, and download and upload information. In the printscape of the late eighteenth-century Atlantic world, these sites were as varied as the era's writing desks, newspaper offices, postal routes, and taverns and public houses.

Across this array of locations, Americans diversified their agency by becoming readers as well as writers, faithful correspondents and also hacks, and forgers in addition to plagiarists. Like the texts they produced and consumed, Americans in the printscape experienced identity as a resource that was constantly shifting and on the move. These fluctuations, however, were not always experienced as pleasant. The preceding chapters have shown how neither Ben Franklin nor George Washington, for instance, found the identity of a traitor and schemer to be particularly liberating. Their respective reactions to the attacks on their reputations and characters suggest that they were not uniformly ready to delight in the modern play of identity created by print. Yet even in settings as seemingly old-fashioned as eighteenth-century correspondence networks, the interplay of propagation, mobility, and emotion described in the introduction had the potential to democratize agency. In some instances, the effects were only transitory, perhaps as short-lived as that week's edition of the newspaper. In other cases, especially when writers could claim only weak senses of authorship, the impact proved more lasting. While authorial agents themselves might resist this sort of disintegration, the spread of propaganda relied on identities that had started to dissolve into the printscape. As a network hub, Franklin relayed sensitive correspondence. As a plagiarized author, Warren widened the reach of her patriot dramas. As a pamphleteer, Paine came to understand himself almost completely as a transmitter of transatlantic revolution. As a recycler of a Loyalist counterfeit, Bache propagated a critique of foreign policy and presidential power. As a poet who expressed ambivalence about the fading significance of verse, Freneau uneasily adjusted to narrow commercial interests that, paradoxically, seemed required by the wider world of prose. Editing, copying, letter writing, culling items for a newspaper, and other activities nurtured by the printscape were just as important as being an author.

If agency became scattered and authorship weakened in the printscape, then it is also the case that these nodes of transmission and circulation have been frequently reconsolidated under more familiar signposts. Historians name such points of dissemination "Ben Franklin" or "Sam Adams." Literary scholars, too, often find it convenient to study the single text at rest and not the many works, especially in their many versions and copies, that were once—and, in some cases, still are—in motion. As a diffuse and ungainly type of communication, however, propaganda is rarely convenient. The mess it creates can nurture unguarded ideas about access and public knowledge that are equally difficult to manage.

{ ACKNOWLEDGMENTS }

In May 1782 while adding to the newspaper installments that would become the *American Crisis*, Tom Paine admitted to being tongue-tied: "We sometimes experience sensations to which language is not equal." Although Paine's words were composed in a very different context from this one, I nonetheless find them fitting when it comes to expressing my sensations of gratitude for all those who have helped with the research and writing of this book.

Friends and colleagues have made this project a better book than it would have been otherwise. I owe much to their collective insight, suggestions, and good cheer. Lauren Berlant, Christopher Breu, Colleen Boggs, Chris Castiglia, Elizabeth Maddock Dillon, Wai Chee Dimock, Andy Doolen, Janet Downie, Brian Edwards, Travis Foster, Greg Jackson, Susan Gillman, David Glimp, Patrick Jagoda, Lynn Keller, Ed Larkin, Caroline Levander, Mark McGurl, W. J. T. Mitchell, Dana Nelson, Susan Scott Parrish, Donald Pease, Maria Teresa Prendergast, Tom Prendergast, Shirley Samuels, Xiomara Santamarina, Ivy Schweitzer, Harry Stecopolous, Elisa Tamarkin, Bryce Traister, Jay Williams, Ivy Wilson, and Sarah Wilson responded to parts of this project in ways that have encouraged the whole. Jonathan Auerbach, Leslie Bow, Gordon Hutner, and Bob Levine helped me with some of the thornier parts of my argument, and I am especially grateful for their careful readings of its chapters.

At the University of Wisconsin-Madison, Anne McClintock, Rob Nixon, and David Zimmerman have been invaluable sources of friendship and intellectual community. I am not alone in being indebted to Theresa Kelley and Caroline Levine for fostering a departmental culture in which academic research can thrive. I had the good fortune to spend a semester at the Institute for Research in the Humanities, and its director, Susan Stanford Friedman, deserves thanks for creating an environment that is as rigorous as it is rewarding. Philip Bandy, Zach Marshall, Rosanna Oh, and Deidre Stuffer provided excellent research assistance. The generous support of the Dorothy Draheim-Bascom Fund has been a significant resource in enabling me to consult archival collections at the American Antiquarian Society, the New York Public Library, the Huntington Library, the Milton Historical Society, and the Massachusetts Historical Society. Librarians at these institutions helped me gain access to many of the documents and images that have received discussion in the preceding pages.

At Oxford University Press, Brendan O'Neill was convinced of the book's potential even before I was. I've been buoyed by his combination of good-natured irreverence and professionalism. My experience with the press has been enhanced by my book's inclusion in the Oxford Studies in American Literary History, which has afforded me the immense benefit of working closely with the series editor, Gordon Hutner. The three anonymous readers for Oxford University Press provided me with criticism that was truly constructive. At my request, one of these reviewers revealed his identity, and I am pleased to have the chance to thank Konstantin Dierks now.

This book was greatly aided by the feedback I received from editorial boards whose journals published parts of the manuscript. While I have since expanded and made significant changes to these articles as they evolved into chapters, the arguments still bear the helpful imprint of readers' suggestions at *American Literary History*, *Critical Inquiry*, and *boundary* 2. I was given a boost at a preliminary stage when Caroline Levander and Bob Levine invited me to contribute a chapter to *A Companion to American Literary Study*. Those pages later developed into the book's final chapter. Portions of the book had their test runs as talks, and these events proved particularly enriching in generating incisive comments and useful suggestions. My thinking has been enlivened by the responses I received from audiences at the University of Western Ontario, the Futures of American Studies Institute at Dartmouth College, Fordham University, Illinois State University, Pennsylvania State University, Northern Illinois University, Northwestern University, Rice University, University of California, Berkeley, University of California, Los Angeles, University of Colorado, Boulder, University of Iowa, University of Michigan, University of Toronto, Vanderbilt University, and Wooster College.

This book is dedicated to the memory of my parents, Frances Abelson Castronovo and Michael Castronovo. Not long after I became an orphan, as it were, I found at my parents' home a box containing papers I had never seen before, papers giving evidence of memories that precede mine. Among my mother's things, many of which would be discarded, I chanced upon her college term paper from the early 1950s that she had written in part about the poetry of Louis Untermeyer. I like to think that this woman, not yet my mother, who wrote about "the expression of ideas in various changing media" would have recognized something of herself in this book.

My deepest and most enduring gratitude goes to Leslie, Julian, and Maya. So deep is this gratitude that the better name for it is love.

# { NOTES }

## Introduction

1. Edward L. Bernays, *Public Relations* (Norman: U of Oklahoma P, 1952), 33–34.

2. See Edward L. Bernays, "The Engineering of Consent," *Annals of the American Academy of Political and Social Science* 250 (March 1947): 113–20.

3. Edward L. Bernays, *Propaganda* (Brooklyn, NY: Ig, 2005), 37.

4. My approach here might be usefully compared to Gordon Wood's *The Radicalism of the American Revolution* (New York: Knopf, 1992), which examines how changing ideas about education, property, and religion imbued the American Revolution with a radical social character. Other important studies of Revolutionary ideology include Hannah Arendt, *On Revolution* (New York: Viking, 1965); Pauline Maier, *From Resistance to Revolution: Colonial Radicals and the Development of American Opposition to Britain, 1765–1776* (New York: Vintage, 1972); Bernard Bailyn, *The Ideological Origins of the American Revolution* (Cambridge, MA: Harvard UP, 1967).

5. See Frederick R. Goff, *The John Dunlap Broadside: The First Printing of the Declaration of Independence* (Washington, DC: Library of Congress, 1976), 11. See also Ray Raphael's chapter "Storybook Nation" in *Founding Myths: Stories That Hide Our Patriotic Past*, rev. ed. (New York: New P, 2014).

6. Bailyn, *Ideological Origins* viii. From the hundreds of pamphlets that he examined, Bailyn adduces a "harmonizing force" that generated "a comprehensive theory of politics" (53–54). In other words, by dismissing propaganda as simply hollow rhetoric, Bailyn is able to posit a more-or-less unified ideological outlook among white colonials in the years immediately preceding the Revolution.

7. D. F. McKenzie, *Bibliography and the Sociology of Texts* (London: British Library, 1986).

8. Bailyn, *Ideological Origins* ix. Bailyn is presenting an alternative to Charles Beard's *An Economic Interpretation of the Constitution of the United States* (1913), which presents an "interpretation of the American Revolution as propaganda," according to Nicholas J. Cull et al., eds., *Propaganda and Mass Persuasion: A Historical Encyclopedia, 1500 to the Present* (Santa Barbara, CA: ABC-Clio, 2003), 346. Andy Doolen sketches changing historical approaches to early American political culture in "Early American Civics: Rehistoricizing the Power of Republicanism," *American Literary History* 19.1 (2007): 120–40.

9. Arjun Appadurai, "Disjuncture and Difference in the Global Culture Economy," *Public Culture* 2 (Spring 1990): 7.

10. See Lisa Parks, "Stuff You Can Kick: Toward a Theory of Media Infrastructures," in *Humanities and the Digital*, ed. David Theo Goldberg and Patrik Svensson (Cambridge, MA: MIT P, 2014).

11. Natalie Zemon Davis, "Printing and the People," in *Society and Culture in Early Modern France: Eight Essays by Natalie Zemon Davis* (Stanford, CA: Stanford UP, 1975), 218.

12. On the quick production time of propaganda, see Lynn Hunt, "Engraving the Republic: Prints and Propaganda in the French Revolution," *History Today* 30 (October 1980): 13.

13. Adrian Johns, *The Nature of the Book: Print and Knowledge in the Making* (Chicago: U of Chicago P, 1998), 445. See also Christian Thorne, who describes the view among eighteenth-century Tory satirists that print "leads not to a definitive corpus of common knowledge but to an insane proliferation of argumentative standpoints" (*The Dialectic of Counter-Enlightenment* [Cambridge, MA: Harvard UP, 2009], 230).

14. Michael Warner, *The Letters of the Republic: Publication and the Public Sphere in 18th-Century America* (Cambridge, MA: Harvard UP, 1991), 61. For an extension of Warner's work in examining the connections between print and republicanism, see Trish Loughran, *The Republic in Print: Print Culture in the Age of U.S. Nationalism, 1770–1870* (New York: Columbia UP, 2007). Carroll Smith-Rosenberg discusses the importance of colonial newspapers and the political magazine to early American society (*This Violent Empire: The Birth of an American National Identity* [Chapel Hill: U of North Carolina Press, 2010], 23–29) as does Arthur M. Schlesinger in *Prelude to Independence: The Newspaper War on Britain, 1764–1776* (New York: Knopf, 1958). On communities of citizen-readers created by print in the early Republic, see Seth Cotlar, *Tom Paine's America: The Rise and Fall of Transatlantic Republicanism* (Charlottesville: U of Virginia P, 2011).

15. Michael Warner, *Publics and Counterpublics* (New York: Zone, 2002), 67.

16. Robert E. Shallhope, "Republicanism," in *A Companion to the American Revolution*, ed. Jack P. Greene and J. R. Pole (Malden, MA: Blackwell, 2000), 670. Daniel Marcus discusses the inadequacy of locating eighteenth-century American journalism within the framework of classical republicanism (*Scandal and Civility: Journalism and the Birth of American Democracy* [New York: Oxford UP, 2009], 16–17).

17. John Adams, "Novanglus," in *The Works of John Adams, Second President of the United States* (Boston: Little, Brown, 1865), 4:31.

18. Jay Fliegelman, *Declaring Independence: Jefferson, Natural Language, and the Culture of Performance* (Stanford, CA: Stanford UP, 1993), 29. For Benjamin Franklin Bache's complaints about Federalist printers, see his *Remarks Occasioned by the Late Conduct of Mr. Washington as President of the United States* (Philadelphia: Bache, 1797), iv.

19. Charles Inglis, *The Deceiver Unmasked; or, Loyalty and Interest United: In Answer to a Pamphlet Entitled "Common Sense"* (New York: Loudon, 1776), v.

20. This definition is drawn from Jonathan Auerbach and Russ Castronovo, "Thirteen Propositions about Propaganda," in *The Oxford Handbook of Propaganda Studies*, ed. Jonathan Auerbach and Russ Castronovo (New York: Oxford UP, 2014), 1–16.

21. The story hinged on "a deliberate mistranslation of the German word *Kadaver* which, although it literally means 'a corpse,' is used in German to refer only to the body of an animal, never to that of a human" (Terence H. Qualter, *Opinion Control in the Democracies* [London: MacMillan, 1985], 175). The factory was rendering fat from animal bodies, not human corpses.

22. In addition to Bailyn's dismissal of "mere rhetoric and propaganda," see Richard D. Brown, who usefully focuses on communication strategies and protocols but resists seeing such activities as evidence of propaganda or manipulation (*Revolutionary Politics in Massachusetts: The Boston Committee of Correspondence and the Towns, 1772–1774* [Cambridge, MA: Harvard UP, 1970], 244–45).

23. See Maria Teresa Prendergast and Thomas A. Prendergast, "The Invention of Propaganda: A Critical Commentary on *Inscrutabili Divinae Providentiae Arcano*," in Auerbach and Castronovo, *Oxford Handbook to Propaganda Studies*, 19–27.

24. George III, "A Proclamation by the King for Suppressing Rebellion and Sedition," in *Documents of American History*, ed. Henry Steele Commager (New York: Appleton-Century-Crofts, 1958), 96. For the context and significance of this proclamation, see Maier 257.

25. Bernays, *Propaganda* 79.

26. See Bernays, *Public Relations* 30.

27. George III 96. Oral transmission also facilitated dissent and early nationalism. See Sandra Gustafson, *Eloquence Is Power: Oratory and Performance in Early America* (Chapel Hill: U of North Carolina P, 2000); Fliegelman; andChristopher Looby, *Voicing America: Language, Literary Form, and the Origins of the United States* (Chicago: U of Chicago P, 1998).

28. George III 96.

29. Hampden [Benjamin Rush?], *The Alarm, Number V* (New York, 1773), 3, accessed August 2, 2008 <http://memory.loc.gov>.

30. T. H. Breen, *American Insurgents, American Patriots: The Revolution of the People* (New York: Hill and Wang, 2010), 17.

31. On the "complex system of links" set up by printers, see M. Warner, *Letters of the Republic* 68. The spread of information via committees of correspondence is described by R. Brown; William B. Warner, "The Invention of a Public Machine for Revolutionary Sentiment: The Boston Committee of Correspondence," *Eighteenth Century* 50 (Summer–Fall 2009): 145–64; and Richard Alan Ryerson, *The Revolution Is Now Begun: The Radical Committees of Philadelphia, 1765–1776* (Philadelphia: U of Pennsylvania P, 1978). Jeffrey L. Pasley discusses the range of venues for creating and contesting public opinion, including "holiday celebrations, parades, taverns, toasts, songs, town meetings, petitions, militia company training days, and various products of local printing presses, including broadsides, handbills, almanacs, poems, pamphlets, and, especially, the small-circulation local and regional newspapers that sprang up everywhere after the Revolution" ("The Cheese and the Words: Popular Political Culture and Participatory Democracy in the Early American Republic," in *Beyond the Founders: New Approaches to the Political History of the Early American Republic*, ed. Jeffrey L. Pasley, Andrew W. Robertson, and David Waldstreicher [Chapel Hill: U of North Carolina P, 2004], 39).

32. See Stephen Botein, "Printers and the American Revolution," in *The Press and the American Revolution*, ed. Bernard Bailyn and John B. Hench (Worcester, MA: American Antiquarian Society, 1980), 41. See also G. Thomas Tanselle, "Some Statistics on American Printing, 1764–1783," in Bailyn and Hench, *The Press and the American Revolution*, 315–64; and Charles E. Clarke, "Early American Journalism: News and Opinion in the Popular Press," in *A History of the Book in America*, ed. Hugh Amory and David D. Hall (Worcester, MA: American Antiquarian Society, 2007–10), 1:347–66. Urban centers in Massachusetts, New York, and Philadelphia were key sites of propagation, but see Tanselle for figures on printing in the southern colonies as well as Calhoun Winton, "The Southern Printer as Agent of Change in the American Revolution," in *Agent of Change: Print Culture Studies after Elizabeth L. Eisenstein*, ed. Sabrina Alcorn Baron, Eric N. Lindquist, and Eleanor F. Shelvin (Amherst: U of Massachusetts P, 2007), 238–49.

33. Oliver makes this comment about Franklin in his "Origin and Progress of the *American* Rebellion" (1781) in Douglass Adair and John A. Schutz, eds., *Peter Oliver's Origin and Progress of the American Rebellion: A Tory View* (San Marino: Huntington Library, 1961) 79.

34. Oliver 106, 144.

35. Clarke 365.

36. Clarke 364. See Tanselle on the decline of religious items (327), as well as David D. Hall, who describes how "a veritable revolution in reading was carrying cosmopolitan culture to supremacy over 'sermons' and other religious texts" (*Cultures of Print: Essays in the History of the Book* [Amherst: U of Massachusetts P, 1996], 159).

37. Paul Virilio, *Speed and Politics: An Essay on Dromology*, trans. Mark Polizzotti (New York: Semiotext(e), 1986) [1977], 5.

38. Joseph Goebbels, *My Part in Germany's Fight*, trans. Kurt Fielder (London: Hurst and Blackett, 1940), 7, 14, 38, 60.

39. On the delays and slowness of mail, printing, and newspaper production in early America, see Loughran, *Republic in Print* 7–21.

40. Philip Davidson, *Propaganda and the American Revolution, 1763–1783* (Chapel Hill: U of North Carolina P, 1941), xiv.

41. Bernays, *Public Relations* 33. Colonial leaders used print and public spectacles as they "deliberately engineered" and incited mob action, as Arthur Meier Schlesinger noted some time ago ("Political Mobs and the American Revolution, 1765–1776," *Proceedings of the American Philosophical Society* 99 [August 1955], 244). But drawing an exact correlation between print and action, as in the efforts of social scientists and psychologists to quantify the effects of propaganda, is impossible. For social scientists, the problem has been the lack of a control group (i.e., a set of individuals who are unexposed to mass persuasion) who could then be compared to people who are subjected to propaganda. How can the effects of mass persuasion be measured when people are never not exposed to its influence?

42. John Dewey, "Public Opinion," *New Republic* May 3, 1922: 286. Brett Gary discusses the significance of the Dewey-Lippmann debates for understandings of publics' capacity for representative democracy (*The Nervous Liberals: Propaganda Anxieties from World War I to the Cold War* [New York: Columbia UP, 1999]).

43. John Dewey, *The Public and Its Problems* (New York: Holt, 1927), 177.

44. Dewey, *The Public and Its Problems* 137. In her work on deliberative democracy in early America, Sandra Gustafson examines the Dewey-Lippmann debates (*Imagining Deliberative Democracy in the Early American Republic* [Chicago: U of Chicago P, 2011]). Jonathan Auerbach has suggested that more continuity exists between Lippmann's and Dewey's respective positions than scholars have generally acknowledged ("Weapons of Democracy: Propaganda, Progressivism, and the American Public," [2014, MS.]). Dewey's nostalgia, Gustafson notes, led him to romanticize formal deliberation and other types of unmediated communication, but he also acknowledged that "the local face-to-face community has been invaded by forces so vast, so remote" that citizens lack the necessary information for democratic decision making (Dewey, *Public* 131). To what extent, then, is the ideal of deliberative democracy unequipped to deal with print and other media?

45. Stanley B. Cunningham, *The Idea of Propaganda: A Reconstruction* (Westport, CT: Praeger, 2002), 176.

46. Oliver Thomson, *Easily Led: A History of Propaganda* (Stroud, UK: Sutton, 1999). On the "fear" that stands behind most studies of propaganda, see Garth S. Jowett and Victoria O'Donnell, introduction to *Readings in Propaganda and Persuasion: New and Classic Essays*, ed. Garth S. Jowett and Victoria O'Donnell (Thousand Oaks, CA: Sage, 2006), ix.

47. Harold D. Lasswell, "The Theory of Propaganda," *American Political Science Review* 21 (August 1927): 627; Randal Marlin, *Propaganda and the Ethics of Persuasion* (Peterborough,

ON: Broadview 2002), 18; Susan A. Brewer, *Why America Fights: Patriotism and War Propaganda from the Philippines to Iraq* (New York: Oxford UP, 2009), 279; Frank Rich, *The Greatest Story Ever Sold: The Decline and Fall of Truth from 9/11 to Katrina* (New York: Penguin, 2006), 2.

48. Qualter 123. This custodial approach is an inheritance from the Progressive social criticism of muckrakers who attempted "to modify democracy's rank and file" by giving them the analytic tools to withstand media manipulation (J. Michael Sproule, *Propaganda and Democracy: The American Experience of Media and Mass Persuasion* [Cambridge: Cambridge UP, 1997], 269).

49. Carl Berger, *Broadsides and Bayonets: The Propaganda War of the American Revolution* (Philadelphia: U of Pennsylvania P, 1961), 18.

50. Robert Darnton, "What Is the History of Books?," in *The Book History Reader*, 2nd ed., ed. David Finkelstein and Alistair McCleery (New York: Routledge, 2006), 17.

51. Darnton 17, 22.

52. Peter Stallybrass, "'Little Jobs': Broadsides and the Printing Revolution," in Baron, Lindquist, and Shelvin, *Agent of Change* 315.

53. Samuel Adams, letter to Elbridge Gerry, November 5, 1772, in *The Writings of Samuel Adams*, ed. Harry Alonzo Cushing (New York: Putnam's, 1906), 2:346. On the importance of the postal system in early American politics, see Konstantin Dierks, *In My Power: Letter Writing and Communication in Early America* (Philadelphia: U of Pennsylvania P, 2009), xiii, 189–96. For more on emotion in late eighteenth-century America and the early republic, see Justine Murison, *The Politics of Anxiety in Nineteenth-Century American Literature* (Cambridge: Cambridge UP, 2011); Julia Stern, *The Plight of Feeling: Sympathy and Dissent in the Early American Novel* (Chicago: U of Chicago P, 1997); and Cathy N. Davidson, *Revolution and the Word: The Rise of the Novel in America* (New York: Oxford UP, 1986).

54. John C. Miller, *Sam Adams: Pioneer in Propaganda* (Stanford, CA: Stanford UP, 1936); Hanno Hardt, *Myths for the Masses: An Essay on Mass Communication* (Malden, MA: Blackwell, 2004), 7.

55. Maier xvii–xviii.

56. S. Adams, letter to Geary 2:346.

57. David Barsamian and Noam Chomsky, *Propaganda and the Public Mind: Conversations with Noam Chomsky* (Cambridge, MA: South End Press, 2001), 152.

58. Jacques Ellul, *Propaganda: The Formation of Men's Attitudes*, trans. Konrad Kellen and Jean Lerner (New York: Vintage, 1965), 121. For Ellul, propaganda comprises not only the messages of a specific political program but a broader sociological phenomenon of internal adjustment.

59. Ellul 132.

60. Ellul 119.

61. Frederick E. Lumley, *The Propaganda Menace* (New York: Century, 1933) 380. The currency of this view is suggested in part by the fact that the edition I consulted is presented as a "Student's Edition."

62. Mark Wollaeger, *Modernism, Media, and Propaganda: British Narrative Form from 1900 to 1945* (Princeton, NJ: Princeton UP, 2006) 10.

63. Ellul 145.

64. Thomas Paine, "Liberty Tree," in *The Thomas Paine Reader*, ed. Michael Foot and Isaac Kramnick (New York: Penguin, 1987), 63. John Dickinson also tried his hand at adapting

recognizable compositions to patriotic song by writing "Liberty Song" to the tune of "Hearts of Oak." On the importance of tavern culture to late eighteenth-century American politics, see Peter Thompson, *Rum Punch and Revolution: Taverngoing and Public Life in Eighteenth-Century Philadelphia* (Philadelphia: U of Pennsylvania P, 1999). Although newspapers and broadsides readily found their way into drinking establishments, Thompson suggests that the circulation of printed material gradually watered down the meaning of political speech and behavior in taverns (179–81).

65. George Alexander Stevens, "The Origin of English Liberty," in *The Choice Spirit's Chaplet; or, A Poesy from Parnassus. Being a select collection of songs, from the most approved Authors; Many of them Written and the Whole compiled by George Alexander Stevens, Esq.* (London: Whitehaven, 1771), 162.

66. Robert S. Levine, *Dislocating Race and Nation: Episodes in Nineteenth-Century Literary Nationalism* (Chapel Hill: U of North Carolina P, 2008), 11.

67. See Sahar Khamis, Paul B. Gold, and Katherine Vaughn, "Propaganda in Egypt and Syria's 'Cyberwars': Contexts, Actors, Tools, and Tactics" in Auerbach and Castronovo, *Oxford Handbook of Propaganda Studies* 418–38; David Yanagizawa-Drott, "Propaganda vs. Education: A Case Study of Hate Radio in Rwanda," in Auerbach and Castronovo, *Oxford Handbook of Propaganda Studies* 378–95; Philip N. Howard, *The Digital Origins of Dictatorship and Democracy: Information Technology and Political Islam* (New York: Oxford UP, 2010). On the relationship of printed matter to digital forms, see David J. Gunkel, "What's the Matter with Books?" *Configurations* 11 (Fall 2003): 277–303.

68. Quoted in Clyde Augustus Duniway, *The Development of Freedom of the Press in Massachusetts* (Cambridge, MA: Harvard UP, 1906) 136n.

69. Edmund S. Morgan, *Inventing the People: The Rise of Popular Sovereignty in England and America* (New York: Norton, 1989), 233. On retrenchments after the Revolution, see Gary B. Nash, *The Unknown American Revolution: The Unruly Birth of Democracy and the Struggle to Create America* (New York: Viking, 2005), 423–45; and Larry E. Tise, *The American Counterrevolution: A Retreat from Liberty, 1783–1800* (Mechanicsburg, PA: Stackpole, 1998). For a contrasting view, see Wood's *Radicalism of the American Revolution*, which argues that the political revolution of 1776 set in motion social radicalism that continued into the nineteenth century.

70. W. Warner, "Invention of a Public Machine" 162.

71. P. Davidson 13.

72. See Berger 213.

73. Henry Adams, *The Education of Henry Adams* (New York: Modern Library, 1931), 382.

## Chapter 1

1. The video is widely available on the Web, most notably at collateralmuder.com.

2. Manuel Castells, *The Rise of the Network Society*, 2nd ed. (Malden, MA: Wiley-Blackwell, 2000).

3. See Arendt 49, 65.

4. Friedrich A. Kittler, *Discourse Networks, 1800/1900*, trans. Michael Metteer (Stanford, CA: Stanford UP, 1990), 119.

5. For more on these formulations, see Auerbach and Castronovo.

6. Bill Keller, executive editor of the *New York Times*, makes the argument that "if the freedom of the press makes some Americans uneasy, it is anathema to the ideologists of terror" ("The Boy Who Kicked the Hornet's Nest," in *Open Secrets: WikiLeaks, War, and American Diplomacy*, ed. Alexander Star (New York: Grove, 2011), 17). On Assange's appeal to American values, see http://www.wikileaks.ch/About.html. Daniel Domscheit-Berg dedicates his *Inside WikiLeaks: My Time with Julian Assange at the World's Most Dangerous Website* (New York: Crown, 2011) to "the First Amendment and those defending the world's most precious bastion of freedom of speech" (iv). For comprehensive treatment of these and other issues involving the "networked fourth estate," see Yochai Benkler, "A Free Irresponsible Press: Wikileaks and the Battle over the Soul of the Networked Fourth Estate," *Harvard Civil Rights–Civil Liberties Law Review* 46.2 (2011): 311–97.

7. Slavoj Žižek, "Good Manners in the Age of WikiLeaks," *London Review of Books* January 20, 2011, accessed March 11, 2011 <http://www.lrb.co.uk/v33/n02/slavoj-zizek/good-manners-in-the-age-of-wikileaks>.

8. Palin quoted in Martin Beckford, "Sarah Palin: Hunt WikiLeaks Founder like al-Qaeda and Taliban Leaders," *Telegraph* November 30, 2010, accessed April 1, 2011 <http://www.telegraph.co.uk/news/worldnews/wikileaks/8171269/Sarah-Palin-hunt-WikiLeaks-founder-like-al-Qaeda-and-Taliban-leaders.html>. It is worth remembering that WikiLeaks also released Palin's hacked e-mails. Bob Beckel (Walter Mondale's 1984 campaign manager) is quoted by filmmaker Michael Moore in "Why I'm Posting Bail Money for Julian Assange," *Huffington Post*, December 14, 2010, accessed March 11, 2011 <http://www.huffingtonpost.com/michael-moore/why-im-posting-bail-money_b_796319.html>.

9. Quoted at http://www.wikileaks.ch/About.html. For a related critique, see Bodó Balázs, who argues that WikiLeaks, or "Wikileakistan," as he calls it, re-creates the very sovereignty that it attacks ("Wikileaks and Freedom, Autonomy and Sovereignty in the Cloud," *Center for Internet and Society*, March 11, 2011, accessed July 5, 2011 <http://cyberlaw.stanford.edu/node/6635>.

10. The field is diverse and growing, and has spread across disciplines to include work by sociologists (Castells plus Bruno Latour, *Reassembling the Social: An Introduction to Actor-Network-Theory* [Oxford: Oxford UP, 2005]); physicists (Albert-László Barabási, *Linked: The New Science of Networks* [Cambridge, MA: Perseus, 2002]); literary critics (Steven Shaviro, *Connected, or, What It Means to Live in the Network Society* [Minneapolis: U of Minnesota P, 1999]) and Matt Cohen, *The Networked Wilderness: Communications in Early New England* [Minneapolis: U of Minnesota P, 2010]); medical sociologists (Nicholas A. Christakis and James H. Fowler, *Connected: The Surprising Power of Our Social Networks and How They Shape Our Lives* [New York: Little, Brown, 2009]); and filmmakers (James Der Derian, "9.11: Before, After, and In Between," *Social Science Research Council/After Sept. 11*, Social Science Research Council, accessed May 23, 2011 <http://essays.ssrc.org/sept11/essays/der_derian.htm>).

11. John F. Burns and Ravu Somaiya, "Who Is Julian Assange?" in Star, *Open Secrets*, 26. For comparisons of Assange and Ellsberg, see Micah L. Sifry, *WikiLeaks and the Age of Transparency* (Berkeley, CA: Counterpoint, 2011), 28–32.

12. Scott Shane, "Can the Government Keep a Secret?" in Star, *Open Secrets* 338.

13. Seen from this perspective, the correlation between WikiLeaks and democratic agency falls prey to the critique of "technodeterminism" that Michael Warner makes (*Letters of the Republic* 6). Given my pairings here, the continued applicability of Warner's critique is striking since his context is eighteenth-century America.

14. Amy Goodman, July 5, 2011. All quotations from this event are from the transcript (and video) available at http://www.democracynow.org/blog/2011/7/5/watch_full_video_of_wikileaks_julian_assange_philosopher_slavoj_iek_with_amy_goodman.

15. Slavoj Žižek, *Living in the End of Times* (New York: Verso, 2011), 408. This work reframes and adds to Žižek's earlier comments on WikiLeaks ("Good Manners") published in the *London Review of Books*.

16. Žižek, *Living in the End of Times* 408.

17. Indeed, the scenario that Žižek conjures up seems borrowed from Pierre Morel's film *Taken* (2008), in which the daughter of a former CIA operative is abducted into white slavery. The hero, played by Liam Neeson, tortures or kills anyone who may have information about his daughter's whereabouts.

18. For a list of some of WikiLeaks' disclosures prior to Cablegate, see David Kushner, "Click and Dagger," *Mother Jones* July–August 2010, accessed June 12, 2013 <http://www.motherjones.com/politics/2010/07/click-and-dagger-wikileaks-julian-assange-iraq-video-updated>. Since Cablegate and at the time of this writing, discussion of WikiLeaks has become embroiled with another leaker of secret information, Eric Snowden.

19. See David Leigh and Luke Harding, *WikiLeaks: Inside Julian Assange's War on Secrecy* (New York: Perseus, 2011), 53–54, as well as http://www.torproject.org.

20. Thomas Friedman, "We've Only Got America A," in Star, *Open Secrets* 399.

21. Leigh and Harding 6. "Why is the coverage of Julian Assange so personal?" asks C. W. Anderson in a Web installation on "Politics in the Age of Secrecy and Transparency" ("Spotlights and Shadows Revisited: The Case of Julian Assange," *The New Everyday: A Media Commons Project*, April 22, 2011, accessed October 1, 2013 <http://mediacommons.futureofthebook.org/tne/pieces/spotlights-and-shadows-revisited-case-julian-assange>. Anderson's answer is that Assange, like many iconic figures of the cultural Left in the 1960s, consents to journalistic celebrity in order to secure an audience for scoops and exposés.

22. Saroj Giri, "WikiLeaks beyond WikiLeaks," *Mute: Culture and Politics after the Net*, Mute, December 16, 2010, accessed November 3, 2012 <http://www.metamute.org/en/articles/WikiLeaks_beyond_WikiLeaks>. See also Finn Burton, who argues that the "least interesting things about WikiLeaks" may be WikiLeaks itself ("After WikiLeaks, Us," *The New Everyday: A Media Commons Project*, April 4, 2011, accessed October 1, 2013 <http://mediacommons.futureofthebook.org/tne/pieces/after-wikileaks-us>.

23. Julian Assange, "Don't Shoot the Messenger for Revealing Uncomfortable Truths," *Australian*, December 8, 2010, accessed March 1, 2012 <http://www.theaustralian.com.au/in-depth/wikileaks/dont-shoot-messenger-for-revealing-uncomfortable-truths/story-fn775xjq-1225967241332>.

24. Marshall McLuhan, "The Medium Is the Message," in *Understanding Media* (Cambridge, MA: MIT P, 1964), 9. See also Kittler's version of this idea: "Not content or message but the medium itself" signaled the end of German romantic idealism (178).

25. Giri.

26. Žižek, *Living in the End of Times* 408.

27. Caroline Levine, "Narrative Networks: *Bleak House* and the Affordances of Form," *Novel* 42.3 (2009): 517–23; Patrick Jagoda, "Terror Networks and the Aesthetics of Interconnection," *Social Text* 105 (Winter 2010): 65–89.

28. Bernays, *Propaganda* 44, 55.

29. Shaviro 24.

30. Shaviro 24.

31. See Bryce Traister, "Criminal Correspondence: Loyalism, Espionage, and Creve-coeur," *Early American Literature* 27 (2002): 469–96.

32. Dierks describes letters as constituting "an exceptionally potent mode of communi-cation," one in which they function as "instruments of political action" (xiii). For more on this point, see Dierks 189–234; W. Warner, "Invention of a Public Machine"; and Loughran, *Republic in Print*.

33. Eve Tavor Bannet, *Empire of Letters: Letter Manuals and Transatlantic Correspondence, 1688–1820* (Cambridge: Cambridge UP, 2005), 25. Letters were routinely stolen, intercepted, forged, or reprinted with unauthorized interpolations. So commonplace were counterfeit-ing and privacy that print culture became a zone that both confirmed and called into ques-tion the status of written knowledge. On this point, see Johns's comprehensive *Nature of the Book*. In this context, Tory writers like Swift and Pope expressed apprehension that the wid-ening of print culture generated "an insane proliferation" of opinions and viewpoints (Thorne 223).

34. Bannet x. See also W. Warner on colonial committees of correspondence as a "com-munication network" ("Invention of a Public Machine" 161); Cohen on encounters between European and Native American communication networks; Bryan Waterman on transat-lantic intellectual networks (*The Republic of Intellect: The Friendly Club of New York City and the Making of American Literature* [Baltimore: Johns Hopkins UP, 2007]); Roger Kaplan on spy networks ("The Hidden War: British Intelligence Operations during the American Rev-olution," *William and Mary Quarterly* 47 [January 1990]: 115–38); and William Decker, *Epis-tolary Practices: Letter Writing in America before Telecommunications* (Chapel Hill: U of North Carolina P, 1998).

35. Susan Scott Parrish, *American Curiosity: Cultures of Natural History in the Colonial British Atlantic World* (Chapel Hill: U of North Carolina P, 2006), 106.

36. See Jagoda 75.

37. Levine 520.

38. M. Warner, *Publics and Counterpublics* 90.

39. Qtd. in Allen French, "The First George Washington Scandal," *Proceedings of the Massachusetts Historical Society* 65 (November 1935): 469. See also Schlesinger, *Prelude to Independence* 244–45.

40. Charles Francis Adams, *The Life of John Adams*, in J. Adams, *Works* 1:180. For more on correspondence, interception, and printing in eighteenth-century America, see Jeremy Black, "Eighteenth-Century Intercepted Dispatches," *Journal of the Society of Archivists* 11 (Octo-ber 1990): 138–43; Paul Langford, "British Correspondence in the Colonial Press, 1763–1775: A Study in Anglo-American Misunderstanding before the American Revolution," in *The Press and the American Revolution*, ed. Bernard Bailyn and John B. Hench (Worcester, MA: American Antiquarian Society, 1980), 273–313; Thomas C. Leonard, "News for a Revolution: The Exposé in America, 1768–1773," *Journal of American History* 67 (June 1980): 26–40; Schlesinger, *Prelude to Independence*; and Corrina A. Wagner, "Loyalist Propaganda and the Scandalous Life of Tom Paine," *British Journal for Eighteenth-Century Studies* 28 (2005): 97–115.

41. J. Adams, *Works* 1:179, 2:411.

42. Rush quoted in Schlesinger, *Prelude to Independence* 245.

43. Joseph Warren to John Adams, September 19, 1775, in *Warren-Adams Letters: Being Chiefly a Correspondence among John Adams, Samuel Adams, and James Warren*, vol. 2, *1778–1814* (Boston: Massachusetts Historical Society, 1925), 14.

44. "Genuine Copies of the Intercepted Letters Mentioned in Our Last," *Massachusetts Gazette and Boston News-Letter* August 17, 1775.

45. J. Adams, *Works* 2:412.

46. J. Adams, *Works* 2:412.

47. Bruno Latour, "On Actor-Network Theory: A Few Clarifications," *Centre for Social Theory and Technology*, January 11, 1998, accessed October 5, 2010 <http://www.nettime .org/Lists-Archives/nettime-l-9801/msg00019.html>. But networks also have their exclusions. For a critique of Latour on this point, see Sianne Ngai, "Network Aesthetics: Juliana Spahr's *The Transformation* and Bruno Latour's *Reassembling the Social*," in *American Literature's Aesthetic Dimensions*, ed. Cindy Weinstein and Christopher Looby (New York: Columbia UP, 2012).

48. Latour highlights the associations and connections that dilute the socius (*Reassembling the Social* 5). Critics have argued that actor-network theory, despite emphasizing links and relays, remains committed to identity under the sign of a "distributed actor" and "thereby reverting to a subject who is invisible and autonomous" (Hélène Mialet, "Reincarnating the Knowing Subject: Scientific Rationality and the Situated Body," *Qui Parle* 18 [Fall–Winter 2009]: 61).

49. Thomas Hutchinson et al. in *The Representation of Governor Hutchinson and Others, Contained in Certain Letters Transmitted to England, and Afterwards Returned from Thence, and Laid before the General Assembly of the Massachusetts-Bay*, in *The Papers of Benjamin Franklin*, ed. William Wilcox (New Haven, CT: Yale UP, 1978), 20:516. All further references to *The Papers of Benjamin Franklin* will be noted parenthetically. The theft of letters was hardly an uncommon feature of the Atlantic world. Many of the personages in this book, such as Edmund Burke, John Dickinson, Mercy Otis Warren, and Franklin, sent correspondence that was intercepted. See Julie M. Flavell, "Government Interception of Letters from America and the Quest for Colonial Opinion in 1775," *William and Mary Quarterly* 58 (April 2001): 403–30; Dierks 203–204; Bannet 250–51; and Fliegelman 44.

50. James Kendall Hosmer, *The Life of Thomas Hutchinson, Royal Governor of the Province of Massachusetts Bay* (Boston: Houghton Mifflin, 1896), 278. For the take of later historians on the affair of Hutchinson's letters, see Schlesinger, *Prelude to Independence* 151–52; Bernard Bailyn, *The Ordeal of Thomas Hutchinson* (Cambridge, MA: Harvard UP, 1974); Gordon Wood, *The Americanization of Benjamin Franklin* (New York: Penguin, 2004); and Benjamin Carp, *Defiance of the Patriots: The Boston Tea Party and the Making of America* (New Haven, CT: Yale UP, 2010). See also M. Warner, *Letters of the Republic* 91–96.

51. See Thomas R. Adams, *American Independence: The Growth of an Idea: A Bibliographic Study of the American Political Pamphlets Printed between 1764 and 1776 Dealing with the Dispute between Great Britain and Her Colonies* (Providence, RI: Brown UP, 1965), 72–74; and T. Leonard 35. Such momentum left Americans with little time for reflection when it came to interpreting Hutchinson's intentions. The tempo of politics made them bad readers, who, in Bailyn's summary in *Ordeal*, confused Hutchinson's predictive use of "must"—that is, an abridgement was inevitable given the brittle state of Anglo-American relations—with the less charitable interpretation that the governor was pushing to curtail the traditional rights enjoyed by colonists.

52. *Boston Gazette and Country Journal* June 7, 1773: 3.

53. *Boston Gazette and Country Journal* June 7, 1773: 3.

54. *Boston Gazette and Country Journal* June 7, 1773: 3.

55. Qtd. in Hosmer 285. Hutchinson also might have looked back on the career of his predecessor, Francis Bernard, whose letters also fell into the hands of Whig opponents. See Francis G. Walett, "Governor Bernard's Undoing: An Earlier Hutchinson Letters Affair," *New England Quarterly* 38 (June 1965): 217–26.

56. No stranger to the world of printing shops, Franklin no doubt knew what would happen when the letters turned up in Boston. In a posthumously published pamphlet, "Tract Relative to the Affair of Hutchinson's Letters" (*Papers* 21: 414–35), Franklin claimed that he only engaged in this ethically suspect act of transmitting purloined letters out of the purest motive. If people could see that the scheming against American liberty and adoption of punitive trade policies emanated not from the Crown but from men like Hutchinson in their midst, then colonial resentment would find its proper target. Yet if Franklin truly believed that limited circulation of this correspondence could improve Anglo-American relations, why then did he also think that their disclosure would likely incite riot? The contradiction speaks either to his caginess, as the editors of his collected papers suggest, or it reveals his startling naiveté, as Gordon Wood has concluded. Compare the editors' assessment in *The Papers of Benjamin Franklin* (20:408) to Wood, *Americanization* 143.

57. Latour, "On Actor-Network Theory." See also Latour's reconsideration of action in *Reassembling the Social* 44.

58. According to Laura Rigal, Franklin moved within a "multinational network of correspondences" that anticipates digital communication. The context of Newtonian physics, especially early understandings of fluid dynamics, drew Franklin and his peers to explore relationships between complex systems ranging from natural science to economy. See Rigal, "Benjamin Franklin, the Science of Flow, and the Legacy of the Enlightenment," in *A Companion to Benjamin Franklin*, ed. David Waldstreicher (New York: Wiley-Blackwell, 2011), 309.

59. Wood, *Americanization* 42; and see also Todd Thompson on Franklin's use of personae early in his career ("Representative Nobodies: The Politics of Benjamin Franklin's Satiric Personae, 1722–1757," *Early American Literature* 46.3 [2011]: 449–79).

60. The original of the play has slightly different wording and punctuation. See Edward Young, *The Revenge, a Tragedy as It Is Acted at the Theatre-Royal in Drury-Lane* (London: Chetwood, 1721), 59, accessed at Google Books, October 14, 2010. Wedderburn also took pains to emphasize Franklin's corporeality in order to simplify the network situation. On this point, see M. Warner, *Letters of the Republic* 93.

61. Jagoda 67.

62. Latour, "On Actor-Network Theory."

63. Ngai 15.

64. For this supposed account, see Wood, *Americanization* 147.

65. "Extract of a Letter from a Gentleman in London," *Pennsylvania Gazette* April 20, 1774: 3. The protective buffer of being a "public messenger" was short lived, however. The letter concludes by surmising that Franklin became a target not because of the Hutchinson affair but because certain satirical pamphlets ("Rules by Which a Great Empire May Be Reduced to a Small One" and "An Edict by the King of Prussia") "are suspected to be his" (3)—which indeed they are.

66. M. Warner, *Letters of the Republic* 96.

67. Chelsea E. Manning, "Subject: The Next Stage of My Life," *Today News*, August 22, 2013, accessed September 13, 2013 <http://www.today.com/news/i-am-chelsea-read-mannings-full-statement-6C10974052>.

## Chapter 2

1. Mercy Otis Warren, *The Defeat* (2.1) in *The Plays and Poems of Mercy Otis Warren*, ed. Benjamin Franklin V (Delmar, NY: Scholars' Facsimiles and Reprints, 1980), n.p. The genuineness of the letters had been an issue when reports of their existence first surfaced. See "Boston, June 14," *Boston Gazette and Country Journal* June 1773 14: 3; and "Province of Massachusetts-Bay," *Boston Gazette* June 1773 21:1.

2. Mercy Otis Warren, *History of the Rise, Progress, and Termination of the American Revolution Interspersed with Biographical, Political and Moral Observations* (Indianapolis: Liberty Classics, 1988), 65. Thomas Hutchinson's brother, Foster Hutchinson, served as justice of the common pleas; Thomas, his son, had secured the position of judge of probate; Andrew Oliver, his wife's brother-in-law, was the lieutenant governor; Peter Oliver, his daughter's father-in-law, was chief justice. The crisis over the importation of tea would intensify the appearance of nepotism since two of Hutchinson's sons acted as consignees for the tea while his younger namesake had married into the family of a major tea importer. On the system of patronage in early America, see Wood, *Radicalism* 57–77.

3. Warren, *The Defeat*.

4. Nina Baym, "Mercy Otis Warren's Gendered Melodrama of Revolution," *South Atlantic Quarterly* 90 (Summer 1991): 544. Often overlooked in the historiography that surrounds the founding fathers, Warren, when discussed, is typically described as a propagandist whose artistic ambitions were sacrificed to political conviction. See John L. Teunissen, "Blockheadism and the Propaganda Plays of the American Revolution," *Early American Literature* 7 (Fall 1972): 148–62; Gerald Weales, "*The Adulateur* and How It Grew," *Library Chronicle* 53 (Winter 1979): 106; Jason Shaffer, "Making 'an Excellent Die': Death, Mourning, and Patriotism in the Propaganda Plays of the American Revolution," *Early American Literature* 41.1 (2006): 1–27; Rosemarie Zagarri, *A Woman's Dilemma: Mercy Otis Warren and the American Revolution* (Wheeling, IL.: Harland Davidson, 1965), 77; Carol Berkin, *First Generations: Women in Colonial America* (New York: Hill and Wang, 1997), 171–72.

5. Franklin, "Tract Relative to the Affair," 21:435.

6. See Jeffrey H. Richards, *Mercy Otis Warren* (New York: Twayne, 1995).

7. Kate Davies, *Catharine Macaulay and Mercy Otis Warren: The Revolutionary Atlantic and the Politics of Gender* (New York: Oxford UP, 2005), 11.

8. Richard Dawkins, *The Selfish Gene* (Oxford: Oxford UP, 1976), 206.

9. See Dawkins's use of "meme" (206). Since Dawkins's coinage, the idea and usage of "meme" has been popularized in ways that suggest that "meme" is itself a meme. Different understandings (and misunderstandings) of memes with respect to agency and determinism have arisen; see Jeremy Trevelyan Burman, "The Misunderstanding of Memes: Biography of an Unscientific Object, 1976–1999," *Perspectives on Science* 20.1 (2012): 75–104. If "the original meme" set in motion by Dawkins "was a rhetorical flourish intended to clarify a larger argument" (Burman 77), then it is fitting that the concept be used to track Warren's rhetoric. Memes have been employed to understand broad developments in music and

art history with varying success. See, for instance, Nicholas Tresilian, "The Swarming of Memes," *Technoetic Arts: A Journal of Speculative Research* 6.2 (2008): 115–26; and Steven Jan, "Meme Hunting with the Humdrum Toolkit: Principles, Problems, and Prospects," *Computer Music Journal* 28.4 (Winter 2004): 68–84.

10. Marchamont Needham [pseud.], "Allied Alas! For Ever to the Crime," *Boston Gazette*, June 15, 1772: 2. Needham was a seventeenth-century pamphleteer at the time of the English Civil War. According to results from *America's Historical Newspapers* database, after March 26, 1772 (when the first installment of *The Adulateur* appeared in *The Massachusetts Spy*) through 1777, "rapacious" appeared 118 times and "rapacity" 138. A pamphlet version of the drama appeared in 1773.

11. Warren, *History* 45.

12. Warren, *History* 355.

13. Thomas Hutchinson to Mr. Jackson, December 8, 1772, and Thomas Hutchinson to John Pownal, October 18, 1773, in Mercy Otis Warren, appendix 9, *History* 354–55.

14. Warren, *History* 64.

15. Thomas Hutchinson to Mr. Jackson, Pownal, and others, August 17, 1772, appendix 9 of Warren, *History* 354.

16. Warren, *History* 62.

17. Ruth H. Bloch, "The Gendered Meanings of Virtue in Revolutionary America," in *Gender and Morality in Anglo-American Culture* (Berkeley: U of California P, 2003), 136–53.

18. Thomas Paine, "Crisis III," in *The Complete Writings of Thomas Paine*, ed. Philip Foner (New York: Citadel, 1945), 1:90.

19. See "From the *Newport Mercury*," *New Hampshire Gazette* August 22, 1775: 2 and "At a Legal Meeting of the Daughters of LIBERTY at Constitution Hall, R. Island, April 1, 1774," *Newport Mercury* April 11, 1774: 2. See also Rolla Milton Tryon, *Household Manufactures in the United States, 1640–1860: A Study in Industrial History* (Chicago: U of Chicago P, 1917), 106–107.

20. Linda Kerber, *Women of the Republic: Intellect and Ideology in Revolutionary America* (New York: Norton, 1986), 85. Readers have challenged Kerber's notion of republican motherhood as essentially private. For Rosemarie Zagarri, "Republican motherhood thus represented a moderate, non-threatening response to the challenge of the Revolution for women. It was a formulation that kept the gender status quo intact" (*Revolutionary Backlash: Women and Politics in the Early Republic* [Philadelphia: U of Pennsylvania P, 2007], 5).

21. Davies 212. For more on gender and letter writing, see Frank Shuffelton, "In Different Voices: Gender in the American Republic of Letters," *Early American Literature* 25 (1990): 289–304; Rebecca Earle, "Introduction: Letters, Writers, and the Historian," in *Epistolary Selves: Letters and Letter-Writers, 1600–1945* (Brookfield, VT: Ashgate, 1999), 4–7; and Mary Kelly, "'The Need of Their Genius': Women's Reading and Writing Practices in Early America," *Journal of the Early Republic* 28 (Spring 2008): 7.

22. Zagarri observes that the "extensive use of print media" often appealed to women as readers in which "male political leaders" invited women to the Revolutionary cause (*Revolutionary Backlash* 22). While documenting the growing awareness in the late eighteenth century of literate white women's political subjectivity, this account remains somewhat unidirectional since it positions women more as consumers than as participants in the public print sphere. For more on women's networks in general and women's correspondence networks in early America, see Nancy F. Cott, *The Bonds of Womanhood: Woman's Sphere in New England,*

*1780–1835* (New Haven, CT: Yale UP, 1997); andMary Beth Norton, *Liberty's Daughters: The Revolutionary Experience of American Women, 1750–1800* (Boston: Little, Brown, 1980).

23. Davies 209. See also Peter C. Messer, "Writing Women into History: Defining Gender and Citizenship in Post-Revolutionary America," *Studies in Eighteenth Century Culture* 28 (1999): 341–60; and Pauline Schloesser, *The Fair Sex: White Women and Racial Patriarchy in the Early American Republic* (New York: New York UP, 2002), 95–96.

24. Bloch 150. See also Sarah Richardson, "'Well-Neighboured Houses': The Political Networks of Elite Women, 1780–1860," in *The Power of the Petticoat*, ed. Kathryn Gleadle and Sarah Richardson (New York: St. Martins, 2000), 56–73.

25. John Adams to Mercy Otis Warren, July 15, 1814, in Adams, *Works*. 10:99.

26. Richardson 60.

27. Davies 185. Bailyn describes the prevalence of classical references in the literature of the American Revolution (*Ideological Origins* 23–26). On classical republicanism in colonial America and the early United States, see J. G. A Pocock, *The Machiavellian Moment: Florentine Political Thought and the Atlantic Republican Tradition* (Princeton, NJ: Princeton UP, 1975); and Paul A. Rahe, *Republics Ancient and Modern: Classical Republicanism and the American Revolution* (Chapel Hill: U of North Carolina P, 1992). Elizabeth Maddock Dillon discusses how notions of republicanism were modified by Lockean liberalism, arguing that the divide between the two ideologies is not as distinct or as total as many critics, such as Pocock, suggest. For eighteenth-century white women, in particular, gendered expectations of virtue made women's privacy an important component of republicanism (*The Gender of Freedom: Fictions of Liberalism and the Literary Public Sphere* [Stanford, CA: Stanford UP, 2004], 142–45). On the appearance of classical republicanism in letter writing, see Mary Kelley, "'While Pen, Ink & Paper Can Be Had': Reading and Writing in a Time of Revolution," *Early American Studies* (Fall 2012): 442–45.

28. Samuel Adams, *The Writings of Samuel Adams* (Teddington, UK: Echo Library, 2006), 3:57. Ann Fairfax Withington describes the interconnections between a renewed emphasis on moral behavior in Revolutionary America, seen in the prohibitions against cockfighting and other displays, and the cultural dimensions of republican virtue (*Toward a More Perfect Union: Virtue and the Formation of American Republics* [New York: Oxford UP, 1991], 11–18).

29. Warren, *History* 62.

30. Warren, *History* 62.

31. Janet Gurkin Altman, *Epistolarity: Approaches to a Form* (Columbus: Ohio State UP, 1982), 48.

32. Davies 185. In addition to this sort of performance, there is also evidence that her dramatic sketches were read aloud in "clandestine gatherings" (S. E. Wilmer, *Theatre, Society, and the Nation: Staging American Identities* [Cambridge: Cambridge UP, 2002], 46).

33. Davies 218.

34. Mercy Otis Warren to Abigail Adams, February 7, 1776, *Warren-Adams Letters* 1:205.

35. Abigail Adams to Mercy Otis Warren, January 16, 1803, *Warren-Adams Letters* 2:342.

36. Abigail Adams to Mercy Otis Warren, January 8, 1781, *Warren-Adams Letters* 2:164.

37. Mercy Otis Warren to John Adams, January 30, 1775, *Warren-Adams Letters* 1:38.

38. Walter Benjamin, "The Author as Producer," in *Reflections: Essays, Aphorisms, Auto-biographical Writings*, trans. Edmund Jephcott (New York: Schocken, 1986), 225. Despite limitations on literacy, researchers have suggested, New England white women "may actually have been *nearing* something like universal literacy" toward the close of the eighteenth century (Joel Perlmann and Dennis Shirley, "When Did New England Women Acquire Literacy?," *William and Mary Quarterly* 48 [January 1991]: 64).

39. Benjamin 225.

40. Benjamin 225.

41. McKenzie, *Bibliography and the Sociology of Texts.*

42. James Warren to John Adams, February 20, 1775, in *Warren-Adams Letters* 1:41.

43. *Boston Gazette and Country Journal* June 7, 1773: 3.

44. "A Soliloquy," *Boston Gazette and Country Journal*, June 7, 1773: 3. Although "Rapatio" does not appear by name as the soliloquy's speaker, there is reference to Hazelrod, who appears in *The Adulateur* and *The Group* as his chief henchman. Hazelrod is a screen for Peter Oliver, whom Hutchinson had appointed to the post of chief justice of Massachusetts. Oliver's letters were among those in the packet of Hutchinson's letters that had been passed on to Franklin.

45. "A Soliloquy." The phrase "adulating tongue" can be found in *The Adulateur* as well. The coincident publication of the news of the Hutchinson letters and this poem suggests that it was written by someone who had both intimate knowledge of the closed proceedings in the Massachusetts house and ready access to John Gill and Benjamin Edes at the *Boston Gazette*. It might seem doubtful that a woman from the outlying town of Plymouth would have been privy to the scandal before it broke and that she would have been able to get her composition to the paper in quick order. Then again, Warren, by virtue of her and her husband's connections to men like John and Sam Adams, was in as good a position as anyone to learn about the letters and then get these verses to the printer so that they would appear just as the existence of Hutchinson's letters was coming to light.

46. In a letter of a August 17, 1814, in *Warren-Adams Letters* 2:396. Adams confirms Warren and not "Bishop Barrett" as the play's author. This ecclesiastical reference is puzzling since among the several Samuel Barretts that I could find in the historical record, none seems to have had a church connection, save a "Rev. Samuel Barrett" who died in 1772 before *The Group* was published. The best candidate seems to be a Samuel Barrett who was secretary of the Massachusetts Constitutional Convention. As a delegate from Boston, he was acquainted with Adams.

47. According to Richards, "We can best categorize this play as inspired, but not written, by Mercy Warren" (104).

48. Weales offers a comprehensive textual history of the play. On the identities of characters in *The Adulateur*, see "Editor's Preface," *Magazine of History* 63 (1918): 190; as well as Weales. Like the increased frequency of "rapacity" and "rapacious," variants of "adulateur" such as "adulatory" and "adulation" also experienced a significant uptick in usage.

49. Quoted in Alice Brown, *Mercy Warren* (New York: Scribner's, 1896), 178.

50. Weales 106.

51. Tenuissen 154.

52. John Adams to Mercy Warren, *Works* 10:99–100.

53. A. Brown 156.

54. Adams, "Novanglus," 4:30. "Novanglus" first appeared in 1774.

55. Daniel Leonard, *Massachusettensis; or, A Series of Letters, Containing a Faithful State of Many Important and Striking Facts, Which Laid the foundation of the Present Troubles in the Province of Massachusetts-Bay; Interspersed with Animadversions and Reflections, Originally Addressed to the People of That Province, and Worthy the Consideration of the True Patriots of This Country* (Boston, 1776), 36. The letters first appeared serially from 1774 to 1775. Adams, incorrect in his supposition that Sewall was the author, composed a response with the title *Novanglus* printed in the same issues of the *Boston Gazette* that contained scenes from *The Group*. On the parallel publication histories of Adams's "Novanglus" and Warren's play, see Sandra J. Sarkela, "Freedom's Call: The Persuasive Power of Mercy Otis Warren's Dramatic Sketches, 1772–1775," *Early American Literature* 44.3 (2009): 557–58.

56. D. Leonard 34.

57. Warren regularly associated adulation with Hutchinson. An unpublished poem indicts orators who "Their adulating strains express / With servile flattery flattery's address" in celebration of Hutchinson while another composition takes aim at "adulations" dedicated to "Massachusetts [sic] mimic king" ("An Extempore Thought on Some Servile Addresses from the Long Venerated Seminary of Harvard College" and "A Solemn Debate of a Certain Bench of Justice [illegible words] Are Addressed to Governor Hutchinson Just before He Left the Chair," Mercy Otis Warren Papers, Massachusetts Historical Society, Boston).

58. Aristotle, *The Rhetoric and Poetics of Aristotle*, trans. W. Rhys Roberts (New York: Random House, 1984), 22. For more on the dialogic and emotive nature of enthymemes, see Jeffrey Walker, "The Body of Persuasion: A Theory of the Enthymeme," *College English* 56 (January 1994): 46–65.

59. Aristotle 26.

60. Sarkela 546.

61. Garry Marshall, "The Internet and Memetics," accessed March 20, 2012 <http://pespmc1.vub.ac.be/Conf/MemePap/Marshall.html>. As a woman writer, Warren may have been particularly susceptible to this narrowed print sphere. Newspapers in the eighteenth century and through the first decades of the nineteenth century gave space to the public political presence of women writers. With the growing popularity of domestic ideology and literary sentimentality after the 1820s, however, this space narrowed, often limiting women's "personal expression to individual experience" (Paula Bernat Bennett, *Poets in the Public Sphere: The Emancipatory Project of American Women's Poetry, 1800–1900* [Princeton, NJ: Princeton UP, 2003], 30). For this reason, women often continued to write in eighteenth-century modes well into the nineteenth century in order to resist this sort of private lyricism (Bennett 31).

62. Warren, *History* 646.

63. Mercy Otis Warren, *Observations on the New Constitution, and on the Federal and State Conventions. By a Columbian Patriot* (Boston, 1788). The pamphlet is republished in *Pamphlets on the Constitution of the United States, Published during Its Discussion by the People, 1787–1788*, ed. Paul Leicester Ford (Brooklyn, 1888). Ford incorrectly identifies Elbridge Gerry as the pamphlet's author.

64. Tise, *American Counterrevolution* 81, 86.

65. Warren, *History* 694.

66. Albany Committee to New York Committee, April 12, 1788, is quoted in Ford's headnote to Warren, *Observations*, in *Pamphlets on the Constitution of the United States* 2.

67. Warren, *History* 694.

## Chapter 3

1. Warren, *History* 698.

2. Warren, *History* 573, 596.

3. J. Adams, "Novanglus" 167.

4. A Tradesman, "For the Pennsylvania Evening Post," *Pennsylvania Evening Post* April 30, 1776, 218.

5. Mercy Otis Warren to Catharine Sawbridge Macaulay, December 29, 1774, in *Mercy Otis Warren: Selected Letters*, ed. Jeffrey H. Richards and Sharon M. Harris (Athens: U of Georgia P, 2009), 37.

6. "Messieurs Printers," *Boston Gazette*, October 19, 1772. Patricia Bradley discusses the rhetorical deployment of slavery in *Slavery, Propaganda, and the American Revolution* (Jackson: U of Mississippi P, 1998). While Bradley does not treat imperial contexts, her study focuses on metaphors of domestic slavery, which, she argues, had the effect of hardening racist attitudes toward blacks in the American colonies.

7. See Gustafson, *Imagining Deliberative Democracy*.

8. Dewey, *Public and Its Problems* 131. For Dewey's invocation of Jefferson, see his review of Lippmann ("Public Opinion").

9. Walter Lippmann, *Public Opinion* (New York: Free P, 1997), 165.

10. Ellul 25. This comparison should not obscure the pronounced differences between Lippmann and Ellul. Propaganda, Ellul asserted, "is not simply a matter of public opinion" because of its capacity to impel action (26). In a generative study, Marc Wollaeger suggests September 22, 1914, as the inauguration of modern literary propaganda when a host of writers, including Rudyard Kipling, Arthur Conan Doyle, H. G. Wells, and Thomas Hardy were recruited to lend their talents to British propaganda efforts (14).

11. Lippmann 163.

12. For this confusion between an independent press and a paid one, see Jeff Gerth and Scott Shane, "U.S. Is Said to Pay to Plant Articles in Iraq Papers," *New York Times* December 10, 2005.

13. Ellul 74.

14. Ellul 148.

15. Ellul 132.

16. Ellul 72.

17. Jack P. Greene, "Colonial History and National History: Reflections on a Continuing Problem." *William and Mary Quarterly* 64 (April 2007) 235. The same often holds true in literary studies. As Michael Warner argues, a "nationalist impulse is an almost preinterpretative commitment for the discipline" of early Anglo-American literature ("What's Colonial about Colonial America?," in *Possible Pasts: Becoming Colonial in Early America*, ed. Robert Blair St. George [Ithaca, NY: Cornell UP, 2000], 50).

18. As Greene argues, settlement does not so much proceed from "nation-building impulses" as from other motives typically associated with land, profit, and exploitation (247). Greene sees a remedy in postcolonial approaches to national history, a view shared by Lawrence Buell, "American Literary Emergence as a Postcolonial Phenomenon," *American Literary History* 4 (Autumn 1992): 411–42; and Peter Hulme, "Postcolonial Theory and Early America: An Approach from the Caribbean," in Blair St. George 33–48. Kariann Yokota suggests that such a postcolonial perspective, unlike a national focus, results in sharper attention to the history of racial oppression ("Postcolonialism and Material Culture in the Early United

States," *William and Mary Quarterly* 64 (April 2007): 264–65). On the difficulty of incorporating postcolonial perspectives into American studies, see Brian T. Edwards, "Preposterous Encounters: Interrupting American Studies with the (Post)Colonial, or Casablanca in the American Century," *Comparative Studies of South Asia, Africa and the Middle East* 23 (2003): 70–86.

19. This formulation draws on and adapts an argument by Frederick Cooper, who calls for "a history that compares" rather than "Comparative History" ("Race, Ideology, and the Perils of Comparative History," *American Historical Review* 101 [October 1996]: 1135). For Cooper, Comparative History (his example is George Fredrickson's *Black Liberation: A Comparative History of Black Ideologies in the United States and South Africa*) results in static explanations that cannot take account of transatlantic or global situations.

20. Hampden [Benjamin Rush?], *The Alarm. Number II* (New York, 1773), 2, Library of Congress, Printed Ephemera Collection, portfolio 105, folder 9a, accessed March 1, 2007 <memory.loc.gov>. P. Davidson identifies "Hampden" as Rush (242n34). This choice of pseudonym refers to a "popular hero in Cromwellian England," indicating how early American nationalism still relied on English revolutionary history (David Freeman Hawke, *Benjamin Rush: Revolutionary Gadfly* [Indianapolis: Bobbs-Merrill, 1971], 109). According to the *Historical Dictionary of Revolutionary America*, however, Rush wrote under the pseudonym "Hamden" and should not be confused with the writer who used "Hampden." (Terry M. Mays, *Historical Dictionary of Revolutionary America* [Oxford: Scarecrow P, 2005], 124). Thanks to Julia Dauer for pointing out these inconsistencies.

21. "*A New* SONG, *to the Plaintive Tune of* Hosier's Ghost," *Virginia Gazette* January 20, 1774, reprinted in Arthur M. Schlesinger, "A Note on Songs as Patriot Propaganda, 1765–1776," *William and Mary Quarterly* 11.1 (1954): 80. Ballads were frequently reprinted and their length was convenient for broadsides.

22. Edmund Burke, "Letter to John Farr and John Harris, Esqrs., Sheriffs of the City of Bristol, on the Affairs of America," in *The Works of the Right Honourable Edmund Burke* (London: Nimmo, 1887), 2:191.

23. William B. Warner, "Communicating Liberty: The Newspapers of the British Empire as a Matrix for the American Revolution," *ELH* 72.2 (2005): 350.

24. Benjamin L. Carp, *Rebels Rising: Cities and the American Revolution* (New York: Oxford UP, 2007), 5, 57, 61.

25. Peter Linebaugh and Marcus Rediker, *The Many-Headed Hydra: Sailors, Slaves, Commoners, and the Hidden History of the Revolutionary Atlantic* (Boston: Beacon, 2000), 4. See also Steven Shapiro on the "geoculture" of the late eighteenth century that partially gave rise to the early American novel (*The Culture and Commerce of the Early American Novel: Reading the Atlantic World-System* [University Park: Pennsylvania State UP, 2006]).

26. "The Tea Act," May 10, 1773, *USHistory.org*, accessed April 22, 2013 <http://www.ushistory.org/declaration/related/teaact.htm>.

27. Wood, *Americanization* 91. Wood follows up with a caution against protonationalist readings: because we know that Franklin becomes an American patriot, we construct him as having been an American patriot (and not a British imperialist) all along. Nationalist history occludes the past: "Knowing what happened in 1776 as we do makes it difficult for us to interpret American thinking in 1760" (93). See also T. H. Breen, "Ideology and Nationalism on the Eve of the American Revolution: Revisions Once More in Need of Revising," *Journal of American History* 84 (June 1997): 13–39; and Edmund S. Morgan, who notes the

propensity of Americans, along with whites in Florida, Canada, and the East and West Indies, to identify as British subjects (*The Birth of the Republic, 1763–89*, 3rd ed. [Chicago: U of Chicago P, 1992], 8). These imperial identifications make it difficult to locate Loyalist writing with respect to national literary traditions. On this point, see Philip Gould, "Wit and Politics in Revolutionary British America: The Case of Samuel Seabury and Alexander Hamilton," *Eighteenth-Century Studies* 41.3 (2008): 383–403.

28. Q.E.D. [Benjamin Franklin], "Rules by Which a Great Empire May Be Reduced to a Small One," *Massachusetts Spy* December 16, 1773: 1.

29. "Tuesday, December 14, BOSTON," *Massachusetts Spy* December 16, 1773: 2.

30. "Tuesday, December 14, BOSTON."

31. Thomas Bender, *A Nation among Nations: America's Place in World History* (New York: Hill and Wang, 2006), ix. Discussing revolts in Peru and elsewhere in Latin America that were contemporaneous with the American Revolution, Bender writes American history in the context of world history, but national metrics remain indispensable in the overall economy of his account. While his focus on the thirteen colonies and then the United States as one nation among European powers repositions American history along an international axis, it is also the case that an international perspective still presumes a strong sense of nation. When it comes to writing colonial history, Bender highlights the importance of international diplomacy but that emphasis is too official and state-centered to express the global sensibilities articulated in American Revolutionary print culture. Still, for Bender, there is good reason for using national units since human rights, in his view, are best secured by nation-states (8, 298). For a contrasting view, see the discussion of Nancy Fraser below in this chapter.

32. Like propaganda, comparative history often presumes nation-states. This is not to imply that comparative history functions as propaganda, but only to say that just as the state seems indispensable to the functioning of modern propaganda, so too nations have remained central to the methods of comparative history. Micol Seigel has made this critique in asserting that historians frequently do not question their reliance on nations as a starting point. The result is that comparisons take for granted notions of national difference and end up reifying not just the concept of nation but the particular subjects who inhabit those entities. "Comparisons obscure the workings of power" because their effect is to accept without question the prior interpretative frames that saddle subjects with national characteristics and traits ("Beyond Compare: Comparative Method after the Transnational Turn," *Radical History Review* 91 [Winter 2005]: 65).

33. Despite Americans' claims to Britishness, back in England "metropolitan measures... seemed to call into question colonial claims to a British identity" (Jack P. Greene, "Identity and Independence," in *A Companion to the American Revolution*, ed. Jack P. Greene and J. R. Pole [Malden, MA: Blackwell, 2000], 234). This difference was accentuated by the contrasting ideas that American and Britons had about "how Britain's empire ought to work" (Eliga H. Gould, "Fears of War, Fantasies of Peace: British Politics and the Coming of the American Revolution," in *Empire and Nation: The American Revolution in the Atlantic World*, ed. Eliga H. Gould and Peter S. Onuf [Baltimore: Johns Hopkins UP, 2005], 24).

34. Immanuel Wallerstein, *The Modern World System III: The Second Era of Great Expansion of the Capitalist World-Economy, 1730s–1840s* (San Diego: Academic, 1989), 145. On the importance of Asia to identity and literature within the eighteenth-century world-system, see Chi-ming Yang, "Asia out of Place: The Aesthetics of Incorruptibilty in Behn's

*Oronooko" Eighteenth-Century Studies* 42.2 (2009): 235–53; Philip J. Stern, "British Asia and British Atlantic: Comparisons and Connections," *William and Mary Quarterly* 3rd ser., 63. (October 2006): 693–712; and James McCutcheon, "The Asian Dimension in the American Revolutionary Period," in *The American Revolution: Its Meaning to Asians and Americans,* ed. Cedric B. Cowing (Honolulu: East-West Center, 1977), 87–107.

35. Carole Shammas, "The Revolutionary Impact of European Demand for Tropical Goods," in *The Early Modern Atlantic Economy,* ed. John J. McCusker and Kenneth Morgan (Cambridge: Cambridge UP, 2000), 180.

36. Arendt 49. After mentioning Arendt at the outset, Wood critiques the tendency "to think of the American Revolution as having no social character, as having no social consequences" (*Radicalism* 4).

37. Linebaugh and Rediker 212.

38. Hampden [Benjamin Rush?], "On Patriotism," *Pennsylvania Journal* October 20, 1773: 1.

39. "Philadelphia," *Pennsylvania Journal,* October 20, 1773: 3–4.

40. Benedict Anderson, *Imagined Communities: Reflections on the Origin and Spread of Nationalism,* rev. and exp. ed. (New York: Verso, 2006).

41. Yokota argues that Americans' "sense of nationhood remained inchoate throughout the early national period....These colonials-turned-citizens had to create an interstitial space between their former identity as British subjects and the new political and cultural context in which they now found themselves" (*Unbecoming British: How Revolutionary America Became a Postcolonial Nation* [New York: Oxford UP, 2011], 10–11).

42. See Shammas 181. For estimates of military spending by the United States, see Anup Shah, "World Military Spending," *Global Issues,* June 30, 2013, accessed March 21, 2007 <www.globalissues.org/Geopolitics/ArmsTrade/Spending.asp#USMilitarySpending>; and War Resisters League, "Where Your Income Tax Money Really Goes," *War Resisters,* accessed 21 March 2007 <www.warresisters.org/piechart.htm>.

43. For estimates of Department of Defense spending, see www.globalissues.org/Geopolitics/ArmsTrade/Spending.asp#USMilitarySpending and www.warresisters.org/piechart.htm, both accessed March 21, 2007.

44. Breen, "Ideology and Nationalism" 16. On Britain's unprecedented and intense mobilization for war, an operation aided by the fiscal-military state, see the figures and conclusions supplied by John Brewer, "The Eighteenth-Century British State: Contexts and Issues," in *An Imperial State at War: Britain from 1689 to 1815,* ed. Lawrence Stone (London: Routledge, 1994), 57–61.

45. John Dickinson, "Two Letters on the Tea Tax," in *Memoirs of the Historical Society of Pennsylvania,* vol. 14, *Life and Writings of John Dickinson* (Philadelphia: Historical Society of Pennsylvania, 1895), 2:459.

46. See H. V. Bowen, *The Business of Empire: The East India Company and Imperial Britain, 1756–1833* (Cambridge: Cambridge UP, 2006), 22; Carp, *Defiance of the Patriots* 8; Bruce G. Carruthers, *City of Capital: Politics and Markets in the English Financial Revolution* (Princeton, NJ: Princeton UP, 1996), 5–6; and E. Gould, "Fears of War" 25–33. On the size and implications of the debts of the East India Company, see Benjamin Larabee, *The Boston Tea Party* (New York: Oxford UP, 1964), 58–64. P. J. Marshall describes the British fiscal-military state as a study in contradictions, its enormous power amassing territories that it did not have the complete control to administer ("Britain and the World in the Eighteenth

Century: I, Reshaping the Empire," *Transactions of the Royal Historical Society* 6th ser., 8 [1998]: 1–18).

47. Warren, *History* 596.

48. Dickinson, "Two Letters" 2:459. On the famine, see David Arnold, "Hunger in the Garden of Plenty: The Bengal Famine of 1770," in *Dreadful Visitations: Confronting Natural Catastrophe in the Age of Enlightenment*, ed. Alessa Johns (New York: Routledge, 1999), 85–86; and Lynn Festa, *Sentimental Figures of Empire in Eighteenth-Century Britain and France* (Baltimore: Johns Hopkins UP, 2006), 225. Although Carp adopts a lower estimate, the analogy he offers suggests how the famine might have hit home with Americans: "had it struck the Thirteen Colonies of North America, it would have wiped out half of the entire population" (*Defiance of the Patriots* 11).

49. *To the Tradesmen, Merchants,&c. of the Province of Pennsylvania* (Philadelphia, 1773), accessed March 20, 2007 <memory.loc.gov>.

50. *To the Worthy Inhabitants of New-York* (New York, 1773), accessed March 20, 2007 <memory.loc.gov>. These fears over the close cooperation between Parliament and the East India Company, like Mercy Otis Warren's portraits of Governor Hutchinson's backroom dealings or the plot against American liberties that Americans saw revealed in the Hutchinson letters, fit with what Gordon Wood describes as "American whig conspiratorial thinking" ("Conspiracy and the Paranoid Style: Causality and Deceit in the Eighteenth Century," *William and Mary Quarterly* 39.3 [1982]: 420).

51. T. H. Breen, "'Baubles of Britain': The American and Consumer Revolutions of the Eighteenth Century," *Past and Present* 119 (May 1988): 86. But see Festa on how eighteenth-century commodities and other objects could personalize (and misrepresent) not just national but global connections (114–21).

52. *To the Tradesmen*; and Z, "To the PEOPLE of New York," *New-York Journal* November 25 1773: 3.

53. "For the Massachusetts SPY," *Massachusetts Spy* December 23 1774: 3. Thomas Hutchinson, Jr., and Elisha Hutchinson, sons of the governor, were the consignees for the East India tea awaiting distribution.

54. Robert Middlekauff discusses the issue of colonial salaries in *The Glorious Cause: The American Revolution, 1763–1789* (New York: Oxford UP, 1982), 215.

55. Until recently, when historians of early America have stressed wider contexts, the results often stick close to the smaller theaters of European republicanism and British Enlightenment thinking. For Michael Kammen, the "meaning of colonization" remains tied to North American locales ("The Meaning of Colonization in American Revolutionary Thought," in *The American Enlightenment*, ed. Frank Shuffleton [Rochester, NY: U of Rochester P, 1993], 183–204). See also Bernard Bailyn, who depicts the Revolution as the result of Enlightenment ideas that "had long existed" in the Anglo-American world, which did not necessarily "create new social and political forces in America" ("Political Experience and Enlightenment Ideas in 18th-Century America," *American Historical Review* 67 [1962]: 351). Wood revises this characterization of the Revolution by emphasizing its social radicalism but principally with respect to British monarchical and patriarchal values (*Radicalism* 169–83). David Wootton sketches the development of republican ideology in Anglo-American thinking up to the publication of *Common Sense* ("Introduction: The Republican Tradition: From Commonwealth to Common Sense," in *Republicanism, Liberty, and Commercial Society, 1649–1776* [Stanford, CA: Stanford UP, 1994], 1–41).

56. Thomas Paine, *The Rights of Man* (New York: Penguin, 1984), 228.

57. Dickinson, "Two Letters" 2:459.

58. James Rivington, *Letter to the Inhabitants of the City and Colony of New-York* (New York: Rivington, 1773).

59. Nancy Fraser, "Reframing Justice in a Globalizing World," *New Left Review* 36 (November–December 2005): 71.

60. Fraser 82.

61. Hampden, *The Alarm. Number II*, 2

62. Hampden, *The Alarm. Number V*, 3. For Adams's warning, see "Circular Letter of the Boston Committee of Correspondence; May 13, 1774," in *Writings*.

63. Arjun Appadurai, for instance, explores the connections, facilitated by phone, e-mail, and fax, among antipoverty activists worldwide ("Deep Democracy: Urban Governmentality and the Horizon of Politics," *Public Culture* 14 [Winter 2002]: 21–47, and "Grassroots Globalization and the Research Imagination," *Public Culture* 12 [Winter 2000]: 1–19).

64. *Warren-Adams Letters* 1:363. For additional letters conveying similar intelligence, see James Lovell to James Bowdoin, April 16, 1777, and Oliver Wolcott to George Wylllys, April 17, 1777, in Paul H. Smith, ed., *Letters of the Delegates to Congress, 1774–1789* (Washington, DC: Library of Congress, 1976–2000), 6:596, 609.

65. Anne McClintock, "Paranoid Empire: Specters from Guantánamo and Abu Ghraib," in *States of Emergency: The Object of American Studies*, ed. Russ Castronovo and Susan Gillman (Chapel Hill: U of North Carolina P, 2009), 88.

66. Dickinson, *Letters from a Farmer* 7.

67. P. Smith 17:345–46. On British military operations in India and America, see P. J. Marshall, *Trade and Conquest: Studies on the Rise of British Dominance in India* (Aldershot: Variorum, 1993), 25.

68. Jenkins is quoted in Lucy Stuart, *The East India Company in Eighteenth-Century Politics* (Oxford: Oxford UP, 1952), 315.

69. Nathaniel Smith, *General Remarks on the System of Government in India; with Farther Considerations on the Present State of the Company at Home and Abroad. To Which Is Added, a General Statement and Fair Examination of Their Latest Accounts from the Year 1766. And a Plan for the Mutual Advantage of the Nation and the Company* (London: Nourse, 1773), 64.

70. N. Smith 3.

71. F. P. Robinson, *The Trade of the East India Company from 1709 to 1813* (Cambridge: Cambridge UP, 1912), 179.

72. Robinson 174.

73. Dickinson, "Two Letters" 2:463.

74. Trish Loughran, "Disseminating *Common Sense*: Thomas Paine and the Problems of the Early National Bestseller," *American Literature* 78 (March 2006): 3. The nationalist work of Paine's pamphlet, Loughran points out, is always connected to myths of its incredible popularity. In contradistinction to effusive estimates that *Common Sense* "roused the entire continent" (Foner in Paine, *Complete Writings* 1:49), Loughran argues that the popularity of *Common Sense* is more an idea than an established fact. She suggests that the pamphlet's wide diffusion is "an essentially postcolonial fantasy," which "worked from the outset to naturalize the not-yet realized nation" (20). Loughran extends this insight in *The Republic in Print*.

75. See Arendt 81–82.

76. Thomas Paine, "Reflections on the Life and Death of Lord Clive" in *Complete Writings* 2:23–27. This essay first appeared in *Pennsylvania Magazine* (March 1775). For further treatment of Clive by Paine, see his March 21, 1778, installment of *The American Crisis* (in *Complete Writings* 1:118). Paine might also be playing on the financial sense of "bubble" as a type of unrestrained economic speculation that eventually bursts. The South Sea Bubble was still relatively recent history. Under Paine's editorship, as Edward Larkin documents, the *Pennsylvania Magazine* featured pieces about the dangers that Americans faced in consuming goods imported from elsewhere in the British Empire. See Edward Larkin, *Thomas Paine and the Literature of Revolution* (Cambridge: Cambridge UP, 2005), 36–45.

77. Paine, "A Serious Thought," in *Complete Writings* 2:20. Paine later invoked the "horrid scene that is now acting by the English government in East India" as encouragement for Spain to reconsider the prospect of Latin American independence (*Rights of Man* 267). From the negative example of the British Empire, Spain can learn to pursue an enlightened approach tied to trade in dealing with its colonial possessions in South America, according to Paine.

78. Robert Ferguson, *The American Enlightenment, 1750–1820* (Cambridge, MA: Harvard UP, 1997), 115.

79. Paine, *American Crisis* 1:59. All further references to *The American Crisis* are to this volume and edition, and are cited parenthetically. It is notable that in 1777 he was appointed to the Committee on Foreign Affairs but was soon discharged after conservative elements in the Continental Congress pushed for his removal. On this incident, see Isaac Kramnick, *Republicanism and Bourgeois Radicalism: Political Ideology in Late Eighteeenth-Century England and America* (Ithaca, NY: Cornell UP, 1990), 139. Paine's internationalism extended to his participation in, imprisonment by, and narrow escape from the guillotine of the French Revolutionary government (Harvey J. Kaye, *Thomas Paine and the Promise of America* [New York: Hill and Wang, 2005], 78–89). Yet Kaye still nationalizes Paine as a proponent of American exceptionalism (41).

80. Paine, "Reflections" 2:26–27.

81. M. Warner, *Letters of the Republic* 56. On Paine's efforts to literalize an abstract public sphere in the space of colonial American print culture, see Larkin 24–50. Unlike Mercy Warren with her employment of Roman themes and topoi, Paine was not steeped in "the dominant tradition of classic rhetoric," a fortunate deficiency that allowed him to make his appeal in a popular idiom (Larkin 1).

82. Richard Viscount Howe and William Howe, "Proclamation," *New-York Gazette; and Weekly Mercury* December 30, 1776: 1. Howe's proclamation was issued on November 30, 1776, and appeared in colonial newspapers subsequently. On the Howes' use of the printing press to produce propaganda leaflets advertising clemency and encouraging soldiers' desertion from the rebel forces, see Berger 137–40.

83. Wallerstein 228. Efforts to situate the American Revolution within the context of larger upheavals of Enlightenment reason remain dogged by traces of parochialism. When Wood sets the historical backdrop for the Revolution by observing that all over "the Western world people were making tiny, piecemeal assaults on the ignorance and barbarism of the past" (*Radicalism* 192), the effect is to retract the world-system to Europe.

84. "Extract of a Letter from London, April 19, 1774," *Massachusetts Spy* July 15, 1774: 3. Schlesinger reports that this rumor also circulated as a handbill in New York, setting the bribe at £500 (*Prelude* 184).

85. "To the Public," *Massachusetts Spy* May 3, 1775: 1.

86. The inscription can be found on the copy in the Library of Congress. See "Inscription of Isaiah Thomas," accessed April 18, 2013 <http://www.loc.gov/rr/news/circulars/spy.html>.

## Chapter 4

1. Worthington Chauncey Ford, ed., *The Spurious Letters Attributed to Washington. With a Bibliographic Note by Worthington Chauncey Ford* (Brooklyn, NY: privately printed, 1889), 46.

2. *Letters from General Washington to Several of His Friends in the Year 1776: In Which Are Set Forth a Fairer and Fuller View of American Politics. Than Ever Transpired* (London: Bew, 1777); and *Letters from General Washington to Several of His Friends in the Year 1776: In Which Are Set Forth a Fairer and Fuller View of American Politicks. Than Ever Yet Transpired, or the Public Could Be Made Acquainted with through Any Other Channel* (New York: Rivington, 1778).

3. George Washington to Mathew Carey, October 27, 1788, in *The Writings of George Washington*, 14 vols., ed. Worthington Chauncey Ford (New York: Putnam's, 1889–93), 11:340.

4. Authority, authenticity, and circulation of letter writing are put under pressure in epistolary novels. See Altman 25–26. The epistolary pamphlet was among the "most popular genres for political debate" (M. Warner, *Letters of the Republic* 40).

5. Jared Sparks, *The Life of Washington* (Boston: Little, Brown, 1853), 246. The British press generally portrayed Washington in sympathetic lights, emphasizing his virtue and command. See Troy O. Bickham, "Sympathizing with Sedition: George Washington, the British Press, and British Attitudes during the American War of Independence," *William and Mary Quarterly* 59 (2002): 102–22.

6. Ford 49, Washington quoted by Ford at 50n. Ford's privately printed edition of *The Spurious Letters Attributed to Washington* (1889) correlates the lies of "Washington" with the words truly written by the American general.

7. Washington to Carey 11:340.

8. See Seth Cotlar, "Reading the Foreign News, Imagining an American Public Sphere: Radical and Conservative Visions of 'the Public' in Mid-1790s Newspapers," in *Periodical Literature in Eighteenth-Century America*, ed. Mark L. Kamrath and Sharon M. Harris (Knoxville: U of Tennessee P, 2006), 320. Roughly 100 newspapers existed in 1790, a figure roughly consistent with the 137 newspapers Tanselle finds in existence from 1764 to 1783. See James Breig, "Early American Newspapering," *Colonial Williamsburg Journal* (Spring 2003), accessed March 3, 2014 <http://www.history.org/Foundation/journal/spring03/journalism.cfm>.

9. Lippmann 158.

10. See, for instance, Eric Foner on artisans' support of the Philadelphia press (*Tom Paine and Revolutionary America* [New York: Oxford UP, 1976], 34).

11. Jason Frank, *Constituent Moments: Enacting the People in Postrevolutionary America* (Durham, NC: Duke UP, 2010), 144.

12. Noam Chomsky, "Propaganda, American-Style," *zpub.com*, accessed November 6, 2008 <http://www.zpub.com/un/chomsky.html>. For more on this idea and the influence

of Lippmann, see Edward S. Herman and Noam Chomsky, *Manufacturing Consent: The Political Economy of Mass Media* (New York: Pantheon, 1988).

13. Lippmann 158.

14. Ellul 128.

15. See Bernays, "Engineering of Consent" and *Public Relations* 160. Stewart Ewen considers Bernays's attempts to justify the technocrat's management of public opinion (*Spin! A Social History of Spin* [New York: Basic Books, 1996], 4–35).

16. See Josef Metzler, "Foundation of the Congregation 'de Propaganda Fide' by Gregory XV," in *Sacrae Congregationis de Propaganda Fide Memoria Rerum*, 2 vols. (Rome: Herder, 1971), 1:95. The Church of England operated a similar mission in the colonies under the name of the Society for the Propagation of the Gospel in Foreign Parts. Founded in 1701 to convert American Indians, this propaganda agency of the Church of England by 1763 fell under suspicion as a program for squelching religious diversity in the colonies. See Bailyn, *Ideological Origins* 96–97.

17. Benjamin Franklin Bache, "To the Public," *General Advertiser, Political, Commercial, Agricultural and Literary Journal* October 1, 1790: 1.

18. Benjamin Franklin Bache, "To the Public," *Aurora General Advertiser*, November 8, 1794: 2.

19. "From the *Gazette of the United States*," reprinted in the *Aurora General Advertiser*, November 8, 1794: 2.

20. "For the General Advertiser," *Aurora General Advertiser* November 8, 1794: 2.

21. For more on this formulation, see Auerbach and Castronovo 9–10.

22. W. Warner, "Invention of a Public Machine" 161.

23. W. Warner, "Invention of a Public Machine" 150.

24. Edmund Burke, *Reflections on the Revolution in France* (New Rochelle, NY: Arlington House, 1966), 14, 21.

25. Warren's preface can be found in Catharine Macaulay, *Observations on the Reflections of the Right Hon. Edmund Burke, on the Revolution in France, in a Letter to the Right Hon. the Earl of Stanhope* (Boston: Thomas and Andrews, 1791).

26. Ellul 235.

27. Burke, *Reflections* 126, 187.

28. Ferguson 1.

29. Ferguson 20.

30. Elizabeth Hewitt, "The Authentic Fictional Letters of Charles Brockden Brown" in *Letters and Cultural Transformations in the United States, 1760–1860*, ed. Theresa Strouth Gaul and Sharon M. Harris (Burlington, VT: Ashgate, 2009), 79.

31. Fliegelman 37.

32. This note appears in the Huntington Library copy of *Epistles Domestic, Confidential, and Official, from General Washington, Written about the Commencement of the American Contest, When He Entered on the Command of the Army of the United States. With an Interesting Series of His Letters, Particularly to the British Admirals, Arbuthnot and Digby, to Gen. Sir Henry Clinton, Lord Cornwallis, Sir Guy Carleton, Marquis de la Fayette, &c. &c. To Benjamin Harrison, Esq. Speaker of the House of Delegates in Virginia, to Admiral the Count de Grasse, General Sullivan, Respecting an Attack of New-York; Including Many Application and Addresses Presented to Him with his Answers: Orders and Instructions, on Important Occasions, to His Aids de Camp, &c. &c. &c. None of Which Have Been Printed in the Two Volumes*

*Published a Few Months Ago* (New York: Robinson, 1796). The "Mr. V—" trying to smear Washington has been identified as John Vardill, assistant rector at Trinity Church and propagandist loyal to the Crown (Julian P. Boyd, "Silas Deane: Death by a Kindly Teacher of Treason," *William and Mary Quarterly* 16 [July 1959]: 320). Vardill operated as a spy and on more than one occasion intercepted confidential letters between Franklin and the Continental Congress. In a statement to a postwar parliamentary commission investigating remunerations for Loyalists, Vardill lists the propaganda pamphlets he authored under the names "Poplicola" and "Cassandra" but does not include *Letters from General Washington*. Given that Vardill wanted to impress Parliament with his Tory support, it seems unlikely that he would drop this line from his curriculum vitae of espionage and propaganda. Historians also identify John Randolph as a probable author of *Letters from General Washington*. Not to be confused with John Randolph of Roanoke, this John Randolph was the royal attorney general of Virginia, the last person to hold that post before the Revolution swept away such colonial sinecures.

33. Ford 76.

34. Quoted from an advertisement in the *Aurora General Advertiser* March 19, 1796: 4.

35. Ford 78.

36. Maximilien Robespierre, *Report upon the Principles of Political Morality Which Are to Form the Basis of the Administration of the Interior Concerns of the Republic: Made in the Name of the Committee of Public Safety, the 18th Pluviose, Second Year of the Republic, (February 6th, 1794)* (Philadelphia: Bache, 1794), 10. Yet Bache also expressed reservations about the radical French leader; see Marcus 124–25.

37. C. L. R. James, *The Black Jacobins: Toussaint L'Ouverture and the San Domingo Revolution* (New York: Vintage, 1989). See, for instance, the advertisements in both French and English, *Aurora General Advertiser* November 11, 1794: 4.

38. William Appleman Williams, *America Confronts a Revolutionary World: 1776–1976* (New York: Morrow, 1976), 46.

39. David Waldstreicher, *In the Midst of Perpetual Fetes: The Making of American Nationalism, 1776–1820* (Chapel Hill: U of North Carolina P, 1997), 114–15. David Brion Davis examines how the millennial optimism associated with the French Revolution turned sour in the wake of the slave uprising on Saint-Domingue (*Revolutions: Reflections on American Equality and Foreign Liberations* [Cambridge, MA: Harvard University Press, 1990], 47); and Alfred Young observes the multiple strains of radicalism ("How Radical was the American Revolution," in *Liberty Tree: Ordinary People and the American Revolution* [New York: New York UP, 2006], 227–29). See also Pasley, "Cheese and the Words."

40. Ford 66.

41. In response to the French loss of control on Saint-Domingue, the British order in council implemented a no-sail zone to discourage U.S. merchants from exporting raw materials from or resupplying the island. The plan "was carried out by the British naval officers with even more than their usual callous brutality," according to Stanley Elkins and Eric McKitrick, and soon "succeeded only in enraging every sector of the American republic" (*The Age of Federalism* [New York: Oxford UP, 1993], 403). See also Joseph M. Fewster, "The Jay Treaty and British Ship Seizures: The Martinique Cases," *William and Mary Quarterly* 3rd ser., 45.3 (1988): 426–52.

42. Ford 45–46.

43. Jerald A. Combs, *The Jay Treaty: Political Battleground of the Founding Fathers* (Berkeley: U of California P, 1970), 140.

44. Joyce Appleby, *Capitalism and a New Social Order: The Republican Vision of the 1790s* (New York: New York UP, 1984), 55. Todd Estes provides a comprehensive look at the role of public opinion during the crisis occasioned by the Jay Treaty (*The Jay Treaty, Public Opinion, and the Evolution of Early American Print Culture* [Amherst: U of Massachusetts P, 2006]).

45. Philo-Republicanus, "For the Aurora," *Aurora General Advertiser* November 18, 1794: 3.

46. Philo-Republicanus.

47. Washington quoted in Washington Irving, *Life of George Washington*, 5 vols. (New York: Putnam, 1861), 5:217.

48. On Margaret Bache and her letter to her husband describing public interest in copies of the treaty, see James Tagg, *Benjamin Franklin Bache and the Philadelphia "Aurora"* (Philadelphia: U of Pennsylvania P, 1991), 247; and Jeffrey L. Pasley, *"Tyranny of Printers": Newspaper Politics in the Early American Republic* (Charlottesville: UP of Virginia, 2001), 82. These activities made Bache a "ground-level political activist" (Pasley, *"Tyranny"* 80) and established his *Aurora* as the "leading organ of radical Republicanism" (Paul Starr, *The Creation of the Media: The Political Origins of Modern Communications* [New York: Basic Books, 2004], 77).

49. Lemuel Hopkins, *The Democratiad, a Poem in Retaliation for the "Philadelphia Jockey Club"* in *Magazine of History with Notes and Queries* 29 (1926): 187. For more on the Federalist counteroffensive later in the decade, see Seth Cotlar, "The Federalists' Transatlantic Cultural Offensive of 1798 and the Moderation of American Democratic Discourse," in *Beyond the Founders: New Approaches to the political History of the Early American Republic*, ed. Jeffrey L. Pasley, Andrew W. Robertson, and David Waldstreicher (Chapel Hill: U of North Carolina P, 2004), 274–99.

50. Simon P. Newman, *Parades and the Politics of the Street: Festive Culture in the Early American Republic* (Philadelphia: U of Pennsylvania P, 1997), 135.

51. Hopkins 189.

52. Bache, *Remarks* 38.

53. For more on Bache's foundry, see John Bidwell, "Printers' Supplies and Capitalization," in Hugh Amory and David B. Hall, eds., *A History of the Book in America*, vol. 1, *The Colonial Book in the Atlantic World* (Cambridge: Cambridge UP, 2000), 169.

54. Bache's newspaper became an important hub for "some of the most radical Painite exiles" (Michael Durey, *Transatlantic Radicals and the Early American Republic* [Lawrence: UP of Kansas, 1997], 230–31). These émigrés moved within circles of "transatlantic discourses of radical publicity" (Cotlar, "Reading the Foreign News" 314).

55. Scipio, "For the *Aurora*. To the Representatives of the People. Letter IV," *Aurora* March 3, 1796: 2.

56. Catherine Gallagher, "The Rise of Fictionality," in *The Novel*, vol. 1, *History, Geography, and Culture.*, ed. Franco Moretti (Princeton, NJ: Princeton UP, 2006), 338.

57. *Letters from General Washington* (Philadelphia: Federal P, 1796), vi. The focus on character became a staple of eighteenth-century journalism, which more frequently began to suspect and investigate the private motives of public figures. See Marcus 8–12.

58. Ford 45.

59. Ford 45.

60. Michael McKeon, "*From* Prose Fiction: Great Britain," in *Theory of the Novel: A Historical Approach*, ed. Michael McKeon (Baltimore: Johns Hopkins UP, 2000), 603.

61. William Godwin, "Of History and Romance," Department of English, U of Pennsylvania, accessed October 22, 2009 <http://www.english.upenn.edu/~mgamer/Etexts/godwin .history.html>. All references to Godwin's essay are to this unpaginated electronic source.

62. Ford 9–10.

63. The Jay Treaty provided an early test case over presidential powers. Washington interpreted the Constitution as relegating treaty making to the executive branch in consultation with the "advice and consent" of the Senate. Republicans in the House of Representatives were furious, protesting that these secret proceedings undercut democratic principles. Out of this rancor, the party system was born in the United States. In 1790, Republicans and Federalists in the House crossed still amorphous party lines 42 percent of the time. By the time of the Jay Treaty debates, this number fell to 7 percent (see Joseph Charles, "The Jay Treaty: The Origins of the American Party System," *William and Mary Quarterly* 12 [October 1955]: 583).

64. Estes 3. See also Waldstreicher 113–14 on how the Federalists' enlistment of popular support ultimately led to their defeat.

65. George Washington, "Message to the House Regarding Documents Relative to the Jay Treaty, March 30, 1796," *Avalon Project at Yale Law School*, accessed October 23, 2009 <http://avalon.law.yale.edu/18th_century/gw003.asp>.

66. Thomas Paine, "Letter to George Washington," in *Complete Writings* 1:714.

67. On Bache's reprinting of the spurious letters, see Jeffrey A. Smith, *Franklin and Bache: Envisioning the Enlightened Republic* (New York: Oxford UP, 1990), 140–41.

68. *Letters from General Washington to Several of His Friends, in June and July 1776: In Which Is Set Forth an Interesting View of American Politics, at That All-Important Period* (Philadelphia: Federal P, 1795), 5.

69. "Fourth of July," *Aurora* July 4, 1796: 3. Marcus offers a blow-by-blow account of the *Aurora*'s attack on Washington (109–47).

70. Burke, *Reflections* 168.

71. "Advertisement Extraordinary," *Aurora* March 5, 1796. Bache's paper regularly used farce to convey critique. See, for instance, the farcical pieces written under the name of "Benedict Arnold" and supposedly sent to the editor of the *Gazette of the United States* ("To the Public," *Aurora* January 28, 1795: 3) or the ironic argument for adopting the treaty: "Why should you cry out before you are hurt? Put your necks under the yoke" ("For the *Aurora*," *Aurora* February 11, 1795: 2).

72. Alexander Hamilton, James Madison, and John Jay, *The Federalist* (Cambridge, MA: Harvard UP, 1966), 101. The passage is from "The Federalist No. 4," authored by Jay.

73. "War! War!! War!!!," *Aurora* March 23, 1796: 2.

74. "War! War!! War!!!"

75. "Proposals for Printing, *by Subscription*, the Debates in the Federal House of Representatives, Relative to the Powers of the House on the Subject of TREATIES, and on the British Treaty," *Aurora* March 23, 1796: 1. For the congressional resolution that Washington's papers about the treaty be turned over to the House, see "Federal Legislature," *Aurora* March 7, 1796: 2.

76. "Communication," *Aurora* May 7, 1796: 3.

77. "War! War!! War!!!"

## Chapter 5

1. George Washington, "Letter of the Late President of the United States, to the Secretary of State," *Time Piece*, March 15, 1797: 5.

2. Philip Freneau, "To the Public," *Time Piece*, March 13, 1797: 1.

3. "The preponderance of evidence suggests that the decades from 1790 to 1820 encompassed a massive, multifaceted transformation away from republican traditions and toward modern liberal capitalism in America," writes Steven Watts in *The Republic Reborn: War and the Making of Liberal America, 1790–1820* (Baltimore: Johns Hopkins UP, 1987), xvii. To a certain extent, however, such an opposition is overstated since, as Watts points out, republican ideology fostered the growth of liberal ideas that were to supersede it. On the intertwining of republicanism and liberalism, see also Kramnick; Joyce Appleby, *Liberalism and Republicanism in the Historical Imagination* (Cambridge, MA: Harvard UP, 1992); Daniel T. Rodgers, "Republicanism: The Career of a Concept," *Journal of American History* 79 (June 1992): 11–38; Dillon 145–61; and Shapiro 14–20.

4. Philip Freneau, "Poetic Address," *Time Piece*, March 13, 1797: 4.

5. "*A new* SONG."

6. Schlesinger, "A Note on Songs" 78.

7. Migrations between print and speech flowed both ways. Newspapers such as Freneau's *National Gazette* printed songs that had first been sung in taverns. On the importance of tavern culture to public political discussion, see P. Thompson. Gustafson, *Eloquence Is Power* and Looby examine the often vibrant politics of speech and orality.

8. Philip Freneau, "The Country Printer," in *The Poems of Philip Freneau*, ed. Fred Lewis Pattee (Princeton, NJ: Princeton Historical Society, 1907), 3:61.

9. Freneau, "Country Printer" 64.

10. Freneau, "Country Printer" 62.

11. Thomas Jefferson, *Memoirs, Correspondence, and Private Papers of Thomas Jefferson, Late President of the United States*, ed. Thomas Jefferson Randolph (London: Colburn and Bentley, 1829), 4:503.

12. Bache, "To the Public."

13. Philip Freneau, "To the Public," *National Gazette* October 31, 1791: 4.

14. Hamilton's attack on Freneau as editor of the *National Gazette* appeared in Fenno's *Gazette of the United States* and is quoted in Lewis Leary, *That Rascal Freneau: A Study in Literary Failure* (New Brunswick, NJ: Rutgers UP, 1941), 208.

15. *National Gazette* October 26 1793, 410.

16. See, for instance, Jeffrey L. Pasley, "The Two National *Gazettes*: Newspapers and the Embodiment of American Political Parties," *Early American Literature* 35.1 (2000): 51–86.

17. Vernon Louis Parrington, *Main Currents in American Thought*, vol. 1, *The Colonial Mind, 1620–1800* (New York: Harcourt Brace, 1927), 368. Freneau was not ready for rehabilitation in the context of the Progressive era: "the transatlantic apotheosis of Freneau will doubtless await a more convenient season," wrote a critic of American literature in 1928 (S. B. Hustvedt, "Philippic Freneau," *American Speech* 4 [October 1928]: 2).

18. Freneau, "The Country Printer" 61.

19. Quoted in Leary 204.

20. See Philip Freneau, "Lines Occasioned by a Law Passed by the Corporation of New-York, Early in 1790, for Cutting Down the Trees in the Streets of That City" in *Poems* 3:53–56.

21. Philip Freneau, "The City Poet," in *The Last Poems of Philip Freneau*, ed. Lewis Leary (New Brunswick, NJ: Rutgers UP, 1945), 31.

22. George Creel, *How We Advertised America: The First Telling of the Amazing Story of the Committee on Public Information That Carried the Gospel of Americanism to Every Corner of the Globe* (New York: Harper& Brothers, 1920), 114.

23. Creel 115.

24. Thomas Paine, *The Age of Reason* (New York: Harper& Row, 1974), 50.

25. Philip Freneau, letter to Dr. J. W. Francis, May 15, 1819, in *Unpublished Freneauana*, ed. Charles F. Heartman (New York: printed for the editor, 1918), 14–15.

26. Freneau, letter to Francis 12–13.

27. Freneau, "Country Printer" 63.

28. Philip Freneau, *The Prose of Philip Freneau*, ed. Philip M. Marsh (New Brunswick, NJ: Scarecrow, 1955), 422.

29. Parrington 68.

30. Quoted in Leary 237.

31. Frederic Jameson, *Marxism and Form: Twentieth-Century Dialectical Theories of Literature* (Princeton, NJ: Princeton University Press, 1974), 402–403. Marjorie Perloff offers a similar view of poetry by arguing that the choice of verse or prose is not a matter of individual taste or choice but the result of historical and ideological factors (*Poetry On and Off the Page: Essays for Emergent Occasions* [Evanston, IL: Northwestern UP, 1998], 140–43).

32. Jameson 328–29.

33. Philip Freneau, "Copy of an Intercepted Letter from a New-York Tory, to His Friend in Philadelphia, 1781," in *Poems on Various Subjects, but Being Chiefly Illustrative of the Events and Actors of the American War of Independence* (London: Smith, 1861), 190.

34. Franco Moretti, "The Novel: History and Theory," *New Left Review* 52 (July–August 2008): 111.

35. Moretti, "The Novel: History and Theory" 112.

36. Moretti, "The Novel: History and Theory" 112. "Forward-looking" does not necessarily indicate an emancipatory political agenda. The adventure story, Moretti reminds us, pivots on "a trope of expansion" that is conducive both to "the spirit of capitalism" and war (124). No doubt exceptions to this schema might be cited, but that exercise would shift the discussion to matters of content in particular works when Moretti wants to offer macro-level observations about genres that each have accumulated hundreds, if not thousands, of years of history. Moretti addresses the critical predisposition that reads for such exceptions in *Signs Taken for Wonders: Essays in the Sociology of Literary Forms*, trans. Susan Fischer, David Forgacs, and David Miller (London: New Left Books, 1983): "In what sense does Shakespeare 'violate' the conventions of Elizabethan tragedy? Why not say the opposite: that he was the only writer able to realize them fully, establishing as it were the 'ideal type' of an entire genre? Does *Wilhelm Meister's Apprenticeship* 'defamiliarize' the conventions of the *Bildungsroman*? Is not the opposite the case: that with his novel Goethe founds them and makes them reproducible?" (13).

37. Harry Hayden Clark, "What Made Freneau the Father of American Poetry?," *Studies in Philology* 26 (January 1929): 1–22, and "What Made Freneau the Father of American Prose?," *Transactions of the Wisconsin Academy of Sciences, Arts and Letters* 25 (1930): 39–50.

38. Hustvedt 1.

39. Robert Pinsky, "American Poetry and American Life: Freneau, Whitman, Williams," *Shenandoah* 37.1 (1987): 10.

40. Parrington 379.

41. Leary 99.

42. The first assessment comes from the *Pennsylvania Democrat* of 1809 and is quoted in Leary 329; the second is Clark's in "What Made Freneau the Father of American Poetry?" 16.

43. Jefferson 497.

44. Philip Freneau, "American Liberty, a Poem," in *The Poems of Philip Freneau, Poet of the Revolution*, ed. Lewis Leary (Princeton, NJ: U Library, 1902), 1:145.

45. Philip Freneau, *Poems Written and Published during the American Revolutionary War, and Now Published from the Original Manuscripts; Interspersed with Translations from the Ancients, and Other Pieces Not Heretofore in Print*, 3rd ed., 2 vols (Philadelphia: Bailey, 1809), 1:3.

46. Burke, *Reflections* 92.

47. Freneau, Letter to Francis 16.

48. Emory Elliott, *Revolutionary Writers: Literature and Authority in the New Republic, 1724–1810* (New York: Oxford UP, 1982), 136.

49. Kenneth Burke, "Revolutionary Symbolism in America," in *American Writers' Congress*, ed. Henry Hart (New York: International, 1935), 91–93.

50. Philip Freneau, "Lines Occasioned by Mr. Rivington's New Titular Types in his *Royal Gazette*, of 1782," in *Poems* 2:124. Freneau wrote multiple poems attacking Rivington, the king's printer in the colonies. Some recent historical research has suggested, however, that Rivington worked as a spy for Washington as part of the Culper Ring.

51. Philip Freneau, "A Speech That Should Have Been Spoken by the King of the Island of Britain to his Parliament," in *Poems* 2:118.

52. Philip Freneau, "Reflections on Several Subjects," *National Gazette* August 31, 1793: 320.

53. "Discussion and Proceedings," in Hart, *American Writers' Congress* 168. Frank reads Burke's address in the context of post-Revolutionary struggles over popular sovereignty (28).

54. "*For the* National Gazette," *National Gazette* July 31, 1793: 313.

55. Philip Freneau, "Advice to Authors," in *A Freneau Sampler*, ed. Philip M. Marsh (New York: Scarecrow, 1963), 217.

56. "To the Noblesse and Courtiers of the United States," *National Gazette* January 5, 1793: 78.

57. Freneau, "Reflections on Several Subjects" 320.

58. Freneau, "Reflections on Several Subjects" 320.

59. Philip Freneau, ["Royal Dangers in the American Stage"], in *Prose* 295.

60. Theodor Adorno and Max Horkheimer, *Dialectic of Enlightenment: Philosophical Fragments*, trans. Edmund Jephcott (Stanford, CA: Stanford UP, 1997), 96. Elliott discusses Freneau in connection with the culture industry (135).

61. Kramnick 1.

62. The historiography on republicanism and debates over the republicanism synthesis are copious. For starters, see Robert E. Shallope, "Toward a Republican Synthesis: The Emergence of an Understanding of Republicanism in American Historiography," *William and Mary Quarterly*, 29 (January 1972): 49–80, as well his later assessment, "Republicanism."

63. Kramnick 179.

64. Philip Freneau, "Modern Explanation of a Few Terms Commonly Misunderstood," in *Prose* 297–98. On Freneau's opposition to Hamilton and Federalist economic policies, see Mark Schmeller, "The Political Economy of Opinion: Public Credit and Concepts of Public Opinion in the Age of Federalism," *Journal of the Early Republic* 29 (Spring 2009): 55–56.

65. Freneau, "Reflections on Several Subjects" 320.

66. Philip Freneau, "An Author's Soliloquy," in *Poems* 2:334. Freneau further developed this theme in "Epistle to Sylvius: On the Folly of Writing Poetry," comparing authors to tradesmen and concluding "Low in the dust is genius laid— / The *Muses* with the *man in trade*" (*Poems* 2:314).

67. Rosemarie Waldrop, *Dissonance (If You Are Interested)* (Tuscaloosa: U of Alabama P, 2005), 260. For more on the political valence of poetry, see Bennett's work on nineteenth-century U.S. women writers.

68. Philip Freneau, "To the Concealed Royalist on a Virulent Attack," in *Poems* 2:176. The two versions date from 1782 and 1786 respectively.

69. Freneau, "To a New-England Poet," in *Last Poems* 112.

70. Philip Freneau, "Stanzas Occasioned by Certain Absurd, Extravagant, and Even Blasphemous Panegyrics and Encomiums on the Character of the Late Gen. Washington, That Appeared in Several Pamphlets, Journals and Other Periodical Publications, in January, 1800," in *Poems* 3:236.

71. Freneau, "Stanzas Occasioned" 3:237.

72. Philip Freneau, "To the Americans of the United States," in *Poems* 3:188.

## Coda

1. James Warren to Samuel Adams, November 8, 1772, Samuel Adams Papers, New York Public Library.

2. Samuel Adams to James Warren, November 4, 1772, *Warren-Adams Letters* 11–12.

3. James Warren to Samuel Adams, November 17, 1772, Samuel Adams Papers, New York Public Library.

4. Warren to Adams, November 17.

# { WORKS CITED }

Adams, Charles Frances. *The Life of John Adams, Begun by John Quincy Adams and Completed by Charles Francis Adams* and *Works*.

Adams, Henry. *The Education of Henry Adams*. New York: Modern Library, 1931.

Adams, John. "Novanglus; or, a History of the Dispute with America, from Its Origin, in 1754 to the Present Time." In J. Adams, *Works* 4:3–179.

Adams, John. *The Works of John Adams, Second President of the United States*. Edited by Charles Francis Adams. 10 vols. Boston: Little, Brown, 1865.

Adams, Samuel. *The Writings of Samuel Adams*. Edited by Harry Alonzo Cushing. 4 vols. New York: Putnam's, 1906.

Adams, Samuel. *The Writings of Samuel Adams*. Edited by Harry Alonzo Cushing. 4 vols. Teddington, UK: Echo Library, 2006.

Adams, Thomas R. *American Independence: The Growth of an Idea: A Bibliographic Study of the American Political Pamphlets Printed between 1764 and 1776 Dealing with the Dispute between Great Britain and Her Colonies*. Providence, RI: Brown University Press, 1965.

Adorno, Theodor, and Max Horkheimer. *Dialectic of Enlightenment: Philosophical Fragments*. Trans. Edmund Jephcott. Stanford, CA: Stanford University Press, 1997.

"Advertisement." *Aurora General Advertiser* 19 March 1796: 4.

"Advertisement Extraordinary." *Aurora* 5 March 1796: 2.

Altman, Janet Gurkin. *Epistolarity: Approaches to a Form*. Columbus: Ohio State University Press, 1982.

Anderson, Benedict. *Imagined Communities: Reflections on the Origin and Spread of Nationalism*. New ed. New York: Verso, 2006.

Anderson, C. W. "Spotlights and Shadows Revisited: The Case of Julian Assange." *The New Everyday: A Media Commons Project*. 22 April 2011. Accessed October 1, 2013 <http://mediacommons.futureofthebook.org/tne/pieces/spotlights-and-shadows-revisited-case-julian-assange>.

Appadurai, Arjun. "Deep Democracy: Urban Governmentality and the Horizon of Politics." *Public Culture* 14 (Winter 2002): 21–47.

Appadurai, Arjun. "Disjuncture and Difference in the Global Culture Economy." *Public Culture* 2 (Spring 1990): 1–24.

Appadurai, Arjun. "Grassroots Globalization and the Research Imagination." *Public Culture* 12 (Winter 2000): 1–19.

Appleby, Joyce. *Capitalism and a New Social Order: The Republican Vision of the 1790s*. New York: New York University Press, 1984.

Appleby, Joyce. *Liberalism and Republicanism in the Historical Imagination*. Cambridge, MA: Harvard University Press, 1992.

Arendt, Hannah. *On Revolution*. New York: Viking, 1965.

Aristotle. *The Rhetoric and Poetics of Aristotle*. Trans. W. Rhys Roberts. New York: Random House, 1984.

Arnold, David. "Hunger in the Garden of Plenty: The Bengal Famine of 1770." In *Dreadful Visitations: Confronting Natural Catastrophe in the Age of Enlightenment.* Ed. Alessa Johns, 81–112. New York: Routledge, 1999.

Assange, Julian. "Don't Shoot the Messenger for Revealing Uncomfortable Truths." *Australian* 8 December 2010. Accessed 1 March 2012 <http://www.theaustralian.com.au/ in-depth/wikileaks/dont-shoot-messenger-for-revealing-uncomfortable-truths/ story-fn775xjq-1225967241332>.

"At a Legal Meeting of the Daughters of LIBERTY at Constitution Hall, R. Island, April 1, 1774." *Newport Mercury* 11 April 1774: 2.

Auerbach, Jonathan. "Weapons of Democracy: Propaganda, Progressivism, and the American Public." 2014. MS.

Auerbach, Jonathan, and Russ Castronovo. "Thirteen Propositions about Propaganda." In *The Oxford Handbook of Propaganda Studies.* Edited by Jonathan Auerbach and Russ Castronovo, 1–16. New York: Oxford University Press, 2013.

Bache, Benjamin Franklin. *Remarks Occasioned by the Late Conduct of Mr. Washington as President of the United States.* Philadelphia: Bache, 1797.

Bache, Benjamin Franklin. "To the Public." *Aurora General Advertiser* 8 November 1794: 2.

Bache, Benjamin Franklin. "To the Public." *General Advertiser, Political, Commercial, Agricultural and Literary Journal* 1 October 1790: 1.

Bailyn, Bernard. *The Ideological Origins of the American Revolution.* Cambridge, MA: Harvard University Press, 1967.

Bailyn, Bernard. *The Ordeal of Thomas Hutchinson.* Cambridge, MA: Harvard University Press, 1974.

Bailyn, Bernard. "Political Experience and Enlightenment Ideas in 18th-Century America." *American Historical Review* 67 (1962): 331–52.

Balázs, Bodó. "Wikileaks and Freedom, Autonomy and Sovereignty in the Cloud." *The Center for Internet and Society.* 10 March 2011. Accessed 5 July 2011 <http://cyberlaw .stanford.edu/node/6635>.

Bannet, Eve Tavor. *Empire of Letters: Letter Manuals and Transatlantic Correspondence, 1688–1820.* Cambridge: Cambridge University Press, 2005.

Barabási, Albert-László. *Linked: The New Science of Networks.* Cambridge, MA: Perseus, 2002.

Barsamian, David, and Noam Chomsky. *Propaganda and the Public Mind: Conversations with Noam Chomsky.* Cambridge, MA: South End, 2001.

Baym, Nina. "Mercy Otis Warren's Gendered Melodrama of Revolution." *South Atlantic Quarterly* 90 (Summer 1991): 531–54.

Beckford, Martin. "Sarah Palin: Hunt WikiLeaks Founder like al-Qaeda and Taliban Leaders." *Telegraph* 30 November 2010. Accessed 18 February 2011 <http://www.telegraph .co.uk/news/worldnews/wikileaks/8171269/Sarah-Palin-hunt-WikiLeaks-founder-like- al-Qaeda-and-Taliban-leaders.htm>.

Bender, Thomas. *A Nation among Nations: America's Place in World History.* New York: Hill and Wang, 2006.

Benjamin, Walter. *Reflections: Essays, Aphorisms, Autobiographical Writings.* Translated by Edmund Jephcott. New York: Schocken, 1986.

Benkler, Yochai. "A Free Irresponsible Press: Wikileaks and the Battle over the Soul of the Networked Fourth Estate." *Harvard Civil Rights–Civil Liberties Law Review* 46.2 (2011): 311–97.

Bennett, Paula Bernat. *Poets in the Public Sphere: The Emancipatory Project of American Women's Poetry, 1800–1900*. Princeton, NJ: Princeton University Press, 2003.

Berger, Carl. *Broadsides and Bayonets: The Propaganda War of the American Revolution*. Philadelphia: University of Pennsylvania Press, 1961.

Berkin, Carol. *First Generations: Women in Colonial America*. New York: Hill and Wang, 1997.

Bernays, Edward L. "The Engineering of Consent." *Annals of the American Academy of Political and Social Science* 250 (March 1947): 113–20.

Bernays, Edward L. *Propaganda*. Brooklyn, NY: Ig, 2005.

Bernays, Edward L. *Public Relations*. Norman: University of Oklahoma Press, 1952.

Bickham, Troy O. "Sympathizing with Sedition: George Washington, the British Press, and British Attitudes during the American War of Independence." *William and Mary Quarterly* 59 (2002): 102–22.

Bidwell, John. "Printers' Supplies and Capitalization." In *A History of the Book in America*. Volume 1, *The Colonial Book in the Atlantic World*. Edited by Hugh Amory and David B. Hall, 163–83. Cambridge: Cambridge University Press, 2000.

Black, Jeremy. "Eighteenth-Century Intercepted Dispatches." *Journal of the Society of Archivists* 11 (October 1990): 138–43.

Blair St. George, Robert, ed. *Possible Pasts: Becoming Colonial in Early America*. Ithaca, NY: Cornell University Press, 2000.

Bloch, Ruth H. "The Gendered Meanings of Virtue in Revolutionary America." In *Gender and Morality in Anglo-American Culture*, 136–53. Berkeley: University of California Press, 2003.

*Boston Gazette and Country Journal* 7 June 1773.

"Boston, June 14." *Boston Gazette and Country Journal* 14 June 1773: 3.

Botein, Stephen. "Printers and the American Revolution." In *The Press and the American Revolution*. Edited by Bernard Bailyn and John B. Hench, 11–58. Worcester, MA: American Antiquarian Society, 1980.

Bowen, H. V. *The Business of Empire: The East India Company and Imperial Britain, 1756–1833*. Cambridge: Cambridge University Press, 2006.

Boyd, Julian P. "Silas Deane: Death by a Kindly Teacher of Treason." *William and Mary Quarterly* 16 (July 1959): 319–42.

Bradley, Patricia. *Slavery, Propaganda, and the American Revolution*. Jackson: U of Mississippi P, 1998.

Breen, T. H. *American Insurgents, American Patriots: The Revolution of the People*. New York: Hill and Wang, 2010.

Breen, T. H. "'Baubles of Britain': The American and Consumer Revolutions of the Eighteenth Century." *Past and Present* 119 (May 1988): 73–104.

Breen, T. H. "Ideology and Nationalism on the Eve of the American Revolution: Revisions Once More in Need of Revising." *Journal of American History* 84 (June 1997): 13–39.

Breig, James. "Early American Newspapering." *Colonial Williamsburg Journal* (Spring 2003). Accessed 3 March 2014 <http://www.history.org/Foundation/journal/spring03/journalism.cfm>.

Brewer, John. "The Eighteenth-Century British State: Contexts and Issues." In *An Imperial State at War: Britain from 1689 to 1815*. Edited by Lawrence Stone, 52–71. London: Routledge, 1994.

Brewer, Susan A. *Why America Fights: Patriotism and War Propaganda from the Philippines to Iraq.* New York: Oxford University Press, 2009.

Brown, Alice. *Mercy Warren.* New York: Scribner's, 1896.

Brown, Richard D. *Revolutionary Politics in Massachusetts: The Boston Committee of Correspondence and the Towns, 1772–1774.* Cambridge, MA.: Harvard University Press, 1970.

Buell, Lawrence. "American Literary Emergence as a Postcolonial Phenomenon." *American Literary History* 4 (Autumn 1992): 411–42.

Burke, Edmund. "Letter to John Farr and John Harris, Esqrs., Sheriffs of the City of Bristol, on the Affairs of America." In *The Works of the Right Honourable Edmund Burke.* 2:191. London: Nimmo, 1887.

Burke, Edmund. *Reflections on the Revolution in France.* New Rochelle, NY: Arlington House, 1966.

Burke, Kenneth. "Revolutionary Symbolism in America." In *American Writers' Congress.* Edited by Henry Hart, 87–93. New York: International, 1935.

Burman, Jeremy Trevelyan. "The Misunderstanding of Memes: Biography of an Unscientific Object, 1976–1999." *Perspectives on Science* 20.1 (2012): 75–104.

Burns, John F., and Ravu Somaiya. "Who Is Julian Assange?" In *Open Secrets: WikiLeaks, War, and American Diplomacy.* Edited by Alexander Star, 25–44. New York: Grove, 2011.

Burton, Finn. "After WikiLeaks, Us." *The New Everyday: A Media Commons Project.* 4 April 2011. Accessed 17 May 2011. <http://mediacommons.futureofthebook.org/tne/pieces/after-wikileaks-us>.

Carp, Benjamin L. *Defiance of the Patriots: The Boston Tea Party and the Making of America.* New Haven, CT: Yale University Press, 2010.

Carp, Benjamin L. *Rebels Rising: Cities and the American Revolution.* New York: Oxford University Press, 2007.

Carruthers, Bruce G. *City of Capital: Politics and Markets in the English Financial Revolution.* Princeton, NJ: Princeton University Press, 1996.

Castells, Manuel. *The Rise of the Network Society.* 2nd ed. .Malden, MA: Wiley-Blackwell, 2000.

Charles, Joseph. "The Jay Treaty: The Origins of the American Party System." *William and Mary Quarterly* 12 (October 1955): 581–630.

Chomsky, Noam. "Propaganda, American-Style." *zpub.com.* Accessed 6 November 2008 <http://www.zpub.com/un/chomsky.html>.

Christakis, Nicholas A., and James H. Fowler. *Connected: The Surprising Power of Our Social Networks and How They Shape Our Lives.* New York: Little, Brown, 2009.

Clark, Harry Hayden. "What Made Freneau the Father of American Poetry?" *Studies in Philology* 26 (January 1929): 1–22.

Clark, Harry Hayden. "What Made Freneau the Father of American Prose?" *Transactions of the Wisconsin Academy of Sciences, Arts and Letters* 25 (1930): 39–50.

Clarke, Charles E. "Early American Journalism: News and Opinion in the Popular Press." In *A History of the Book in America.* Volume 1, *The Colonial Book in the Atlantic World.* Edited by Hugh Amory and David D. Hall, 347–66. Cambridge: Cambridge University Press, 2000.

Cohen, Matt. *The Networked Wilderness: Communications in Early New England.* Minneapolis: University of Minnesota Press, 2010.

Combs, Jerald A. *The Jay Treaty: Political Battleground of the Founding Fathers.* Berkeley: University of California Press, 1970.

"Communication." *Aurora* 7 May 1796: 3.

Cooper, Frederick. "Race, Ideology, and the Perils of Comparative History." *American Historical Review* 101 (October 1996): 1122–38.

Cotlar, Seth. "The Federalists' Transatlantic Cultural Offensive of 1798 and the Moderation of American Democratic Discourse." In *Beyond the Founders: New Approaches to the political History of the Early American Republic.* Edited by Jeffrey L. Pasley, Andrew W. Robertson, and David Waldstreicher, 274–99. Chapel Hill: University of North Carolina Press, 2004.

Cotlar, Seth. "Reading the Foreign News, Imagining an American Public Sphere: Radical and Conservative Visions of 'the Public' in Mid-1790s Newspapers." In *Periodical Literature in Eighteenth-Century America.* Edited by Mark L. Kamrath and Sharon M. Harris, 307–38. Knoxville: University of Tennessee Press, 2006.

Cotlar, Seth. *Tom Paine's America: The Rise and Fall of Transatlantic Republicanism.* Charlottesville: University of Virginia Press, 2011.

Cott, Nancy F. *The Bonds of Womanhood: Woman's Sphere in New England, 1780–1835.* New Haven, CT: Yale University Press, 1997.

Creel, George. *How We Advertised America: The First Telling of the Amazing Story of the Committee on Public Information That Carried the Gospel of Americanism to Every Corner of the Globe.* New York: Harper& Brothers, 1920.

Cull, Nicholas, et al. *Propaganda and Mass Persuasion: A Historical Encyclopedia, 1500 to the Present.* Santa Barbara, CA: ABC-Clio, 2003.

Cunningham, Stanley B. *The Idea of Propaganda: A Reconstruction.* Westport, CT: Praeger, 2002.

Darnton, Robert. "What Is the History of Books?" In *The Book History Reader.* 2nd ed. Edited by David Finkelstein and Alistair McCleery, 9–26. New York: Routledge, 2006.

Davidson, Cathy N. *Revolution and the Word: The Rise of the Novel in America.* New York: Oxford University Press, 1986.

Davidson, Philip. *Propaganda and the American Revolution, 1763–1783.* Chapel Hill: University of North Carolina Press, 1941.

Davies, Kate. *Catharine Macaulay and Mercy Otis Warren: The Revolutionary Atlantic and the Politics of Gender.* New York: Oxford University Press, 2005.

Davis, David Brion. *Revolutions: Reflections on American Equality and Foreign Liberations.* Cambridge, MA: Harvard University Press, 1990.

Davis, Natalie Zemon. "Printing and the People." In *Society and Culture in Early Modern France: Eight Essays by Natalie Zemon Davis,* 189–226. Stanford, CA: Stanford University Press, 1975.

Dawkins, Richard. *The Selfish Gene.* Oxford: Oxford University Press, 1976.

Decker, William. *Epistolary Practices: Letter Writing in America before Telecommunications.* Chapel Hill: University of North Carolina Press, 1998.

Der Derian, James. "9.11: Before, After, and In Between," *Social Science Research Council/ After Sept. 11.* Social Science Research Council. Accessed 23 May 2011 <http://essays.ssrc .org/sept11/essays/der_derian.htm>.

Dewey, John. *The Public and Its Problems.* New York: Holt, 1927.

Dewey, John. "Public Opinion." *New Republic* 3 May 1922: 286–88.

Dickinson, John. *Letters from a Farmer in Pennsylvania to the Inhabitants of the British Colonies*. New York: Holt, 1768.

Dickinson, John. "Two Letters on the Tea Tax." In *Memoirs of the Historical Society of Pennsylvania*. Volume 14, *Life and Writings of John Dickinson*, 454–63. Philadelphia: Historical Society of Pennsylvania, 1895.

Dierks, Konstantin. *In My Power: Letter Writing and Communication in Early America*. Philadelphia: University of Pennsylvania Press, 2009.

Dillon, Elizabeth Maddock. *The Gender of Freedom: Fictions of Liberalism and the Literary Public Sphere*. Stanford, CA: Stanford University Press, 2004.

"Discussion and Proceedings." In *American Writers' Congress*. Edited by Henry Hart, 165–92. New York: International, 1935.

Domscheit-Berg, Daniel. *Inside WikiLeaks: My Time with Julian Assange at the World's Most Dangerous Website*. New York: Crown, 2011.

Doolen, Andrew. "Early American Civics: Rehistoricizing the Power of Republicanism." *American Literary History* 19.1 (2007): 120–40.

Duniway, Clyde Augustus. *The Development of Freedom of the Press in Massachusetts*. Cambridge, MA: Harvard University Press, 1906.

Durey, Michael. *Transatlantic Radicals and the Early American Republic*. Lawrence: University Press of Kansas, 1997.

Earle, Rebecca. "Introduction: Letters, Writers, and the Historian." In *Epistolary Selves: Letters and Letter-Writers, 1600–1945*, 1–12. Brookfield, VT: Ashgate, 1999.

"Editor's Preface." *Magazine of History* 63 (1918).

Edwards, Brian T. "Preposterous Encounters: Interrupting American Studies with the (Post)Colonial, or Casablanca in the American Century." *Comparative Studies of South Asia, Africa and the Middle East* 23 (2003): 70–86.

Elkins, Stanley, and Eric McKitrick. *The Age of Federalism*. New York: Oxford University Press, 1993.

Elliott, Emory. *Revolutionary Writers: Literature and Authority in the New Republic, 1724–1810*. New York: Oxford University Press, 1982.

Ellul, Jacques. *Propaganda: The Formation of Men's Attitudes*. Translated by Konrad Kellen and Jean Lerner. New York: Vintage, 1965.

*Epistles Domestic, Confidential, and Official, from General Washington, Written about the Commencement of the American Contest, When He Entered on the Command of the Army of the United States. With an Interesting Series of His Letters, Particularly to the British Admirals, Arbuthnot and Digby, to Gen. Sir Henry Clinton, Lord Cornwallis, Sir Guy Carleton, Marquis de la Fayette, &c. &c. To Benjamin Harrison, Esq. Speaker of the House of Delegates in Virginia, to Admiral the Count de Grasse, General Sullivan, Respecting an Attack of New-York; Including Many Application and Addresses Presented to Him with His Answers: Orders and Instructions, on Important Occasions, to His Aids de Camp, &c. &c. &c. None of Which Have Been Printed in the Two Volumes Published a Few Months Ago*. New York: Robinson, 1796.

Estes, Todd. *The Jay Treaty, Public Opinion, and the Evolution of Early American Print Culture*. Amherst: University of Massachusetts Press, 2006.

Ewen, Stewart. *Spin! A Social History of Spin*. New York: Basic, 1996.

"Extract of a Letter from London, April 19, 1774." *Massachusetts Spy* 15 July 1774: 3.

"Federal Legislature." *Aurora* 7 March 1796: 2.

Ferguson, Robert. *The American Enlightenment, 1750–1820.* Cambridge, MA: Harvard University Press, 1997.

Festa, Lynn. *Sentimental Figures of Empire in Eighteenth-Century Britain and France.* Baltimore: Johns Hopkins University Press, 2006.

Fewster, Joseph M. "The Jay Treaty and British Ship Seizures: The Martinique Cases." *William and Mary Quarterly* 3rd ser., 45.3 (1988): 426–52.

Flavell, Julie M. "Government Interception of Letters from America and the Quest for Colonial Opinion in 1775." *William and Mary Quarterly* 58 (April 2001): 403–30.

Fliegelman, Jay. *Declaring Independence: Jefferson, Natural Language, and the Culture of Performance.* Stanford, CA: Stanford University Press, 1993.

Foner, Eric. *Tom Paine and Revolutionary America.* New York: Oxford University Press, 1976.

"*For the* National Gazette." *National Gazette.* 31 July 1793: 313.

Ford, Worthington Chauncey, ed. *The Spurious Letters Attributed to Washington. With a Bibliographic Note by Worthington Chauncey Ford.* Brooklyn, NY: privately printed, 1889.

"For the *Aurora.*" 11 February 1795: 2.

"For the General Advertiser." *Aurora General Advertiser* 8 November 1794: 2.

"For the Massachusetts SPY." *Massachusetts Spy* 23 December 1774: 3.

"Fourth of July." *Aurora* 4 July 1796: 3.

Frank, Jason. *Constituent Moments: Enacting the People in Postrevolutionary America.* Durham, NC: Duke University Press, 2010.

Franklin, Benjamin. "Extract of a Letter from a Gentleman in London." *Pennsylvania Gazette* 20 April 1774: 3.

Franklin, Benjamin. *The Papers of Benjamin Franklin.* Edited by William Wilcox. 40 vols. New Haven, CT: Yale University Press, 1959–2011.

Franklin, Benjamin [as Q.E.D.]. "Rules by Which a Great Empire May Be Reduced to a Small One." *Massachusetts Spy* 16 December 1773: 1.

Fraser, Nancy. "Reframing Justice in a Globalizing World." *New Left Review* 36 (November–December 2005): 69–88.

French, Allen. "The First George Washington Scandal." *Proceedings of the Massachusetts Historical Society* 65 (November 1935): 460–74.

Freneau, Philip. "Advice to Authors." In *A Freneau Sampler.* Edited by Philip M. Marsh. New York: Scarecrow, 1963.

Freneau, Philip. "American Liberty, a Poem." In *The Poems of Philip Freneau, Poet of the Revolution.* Edited by Lewis Leary. 3 vols., 1:145. Princeton, NJ: University Library, 1902.

Freneau, Philip. "Copy of an Intercepted Letter from a New-York Tory, to His Friend in Philadelphia, 1781." In *Poems on Various Subjects, but Being Chiefly Illustrative of the Events and Actors of the American War of Independence,* 190. London: Smith, 1861.

Freneau, Philip. *The Last Poems of Philip Freneau.* Edited by Lewis Leary. New Brunswick, NJ: Rutgers UP, 1945.

Freneau, Philip. Letter to Dr. J. W. Francis. 15 May 1819. In *Unpublished Freneauana.* Edited by Charles F. Heartman. New York: Printed for the editor, 1918.

Freneau, Philip. *The Poems of Philip Freneau.* Edited by Fred Lewis Pattee. 3 vols. Princeton, NJ: Princeton Historical Society, 1907.

Freneau, Philip. *Poems Written and Published during the American Revolutionary War, and Now Published from the Original Manuscripts; Interspersed with Translations from the*

*Ancients, and Other Pieces Not Heretofore in Print.* 3rd ed. 2 vols. Philadelphia: Bailey, 1809.

Freneau, Philip. "Poetic Address." *Time Piece* 13 March 1797: 4.

Freneau, Philip. *The Prose of Philip Freneau.* Ed. Philip M. Marsh. New Brunswick, NJ: Scarecrow, 1955.

Freneau, Philip. "To the Public." *National Gazette* 31 October 1791: 4.

Freneau, Philip. "To the Public." *Time Piece* 13 March 1797: 1.

Friedman, Thomas. "We've Only Got America A." In *Open Secrets: WikiLeaks, War, and American Diplomacy.* Edited by Alexander Star, 399–401. New York: Grove, 2011.

"From the Gazette of the United States." Reprinted in the *Aurora General Advertiser* 8 November 1794: 2.

"From the *Newport Mercury,*" *New Hampshire Gazette* 22 August 1775: 2.

Gallagher, Catherine. "The Rise of Fictionality." In *The Novel.* Volume I, *History, Geography, and Culture.* Edited by Franco Moretti, 336–63. Princeton, NJ: Princeton University Press, 2006.

Gary, Brett. *The Nervous Liberals: Propaganda Anxieties from World War I to the Cold War.* New York: Columbia University Press, 1999.

"Genuine Copies of the Intercepted Letters Mentioned in Our Last." *Massachusetts Gazette and Boston News-Letter* 17 August 17 1775: 1.

George III, King of England. "A Proclamation by the King for Suppressing Rebellion and Sedition." In *Documents of American History.* Edited by Henry Steele Commager, 96. New York: Appleton-Century-Crofts, 1958.

Gerth, Jeff, and Scott Shane, "U.S. Is Said to Pay to Plant Articles in Iraq Papers." *New York Times* 10 December 2005: A1.

Giri, Saroj. "WikiLeaks beyond WikiLeaks." *Mute: Culture and Politics after the Net.* Mute. 16 December 2010. Accessed November 3, 2012 <http://www.metamute.org/en/articles/WikiLeaks_beyond_WikiLeaks>.

Godwin, William. "Of History and Romance." Department of English, University of Pennsylvania. Accessed 22 October 2009 <www.english.upenn.edu/~mgamer/Etexts/godwin.history.html>.

Goebbels, Joseph. *My Part in Germany's Fight.* Translated by Kurt Fielder. London: Hurst and Blackett, 1940.

Goff, Frederick R. *The John Dunlap Broadside: The First Printing of the Declaration of Independence.* Washington, DC: Library of Congress, 1976.

Gould, Eliga H. "Fears of War, Fantasies of Peace: British Politics and the Coming of the American Revolution." In *Empire and Nation: The American Revolution in the Atlantic World.* Ed. Eliga H. Gould and Peter S. Onuf, 19–34. Baltimore: Johns Hopkins University Press, 2005.

Gould, Philip. "Wit and Politics in Revolutionary British America: The Case of Samuel Seabury and Alexander Hamilton." *Eighteenth-Century Studies* 41.3 (2008): 383–403.

Greene, Jack P. "Colonial History and National History: Reflections on a Continuing Problem." *William and Mary Quarterly* 64 (2007): 235–50.

Greene, Jack P. "Identity and Independence." In *A Companion to the American Revolution.* Edited by Jack P. Greene and J.R. Pole, 230–34. Malden, MA: Blackwell, 2000.

Gunkel, David J. "What's the Matter with Books?" *Configurations* 11 (Fall 2003): 277–303.

Gustafson, Sandra. *Eloquence Is Power: Oratory and Performance in Early America.* Chapel Hill: University of North Carolina Press, 2000.

Gustafson, Sandra. *Imagining Deliberative Democracy in the Early American Republic.* Chicago: University of Chicago Press, 2011.

Hall, David D. *Cultures of Print: Essays in the History of the Book.* Amherst: University of Massachusetts Press, 1996.

Hamilton, Alexander, James Madison, and John Jay. *The Federalist.* Cambridge, MA: Harvard University Press, 1966.

Hampden [Benjamin Rush?]. *The Alarm. Number II.* New York, 1773. Library of Congress, Printed Ephemera Collection, portfolio 105, folder 9a. Accessed 1 March 2007 <memory.loc.gov>.

Hampden [Benjamin Rush?]. *The Alarm, Number V.* New York, 1773. Accessed 1 March 2007 <http://memory.loc.gov>.

Hampden [Benjamin Rush?]. "On Patriotism." *Pennsylvania Journal* 20 October 1773: 1.

Hardt, Hanno. *Myths for the Masses: An Essay on Mass Communication.* Malden, MA: Blackwell, 2004.

Hawke, David Freeman. *Benjamin Rush: Revolutionary Gadfly.* Indianapolis: Bobbs-Merrill, 1971.

Herman, Edward S., and Noam Chomsky. *Manufacturing Consent: The Political Economy of Mass Media.* New York: Pantheon, 1988.

Hewitt, Elizabeth. "The Authentic Fictional Letters of Charles Brockden Brown." In *Letters and Cultural Transformations in the United States, 1760–1860.* Edited by Theresa Strouth Gaul and Sharon M. Harris, 79–98. Burlington, VT: Ashgate, 2009.

Hopkins, Lemuel. *The Democratiad, a Poem in Retaliation for the "Philadelphia Jockey Club."* *Magazine of History with Notes and Queries* 29 (1926): 45–68.

Hosmer, James Kendall. *The Life of Thomas Hutchinson, Royal Governor of the Province of Massachusetts Bay.* Boston: Houghton Mifflin, 1896.

Howard, Philip N. *The Digital Origins of Dictatorship and Democracy: Information Technology and Political Islam.* New York: Oxford University Press, 2010.

Howe, Richard Viscount, and William Howe. "Proclamation." *New-York Gazette; and Weekly Mercury* 30 December 30 1776.

Hulme, Peter. "Postcolonial Theory and Early America: An Approach from the Caribbean." In Blair St. George 33–48.

Hunt, Lynn. "Engraving the Republic: Prints and Propaganda in the French Revolution." *History Today* 30 (October 1980): 11–17.

Hustvedt, S. B. "Philippic Freneau." *American Speech* 4 (October 1928): 1–18.

Inglis, Charles. *The Deceiver Unmasked; or Loyalty and Interest United: in Answer to a Pamphlet Entitled "Common Sense."* New York: Loudon, 1776.

"Inscription of Isaiah Thomas." Library of Congress. Accessed 18 April 2013 <http://www.loc.gov/rr/news/circulars/spy.html>.

Irving, Washington. *Life of George Washington.* 5 vols. New York: Putnam, 1861.

Jagoda, Patrick. "Terror Networks and the Aesthetics of Interconnection." *Social Text* 105 (Winter 2010): 65–89.

James, C. L. R. *The Black Jacobins: Toussaint L'Ouverture and the San Domingo Revolution.* New York: Vintage, 1989.

Jameson, Frederic. *Marxism and Form: Twentieth-Century Dialectical Theories of Literature.* Princeton, NJ: Princeton University Press, 1974.

Jan, Steven. "Meme Hunting with the Humdrum Toolkit: Principles, Problems, and Prospects." *Computer Music Journal* 28.4 (2004): 68–84.

Jefferson, Thomas. *Memoirs, Correspondence, and Private Papers of Thomas Jefferson, Late President of the United States*. Edited by Thomas Jefferson Randolph. 4 vols. London: Colburn and Bentley, 1829.

Johns, Adrian. *The Nature of the Book: Print and Knowledge in the Making*. Chicago: University of Chicago Press, 1998.

Jowett, Garth S., and Victoria O'Donnell. Introduction. In *Readings in Propaganda and Persuasion: New and Classic Essays*. Edited by Garth S. Jowett and Victoria O'Donnell, ix–xv. Thousand Oaks, CA: Sage, 2006.

Kammen, Michael. "The Meaning of Colonization in American Revolutionary Thought." In *The American Enlightenment*. Edited by Frank Shuffleton, 183–204. Rochester, NY: University of Rochester Press, 1993.

Kaplan, Roger. "The Hidden War: British Intelligence Operations during the American Revolution." *William and Mary Quarterly* 47 (January 1990): 115–38.

Kaye, Harvey J. *Thomas Paine and the Promise of America*. New York: Hill and Wang, 2005.

Keller, Bill. "The Boy Who Kicked the Hornet's Nest." In *Open Secrets: WikiLeaks, War, and American Diplomacy*. Edited by Alexander Star, 3–22. New York: Grove, 2011.

Kelly, Mary. "'The Need of Their Genius': Women's Reading and Writing Practices in Early America." *Journal of the Early Republic* 28 (Spring 2008): 1–22.

Kelly, Mary. "'While Pen, Ink& Paper Can Be Had': Reading and Writing in a Time of Revolution." *Early American Studies* 10 (Fall 2012): 439–66.

Kerber, Linda. *Women of the Republic: Intellect and Ideology in Revolutionary America*. New York: Norton, 1986.

Khamis, Sahar, Paul B. Gold, and Katherine Vaughn. "Propaganda in Egypt and Syria's 'Cyberwars': Contexts, Actors, Tools, and Tactics." In *The Oxford Handbook of Propaganda Studies*. Edited by Jonathan Auerbach and Russ Castronovo, 418–38. New York: Oxford University Press, 2013.

Kittler, Friedrich A. *Discourse Networks, 1800/1900*. Translated by Michael Metteer. Stanford, CA: Stanford University Press, 1990.

Kramnick, Isaac. *Republicanism and Bourgeois Radicalism: Political Ideology in Late Eighteeenth-Century England and America*. Ithaca, NY: Cornell University Press, 1990.

Kushner, David. "Click and Dagger." *Mother Jones* July–August 2010. Accessed 12 June 2013 <http://www.motherjones.com/politics/2010/07/click-and-dagger-wikileaks-julian-assange-iraq-video-updated>.

Langford, Paul. "British Correspondence in the Colonial Press, 1763–1775: A Study in Anglo-American Misunderstanding before the American Revolution." In *The Press and the American Revolution*. Edited by Bernard Bailyn and John B. Hench, 273–313. Worcester, MA: American Antiquarian Society, 1980.

Larabee, Benjamin. *The Boston Tea Party*. New York: Oxford University Press, 1964.

Larkin, Edward. *Thomas Paine and the Literature of Revolution*. Cambridge: Cambridge University Press, 2005.

Lasswell, Harold D. "The Theory of Propaganda." *American Political Science Review* 21 (August 1927): 627–31.

Latour, Bruno. "On Actor-Network Theory: A Few Clarifications." *Centre for Social Theory and Technology*. January 11, 1998. Accessed 5 October 2010 <http://www.nettime.org/Lists-Archives/nettime-l-9801/msg00019.html>.

Latour, Bruno. *Reassembling the Social: An Introduction to Actor-Network Theory*. Oxford: Oxford University Press, 2005.

Leary, Lewis. *That Rascal Freneau: A Study in Literary Failure.* New Brunswick, NJ: Rutgers University Press, 1941.

Leigh, David, and Luke Harding. *WikiLeaks: Inside Julian Assange's War on Secrecy.* New York: Perseus, 2011.

Leonard, Daniel. *Massachusettensis; or, A Series of Letters, Containing a Faithful State of Many Important and Striking Facts, Which Laid the foundation of the Present Troubles in the Province of Massachusetts-Bay; Interspersed with Animadversions and Reflections, Originally Addressed to the People of That Province, and Worthy the Consideration of the True Patriots of This Country.* Boston, 1776.

Leonard, Thomas C. "News for a Revolution: The Exposé in America, 1768–1773." *Journal of American History* 67 (June 1980): 26–40.

*Letters from General Washington to Several of His Friends in the Year 1776: In Which Are Set Forth a Fairer and Fuller View of American Politics. Than Ever Transpired.* London: Bew, 1777.

*Letters from General Washington to Several of His Friends in the Year 1776: In Which Are Set Forth a Fairer and Fuller View of American Politicks. Than Ever Yet Transpired, or the Public Could Be Made Acquainted with through Any Other Channel.* New York: Rivington, 1778.

*Letters from General Washington to Several of His Friends, in June and July 1776: In Which Is Set Forth an Interesting View of American Politics, at That All-Important Period.* Philadelphia: Federal Press, 1795.

Levine, Caroline. "Narrative Networks: *Bleak House* and the Affordances of Form." *Novel* 42.3 (2009): 517–23.

Levine, Robert S. *Dislocating Race and Nation: Episodes in Nineteenth-Century Literary Nationalism.* Chapel Hill: University of North Carolina Press, 2008.

Linebaugh, Peter, and Marcus Rediker. *The Many-Headed Hydra: Sailors, Slaves, Commoners, and the Hidden History of the Revolutionary Atlantic.* Boston: Beacon, 2000.

Lippmann, Walter. *Public Opinion.* New York: Free Press, 1997.

Looby, Christopher. *Voicing America: Language, Literary Form, and the Origins of the United States.* Chicago: University of Chicago Press, 1998.

Loughran, Trish. "Disseminating *Common Sense*: Thomas Paine and the Problems of the Early National Bestseller." *American Literature* 78 March 2006: 1–28.

Loughran, Trish. *The Republic in Print: Print Culture in the Age of U.S. Nationalism, 1770–1870.* New York: Columbia University Press, 2007.

Lumley, Frederick E. *The Propaganda Menace.* New York: Century, 1933.

Macaulay, Catharine. *Observations on the Reflections of the Right Hon. Edmund Burke, on the Revolution in France, in a Letter to the Right Hon. the Earl of Stanhope.* Boston: Thomas and Andrews, 1791.

Maier, Pauline. *From Resistance to Revolution: Colonial Radicals and the Development of American Opposition to Britain, 1765–1776.* New York: Vintage, 1972.

Manning, Chelsea E. "Subject: The Next Stage of My Life." *Today News.* 22 August 2013. Accessed 13 September 2013 <http://www.today.com/news/i-am-chelsea-read-mannings-full-statement-6C10974052>.

Marcus, Daniel. *Scandal and Civility: Journalism and the Birth of American Democracy.* New York: Oxford University Press, 2009.

Marlin, Randal. *Propaganda and the Ethics of Persuasion.* Peterborough, ON: Broadview 2002.

228 Works Cited

Marshall, Garry. "The Internet and Memetics." Accessed 20 March 2012 <http://pespmc1
.vub.ac.be/Conf/MemePap/Marshall.html>.
Marshall, P. J. "Britain and the World in the Eighteenth Century: I, Reshaping the Empire."
*Transactions of the Royal Historical Society* 6th ser., 8 (1998): 1–18.
Marshall, P. J. *Trade and Conquest: Studies on the Rise of British Dominance in India.*
Aldershot: Variorum, 1993.
Mays, Terry M. *Historical Dictionary of Revolutionary America.* Oxford: Scarecrow, 2005.
McClintock, Anne. "Paranoid Empire: Specters from Guantánamo and Abu Ghraib." In
*States of Emergency: The Object of American Studies.* Edited by Russ Castronovo and
Susan Gillman, 88–115. Chapel Hill: University of North Carolina Press, 2009.
McCutcheon, James. "The Asian Dimension in the American Revolutionary Period." In *The*
*American Revolution: Its Meaning to Asians and Americans.* Edited by Cedric B. Cowing,
87–107. Honolulu: East-West Center, 1977.
McKenzie, D. F. *Bibliography and the Sociology of Texts.* London: British Library, 1986.
McKeon, Michael. "*From* Prose Fiction: Great Britain." In *Theory of the Novel: A Historical
Approach.* Edited by Michael McKeon, 600–12. Baltimore: Johns Hopkins University
Press, 2000.
McLuhan, Marshall. "The Medium Is the Message." In *Understanding Media: The Extensions
of Man,* 7–23. Cambridge, MA: MIT Press, 1964.
Messer, Peter C. "Writing Women into History: Defining Gender and Citizenship in Post-
Revolutionary America." *Studies in Eighteenth Century Culture* 28 (1999): 341–60.
"Messieurs Printers." *Boston Gazette* 19 October 1772.
Metzler, Josef. "Foundation of the Congregation 'de Propaganda Fide' by Gregory XV." In
*Sacrae Congregationis de Propaganda Fide Memoria Rerum.* 2 vols. Rome: Herder, 1971.
Mialet, Hélène. "Reincarnating the Knowing Subject: Scientific Rationality and the Situated
Body." *Qui Parle* 18 (Fall–Winter 2009): 53–73.
Middlekauff, Robert. *The Glorious Cause: The American Revolution, 1763–1789.* New York:
Oxford University Press, 1982.
Miller, John C. *Sam Adams: Pioneer in Propaganda.* Stanford, CA: Stanford University
Press, 1936.
Moore, Michael. "Why I'm Posting Bail Money for Julian Assange." *Huffington Post.* 14
December 2010. Accessed 1 March 2011 <http://www.huffingtonpost.com/michael-moore/
why-im-posting-bail-money_b_796319.html>.
Moretti, Franco. "The Novel: History and Theory." *New Left Review* 52 (July–August 2008):
111–24.
Moretti, Franco. *Signs Taken for Wonders: Essays in the Sociology of Literary Forms.* Translated
by Susan Fischer, David Forgacs, and David Miller. London: New Left Books, 1983.
Morgan, Edmund S. *The Birth of the Republic, 1763–89.* 3rd ed. Chicago: University of
Chicago Press, 1992.
Morgan, Edmund S. *Inventing the People: The Rise of Popular Sovereignty in England and
America.* New York: Norton, 1989.
Murison, Justine. *The Politics of Anxiety in Nineteenth-Century American Literature.*
Cambridge: Cambridge University Press, 2011.
Nash, Gary B. *The Unknown American Revolution: The Unruly Birth of Democracy and the
Struggle to Create America.* New York: Viking, 2005.
*National Gazette* 26 October 1793: 410.

Needham, Marchamont [pseud.]. "Allied Alas! For Ever to the Crime." *Boston Gazette* 15 June 1772: 2.

Newman, Simon P. *Parades and the Politics of the Street: Festive Culture in the Early American Republic*. Philadelphia: University of Pennsylvania Press, 1997.

"*A New* SONG, *to the Plaintive Tune of* Hosier's Ghost." *Virginia Gazette* 20 January 1774. Reprinted in Schlesinger, "A Note on Songs" 80.

Ngai, Sianne. "Network Aesthetics: Juliana Spahr's *The Transformation* and Bruno Latour's *Reassembling the Social*." In *American Literature's Aesthetic Dimensions*. Edited by Cindy Weinstein and Christopher Looby, 367–92. New York: Columbia University Press, 2012.

Norton, Mary Beth. *Liberty's Daughters: The Revolutionary Experience of American Women, 1750–1800*. Boston: Little, Brown, 1980.

Oliver, Peter. "Origin and Progress of the *American* Rebellion." In *Peter Oliver's Origin and Progress of the American Rebellion: A Tory View*. Edited by Douglass Adair and John A. Schutz, 3–168. San Marino, CA: Huntington Library, 1961.

Paine, Thomas. *The Age of Reason*. New York: Harper& Row, 1974.

Paine, Thomas. *The Complete Writings of Thomas Paine*. 2 vols. Edited by Philip S. Foner. New York: Citadel, 1969.

Paine, Thomas. "Liberty Tree." In *The Thomas Paine Reader*. Edited by Michael Foot and Isaac Kramnick, 63–64. New York: Penguin, 1987.

Paine, Thomas.. *The Rights of Man*. New York: Penguin, 1984.

Parks, Lisa. "Stuff You Can Kick: Toward a Theory of Media Infrastructures." In *Humanities and the Digital*. Edited by David Theo Goldberg and Patrik Svensson. Cambridge, MA: MIT Press, forthcoming.

Parrington, Vernon Louis. *Main Currents in American Thought*. Volume 1, *The Colonial Mind, 1620–1800*. New York: Harcourt Brace, 1927.

Parrish, Susan Scott. *American Curiosity: Cultures of Natural History in the Colonial British Atlantic World*. Chapel Hill: University of North Carolina Press, 2006.

Pasley, Jeffrey L. "The Cheese and the Words: Popular Political Culture and Participatory Democracy in the Early American Republic." In *Beyond the Founders: New Approaches to the Political History of the Early American Republic*. Edited by Jeffrey L. Pasley, Andrew W. Robertson, and David Waldstreicher, 31–56. Chapel Hill: University of North Carolina Press, 2004.

Pasley, Jeffrey L. "The Two National *Gazettes*: Newspapers and the Embodiment of American Political Parties." *Early American Literature* 35.1 (2000): 51–86.

Pasley, Jeffrey L. *"Tyranny of Printers": Newspaper Politics in the Early American Republic*. Charlottesville: University Press of Virginia, 2001.

Perlmann, Joel, and Dennis Shirley. "When Did New England Women Acquire Literacy?" *William and Mary Quarterly* 48 (January 1991): 50–67.

Perloff, Marjorie. *Poetry On and Off the Page: Essays for Emergent Occasions*. Evanston, IL: Northwestern University Press, 1998.

"Philadelphia." *Pennsylvania Journal* 20 October 1773: 3–4.

Philo-Republicanus. "For the Aurora." *Aurora General Advertiser* 18 November 1794: 3.

Pinsky, Robert. "American Poetry and American Life: Freneau, Whitman, Williams." *Shenandoah* 37.1 (1987): 3–26.

Pocock, J. G. A. *The Machiavellian Moment: Florentine Political Thought and the Atlantic Republican Tradition*. Princeton, NJ: Princeton University Press, 1975.

Poplicola. *To the Worthy Inhabitants of New-York*. New York: Rivington, 1773. Accessed on 1 March 2007 <memory.loc.gov>.

Prendergast, Maria Teresa, and Thomas A. Prendergast. "Critical Commentary on *Inscrutabili Divinae Providentiae Arcano*." In *The Oxford Handbook of Propaganda Studies*. Edited by Jonathan Auerbach and Russ Castronovo, 19–27. New York: Oxford University Press, 2013.

"Proposals for Printing, *by Subscription*, the Debates in the Federal House of Representatives, Relative to the Powers of the House on the Subject of TREATIES, and on the British Treaty." *Aurora* 23 March 1796: 1.

"Province of Massachusetts-Bay." *Boston Gazette* 21 June 1773: 1.

Qualter, Terence H. *Opinion Control in the Democracies*. London: MacMillan, 1985.

Rahe, Paul A. *Republics Ancient and Modern: Classical Republicanism and the American Revolution*. Chapel Hill: University of North Carolina Press, 1992.

Raphael, Ray. *Founding Myths: Stories That Hide Our Patriotic Past*. Rev. ed. New York: New Press, 2014.

"Reflections on Several Subjects." *National Gazette* 31 August 1793: 320.

*The Representation of Governor Hutchinson and Others, Contained in Certain Letters Transmitted to England, and Afterwards Returned from Thence, and Laid before the General Assembly of the Massachusetts-Bay*. In Franklin, *Papers* 20:539–80.

Rich, Frank. *The Greatest Story Ever Sold: The Decline and Fall of Truth from 9/11 to Katrina*. New York: Penguin, 2006.

Richards, Jeffrey H. *Mercy Otis Warren*. New York: Twayne, 1995.

Richardson, Sarah. "'Well-Neighboured Houses': The Political Networks of Elite Women, 1780–1860." In *The Power of the Petticoat*. Edited by Kathryn Gleadle and Sarah Richardson, 56–73. New York: St. Martins, 2000.

Rigal, Laura. "Benjamin Franklin, the Science of Flow, and the Legacy of the Enlightenment." In *A Companion to Benjamin Franklin*. Edited by David Waldstreicher, 308–34. New York: Wiley-Blackwell, 2011.

Rivington, James. *Letter to the Inhabitants of the City and Colony of New-York*. New York: Rivington, 1773.

Robespierre, Maximilien. *Report upon the Principles of Political Morality Which Are to Form the Basis of the Administration of the Interior Concerns of the Republic: Made in the Name of the Committee of Public Safety, the 18th Pluviose, Second Year of the Republic, (February 6th, 1794)*. Philadelphia: Bache, 1794.

Robinson, F. P. *The Trade of the East India Company from 1709 to 1813*. Cambridge: Cambridge University Press, 1912.

Rodgers, Daniel T. "Republicanism: The Career of a Concept." *Journal of American History* 79 (June 1992): 11–38.

Ryerson, Richard Allen. *The Revolution Is Now Begun: The Radical Committees of Philadelphia, 1765–1776*. Philadelphia: University of Pennsylvania Press, 1978.

Sarkela, Sandra J. "Freedom's Call: The Persuasive Power of Mercy Otis Warren's Dramatic Sketches, 1772–1775." *Early American Literature* 44.3 (2009): 541–68.

Schlesinger, Arthur M. "A Note on Songs as Patriot Propaganda, 1765–1776." *William and Mary Quarterly* 11.1 (1954): 78–88.

Schlesinger, Arthur M. "Political Mobs and the American Revolution, 1765–1776." *Proceedings of the American Philosophical Society* 99 (August 1955): 244–50.

Schlesinger, Arthur M. *Prelude to Independence: The Newspaper War on Britain, 1764–1776*. New York: Knopf, 1958.

Schloesser, Pauline. *The Fair Sex: White Women and Racial Patriarchy in the Early American Republic*. New York: New York University Press, 2002.

Schmeller, Mark. "The Political Economy of Opinion: Public Credit and Concepts of Public Opinion in the Age of Federalism." *Journal of the Early Republic* 29 (Spring 2009): 35–61.

Scipio. "For the *Aurora*. To the Representatives of the People. Letter IV." *Aurora* 3 March 1796: 2.

Seigel, Micol. "Beyond Compare: Comparative Method after the Transnational Turn." *Radical History Review* 91 (Winter 2005): 62–90.

Shaffer, Jason. "Making 'an Excellent Die': Death, Mourning, and Patriotism in the Propaganda Plays of the American Revolution." *Early American Literature* 41.1 (2006): 1–27.

Shah, Anup. "World Military Spending." *Global Issues*. 30 June 2013. Accessed 21 March 2007 <www.globalissues.org/Geopolitics/ArmsTrade/Spending.asp#USMilitarySpending>.

Shallhope, Robert E. "Republicanism." In *A Companion to the American Revolution*. Edited by Jack P. Greene and J. R. Pole, 668–73. Malden, MA: Blackwell, 2000.

Shallhope, Robert E. "Toward a Republican Synthesis: The Emergence of an Understanding of Republicanism in American Historiography." *William and Mary Quarterly* 29 (January 1972): 49–80.

Shammas, Carole. "The Revolutionary Impact of European Demand for Tropical Goods." In *The Early Modern Atlantic Economy*. Edited by John J. McCusker and Kenneth Morgan, 163–85. Cambridge: Cambridge University Press, 2000.

Shane, Scott. "Can the Government Keep a Secret?" In *Open Secrets: WikiLeaks, War, and American Diplomacy*. Edited by Alexander Star, 337–42. New York: Grove, 2011.

Shapiro, Steven. *The Culture and Commerce of the Early American Novel: Reading the Atlantic World-System*. University Park: Pennsylvania State University Press, 2006.

Shaviro, Steven. *Connected, or, What It Means to Live in the Network Society*. Minneapolis: University of Minnesota Press, 1999.

Shuffelton, Frank. "In Different Voices: Gender in the American Republic of Letters." *Early American Literature* 25 (1990): 289–304.

Sifry, Micah L. *WikiLeaks and the Age of Transparency*. Berkeley, CA: Counterpoint, 2011.

Smith, Jeffrey A. *Franklin and Bache: Envisioning the Enlightened Republic*. New York: Oxford University Press, 1990.

Smith, Nathaniel. *General Remarks on the System of Government in India; with Farther Considerations on the Present State of the Company at Home and Abroad. To Which is Added, a General Statement and Fair Examination of Their Latest Accounts from the Year 1766. And a Plan for the Mutual Advantage of the Nation and the Company*. London: Nourse, 1773.

Smith, Paul H., ed. *Letters of the Delegates to Congress, 1774–1789*. 26 vols. Washington, DC: Library of Congress, 1976–2000.

Smith-Rosenberg, Carroll. *This Violent Empire: The Birth of an American National Identity*. Chapel Hill: University of North Carolina Press, 2010.

"A Soliloquy." *Boston Gazette and Country Journal*. 7 June 1773: 3.

Sparks, Jared. *The Life of Washington*. Boston: Little, Brown, 1853.

Sproule, J. Michael. *Propaganda and Democracy: The American Experience of Media and Mass Persuasion*. Cambridge: Cambridge University Press, 1997.

Stallybrass, Peter. "'Little Jobs': Broadsides and the Printing Revolution." In *Agent of Change: Print Culture Studies after Elizabeth L. Eisenstein*. Edited by Sabrina Alcorn Baron, Eric

N. Lindquist, and Eleanor F. Shelvin, 313–41. Amherst: University of Massachusetts Press, 2007.

Starr, Paul. *The Creation of the Media: The Political Origins of Modern Communications*. New York: Basic, 2004.

Stern, Julia. *The Plight of Feeling: Sympathy and Dissent in the Early American Novel*. Chicago: University of Chicago Press, 1997.

Stern, Philip J. "British Asia and British Atlantic: Comparisons and Connections." *William and Mary Quarterly* 3rd ser., 63 (2006): 693–712.

Stevens, George Alexander. "The Origin of English Liberty." In *The Choice Spirit's Chaplet; or, A Poesy from Parnassus. Being a Select Collection of Songs, from the Most Approved Authors; Many of Them Written and the Whole Compiled by George Alexander Stevens, Esq*. London: Whitehaven, 1771.

Stuart, Lucy. *The East India Company in Eighteenth-Century Politics*. Oxford: Oxford University Press, 1952.

Tagg, James. *Benjamin Franklin Bache and the Philadelphia "Aurora."* Philadelphia: University of Pennsylvania Press, 1991.

Tanselle, G. Thomas. "Some Statistics on American Printing, 1764–1783." In *The Press and the American Revolution*. Edited by Bernard Bailyn and John B. Hench, 315–64. Worcester, MA: American Antiquarian Society, 1980.

"The Tea Act." *US History.org*. 10 May 1773. Accessed 22 April 2013 <http://www.ushistory .org/declaration/related/teaact.htm>.

Teunissen, John L. "Blockheadism and the Propaganda Plays of the American Revolution." *Early American Literature* 7 (Fall 1972): 148–62.

Thompson, Peter. *Rum Punch and Revolution: Taverngoing and Public Life in Eighteenth-Century Philadelphia*. Philadelphia: University of Pennsylvania Press, 1999.

Thompson, Todd. "Representative Nobodies: The Politics of Benjamin Franklin's Satiric Personae, 1722–1757." *Early American Literature* 46.3 (2011): 449–79.

Thomson, Oliver. *Easily Led: A History of Propaganda*. Stroud, UK: Sutton, 1999.

Thorne, Christian. *The Dialectic of Counter-Enlightenment*. Cambridge, MA: Harvard University Press, 2009.

Tise, Larry E. *The American Counterrevolution: A Retreat from Liberty, 1783–1800*. Mechanicsburg, PA: Stackpole, 1998.

"To the Noblesse and Courtiers of the United States." *National Gazette* 5 January 1793: 78.

"To the Public." *Aurora* 28 January 1795: 3.

"To the Public." *Massachusetts Spy* 3 May 1775.

*To the Tradesmen, Merchants, &c. of the Province of Pennsylvania*. Philadelphia, 1773. Accessed on 1 March 2007 <memory.loc.gov>.

A Tradesman. "For the Pennsylvania Evening Post." *Pennsylvania Evening Post* 30 April 1776: 218.

Traister, Bryce. "Criminal Correspondence: Loyalism, Espionage, and Crevecoeur." *Early American Literature* 27 (2002): 469–96.

Tresilian, Nicholas. "The Swarming of Memes." *Technoetic Arts: A Journal of Speculative Research* 6.2 (2008): 115–26.

Tryon, Rolla Milton. *Household Manufactures in the United States, 1640–1860: A Study in Industrial History*. Chicago: University of Chicago Press, 1917.

"Tuesday, December 14, BOSTON." *Massachusetts Spy* 16 December 1773: 2.

Virilio, Paul. *Speed and Politics: An Essay on Dromology.* Translated by Mark Polizzotti. New York: Semiotext(e), 1986.

Wagner, Corrina A. "Loyalist Propaganda and the Scandalous Life of Tom Paine." *British Journal for Eighteenth-Century Studies* 28 (2005): 97–115.

Waldrop, Rosemarie. *Dissonance (If You Are Interested).* Tuscaloosa: University of Alabama Press, 2005.

Waldstreicher, David. *In the Midst of Perpetual Fetes: The Making of American Nationalism, 1776–1820.* Chapel Hill: U of North Carolina P, 1997.

Walett, Francis G. "Governor Bernard's Undoing: An Earlier Hutchinson Letters Affair." *New England Quarterly* 38 (June 1965): 217–26.

Walker, Jeffrey. "The Body of Persuasion: A Theory of the Enthymeme." *College English* 56 (January 1994): 46–65.

Wallerstein, Immanuel. *The Modern World System III: The Second Era of Great Expansion of the Capitalist World-Economy, 1730s–1840s.* San Diego: Academic, 1989.

Warner, Michael. *The Letters of the Republic: Publication and the Public Sphere in 18th-Century America.* Cambridge, MA: Harvard University Press, 1991.

Warner, Michael. *Publics and Counterpublics.* New York: Zone, 2002.

Warner, Michael. "What's Colonial about Colonial America?" In Blair St. George: 49–70.

Warner, William B. "Communicating Liberty: The Newspapers of the British Empire as a Matrix for the American Revolution." *ELH* 72.2 (2005): 339–62.

Warner, William B. "The Invention of a Public Machine for Revolutionary Sentiment: The Boston Committee of Correspondence." *Eighteenth Century* 50 (Summer–Fall 2009): 145–64.

*Warren-Adams Letters: Being Chiefly a Correspondence among John Adams, Samuel Adams, and James Warren.* Boston: Massachusetts Historical Society, 1925.

Warren, James. Letter to Samuel Adams. 8 November 1772. Samuel Adams Papers. New York Public Library.

Warren, James. Letter to Samuel Adams. 17 November 1772, Samuel Adams Papers. New York Public Library.

Warren, Mercy Otis. *History of the Rise, Progress, and Termination of the American Revolution Interspersed with Biographical, Political and Moral Observations.* Indianapolis: Liberty Classics, 1988.

Warren, Mercy Otis. *Mercy Otis Warren: Selected Letters.* Edited by Jeffrey H. Richards and Sharon M. Harris. Athens: University of Georgia Press, 2009.

Warren, Mercy Otis. Mercy Otis Warren Papers. Massachusetts Historical Society, Boston.

Warren, Mercy Otis. *Observations on the New Constitution, and on the Federal and State Conventions. By a Columbian Patriot.* Boston: 1788. Reprinted in Paul Leicester Ford, ed., *Pamphlets on the Constitution of the United States, Published during Its Discussion by the People, 1787–1788.* Brooklyn, 1888.

Warren, Mercy Otis. *The Plays and Poems of Mercy Otis Warren.* Edited by Benjamin Franklin V. Delmar, NY: Scholars' Facsimiles and Reprints, 1980.

War Resisters League. "Where Your Income Tax Money Really Goes." *War Resisters.* Accessed 21 March 2007 <www.warresisters.org/piechart.htm>.

"War! War!! War!!!" *Aurora* 23 March 1796: 2.

Washington, George. "Letter of the Late President of the United States, to the Secretary of State." *Time Piece* 15 March 1797: 5.

Washington, George. "Message to the House Regarding Documents Relative to the Jay Treaty, March 30, 1796." *Avalon Project at the Yale Law School,* accessed 18 March 2008 <http://avalon.law.yale.edu/18th_century/gw003.asp>.

Washington, George. *The Writings of George Washington.* Edited by Worthington Chauncey Ford. 14 vols. New York: Putnam's, 1889–93.

Waterman, Bryan. *The Republic of Intellect: The Friendly Club of New York City and the Making of American Literature.* Baltimore: Johns Hopkins University Press, 2007.

Watts, Steven. *The Republic Reborn: War and the Making of Liberal America, 1790–1820.* Baltimore: Johns Hopkins University Press, 1987.

Weales, Gerald. "*The Adulateur* and How It Grew." *Library Chronicle* 53 (Winter 1979): 103–33.

Williams, William Appleman. *America Confronts a Revolutionary World: 1776–1976.* New York: Morrow, 1976.

Wilmer, S. E. *Theatre, Society, and the Nation: Staging American Identities.* Cambridge: Cambridge University Press, 2002.

Winton, Calhoun. "The Southern Printer as Agent of Change in the American Revolution." In *Agent of Change: Print Culture Studies after Elizabeth L. Eisenstein.* Edited by Sabrina Alcorn Baron, Eric N. Lindquist, and Eleanor F. Shelvin, 238–49. Amherst: University of Massachusetts Press, 2007.

Withington, Ann Fairfax. *Toward a More Perfect Union: Virtue and the Formation of American Republics.* New York: Oxford University Press, 1991.

Wollaeger, Mark. *Modernism, Media, and Propaganda: British Narrative Form from 1900 to 1945.* Princeton, NJ: Princeton University Press, 2006.

Wood, Gordon. *The Americanization of Benjamin Franklin.* New York: Penguin, 2004.

Wood, Gordon. "Conspiracy and the Paranoid Style: Causality and Deceit in the Eighteenth Century." *William and Mary Quarterly* 39.3 (1982): 401–41.

Wood, Gordon. *The Radicalism of the American Revolution.* New York: Knopf, 1992.

Wootton, David. "Introduction: The Republican Tradition: From Commonwealth to Common Sense." In *Republicanism, Liberty, and Commercial Society, 1649–1776.* Edited by David Wootton, 1–41. Stanford, CA: Stanford University Press, 1994.

Yanagizawa-Drott, David. "Propaganda vs. Education: A Case Study of Hate Radio in Rwanda." In *The Oxford Handbook of Propaganda Studies.* Edited by Jonathan Auerbach and Russ Castronovo, 378–95. New York: Oxford University Press, 2013.

Yang, Chi-ming. "Asia out of Place: The Aesthetics of Incorruptibility in Behn's *Oroonoko.*" *Eighteenth-Century Studies* 42.2 (2009): 235–53.

Yokota, Kariann. "Postcolonialism and Material Culture in the Early United States." *William and Mary Quarterly* 64 (April 2007): 263–70.

Yokota, Kariann. *Unbecoming British: How Revolutionary America Became a Postcolonial Nation.* New York: Oxford University Press, 2011.

Young, Alfred F. "How Radical was the American Revolution." In *Liberty Tree: Ordinary People and the American Revolution,* 227–29. New York: New York University Press, 2006.

Young, Edward. *The Revenge, a Tragedy as It Is Acted at the Theatre-Royal in Drury-Lane.* London: Chetwood, 1721.

Z. "To the PEOPLE of New York." *New-York Journal* 26 November 1773: 3.

Zagarri, Rosemarie. *Revolutionary Backlash: Women and Politics in the Early Republic.* Philadelphia: University of Pennsylvania Press, 2007.

Zagarri, Rosemarie. *A Woman's Dilemma: Mercy Otis Warren and the American Revolution.* Wheeling, IL: Harland Davidson, 1965.

Žižek, Slavoj. "Good Manners in the Age of WikiLeaks." *London Review of Books* 20 January 2011, accessed on 18 November 2012. <http://www.lrb.co.uk/v33/n02/slavoj-zizek/good-manners-in-the-age-of-wikileaks>.

Žižek, Slavoj. *Living in the End of Times.* New York: Verso, 2011.

# { INDEX }

*Figures are indicated by "f" following the page number.*

CPSIA information can be obtained
at www.ICGtesting.com
Printed in the USA
BVHW072246011118
531727BV00003B/12/P

9 780190 677497